Deceptive Speed

Deceptive Speed is a beautifully detailed, unflinchingly reported account of Eddie Lee Ivery's remarkable journey on and off the football field. Author Jerry Gentry unspools this roller coaster story—from a house without indoor plumbing in small-town Georgia to pro football's pinnacle in Green Bay to the struggles and redemption that followed—with a sure hand and empathetic eye. Humanity shines through on each page. Both inspirational and cautionary, this is a tale for everyone.

—Drew Jubera, award-winning journalist and author of *Must Win: A Season of Survival for a Town and Its Team*

What stands out most about *Deceptive Speed*, beyond the remarkable story itself, is how committed Jerry Gentry was to getting the full story. Often, sports biographers merely let the subject tell the story as they remember it. Gentry's including so many people who have known Eddie Lee Ivery gives readers an in-depth, warts-and-all portrait of the rise, fall, and recovery of an All-American football star. It's a great football story, but virtually anyone will be intrigued by the story of a person who grew up destitute, had football fame thrust upon him as a teenager, endured a heated recruiting battle, achieved college football glory, experienced a heartbreaking NFL career, lost everything to cocaine, then picked up the pieces. Racism, poverty, the South, celebrity, wealth, addiction, family, faith, courage—there's so much more than just football. It's the tale of a fascinating and unique life.

—Ken Sugiura, *Atlanta Journal-Constitution* sports columnist and former Georgia Tech beat reporter

Deceptive Speed, a remarkable intimate look at college and professional football, tells a story of pride, struggle and triumph, perseverance, and great comebacks. As a former Tech lineman who blocked for Eddie Lee Ivery, I saw how his talent and relentless work ethic propelled him to the top, but even as an NFL first-round draft pick, it's hard to make it. The incredible expectations make it even harder to stay there. It takes so much dedication and sacrifice that it stops being "what you do" and becomes "who you are"—and that's a trap. Jerry Gentry takes us through it all: the gifts, grind, injuries, distractions, fall from grace, rehab and redemption, and a family that never stopped praying for Ivery. Gentry has us rooting for the good guy even when he's doing bad things.

—Ben Utt, 8-year NFL offensive lineman for the Indianapolis Colts

Deceptive Speed

Eddie Lee Ivery's Run Through Tech, Titletown, and Temptation

Jerry Gentry

MERCER UNIVERSITY PRESS
Macon, Georgia

MUP/ P724

Published by Mercer University Press
1501 Mercer University Drive
Macon, Georgia 31207

29 28 27 26 25 5 4 3 2 1

Books published by Mercer University Press are printed on acid-free paper that meets the requirements of the American National Standard for Information Sciences—Permanence of Paper for Printed Library Materials.

Printed and bound in the United States.

This book is set in Adobe Garamond.

Cover/jacket design by Burt&Burt.

ISBN 978-0-88146-984-4 (Print)
978-0-88146-985-1 (eBook)

Cataloging-in-Publication Data is available from the Library of Congress

Contents

MERCER UNIVERSITY

MERCER UNIVERSITY PRESS

Endowed by

TOM WATSON BROWN

and

THE WATSON-BROWN FOUNDATION, INC.

Acknowledgments

I am going to thank only a few people who helped me with this book. If I try to name everyone, I will leave some out. If you are not named, you know who you are, and I thank you. First, I am grateful to Eddie Lee Ivery for sharing his life with me so honestly and trusting me with his story. When I first got to know him, I learned his story was one of triumph, loss, heartache, joy, resilience, and faith, and I am fortunate to be able to tell it. May his story inspire others affected by addiction. Thanks to all his family who shared their experiences. They are a strong, loving family.

Thanks to the citizens of Thomson who told me about the importance of football to their town, as well as their amazement as they watched Ivery play sports. John Barnett was particularly helpful with the history of the town and Thomson football. Many of Ivery's teammates at Georgia Tech—and others affiliated with the school and the team, as well as those who played against him—allowed me a great deal of time to ask about their experiences at Tech and with Ivery. That list is long and dear to me. The Green Bay Packers—players, coaches, staff—were extraordinarily helpful to this little-known writer asking for help. Cliff Christl and Bob Harlan were particularly helpful. There are others connected with Ivery who allowed me the time to ask questions. To all of these, I am deeply grateful.

Thank you, Marc Jolley, and everyone at Mercer University Press for believing in this story.

I could not have written this without the phenomenal support of my wife, Tina Pippin, who should get an award for hearing me say "I'm almost finished" too many times.

Chapter 1

Cherokee: Work and Play

In 1949, Thomson, the county seat of McDuffie County, hopefully submitted an entry to Georgia Power Company's Champion Home Town contest, a gambit to encourage electricity use statewide. A total of $4,500 would be awarded to six winning towns. Thomson's submission (glowing descriptions of the town, newspaper clippings, photographs, lists of accomplishments) boasted of the town's history and progress: business, education, agriculture, civic involvement, entertainment, infrastructure, construction, and municipal development. *What a wonderful, productive, hospitable town we have*, the submission declared. One boast was that 100 citizens signed a statement of "regret" that the Ku Klux Klan had formed a chapter there. Several prominent Georgia newspapers praised these citizens; the story made *Time* magazine. Another item lauded a new residential development on a parcel of land once part of the estate of Thomas E. Watson, the wealthy, famously racist 19th-century Populist politician. The neighborhood would include water and sewage service, and the city voted to extend water service to "practically every home within the city limits."

One neighborhood, called Cherokee, though it abutted the city on three sides, was not officially part of the town and thus was excluded from the proud city's water infrastructure initiative. Most of Cherokee's houses would not have indoor plumbing for 30 years. Separated by only a creek and some woods from Watson's opulent, exquisitely maintained historic home and the new plumbing-supplied neighborhood, Cherokee is where Eddie Lee Ivery was born in 1956.

Cherokee, once occupied by sharecroppers, now was a cluster of shabby rental homes owned by E. W. Hawes, a White man who owned rental properties all over the county. Nicknamed "Sheik," reportedly due to raucous living in his twenties, Hawes had built most of the homes with scrap lumber. Many Cherokee residents bought groceries and paid their rent at his store, E. W. Hawes's Commissary. Ivery would walk there and buy his favorite treats: Honeybuns, a Reese's Cup, and a soda. When he had no money, Ivery stuffed goodies in his pockets and walked out. On weekends, he said, stealing was easy; the clerk was always drunk. Some White people in Thomson considered Hawes a slumlord, but Ivery said, "He was like a god or something to us. Here was this rich guy who let us poor people buy food on credit." He provided an affordable (if shoddy) residence and occasionally paid them to work for him. It was, by nature, an unequal relationship. One rumor passed around Cherokee held that a family asked Hawes for plumbing in their house, and, to let everyone else know not to make that request, he installed a toilet in the living room.

Ivery lived with his mother, Thelma; grandmother, Katie Bell; and sister, Bennie Mae (and sometimes an uncle), in a tiny three-room house, where a midwife had helped deliver him. (He was told that soon after he was born, a neighbor called One-Armed Sadie offered to buy him from the Ivery family. His mother, Eddie Lee was told, threw a fit.) Next door lived his aunt and uncle, Naomi and Nether Ivery, and their children. Naomi and Nether's son, Jerry, was just a year older than Eddie Lee, so the cousins grew up much like brothers. Jerry stressed that even those who knew them *well* thought they were brothers. Nether sometimes bought food, clothing, and other necessities for Eddie Lee's family. Naomi, Eddie Lee said, "always treated me like I was her child. What she did for them, she did for me. She always treated us with kindness and respect. She was like my mom."

To Eddie Lee, Naomi and Nether had a real household: a mother and a father who went to work, took care of their children, cooked for the family; the day ended and began with family together. At Christmas, the contrast between the families was stark. Both were poor, but Nether and Naomi were less poor. Christmas morning, Eddie Lee and Bennie Mae might receive peppermint candy, fruitcake, underwear, T-shirts, perhaps blue jeans or shoes—but no toys. Most of their toys they crafted themselves. Some years they received "Jeepers" (knock-offs of highly desired Converse shoes), which needed to last until the next Christmas. They rarely ate fresh fruit, so an apple or orange on Christmas morning was a treat. Eddie Lee recalled entering his aunt and uncle's house after opening his gifts so he could see his cousins' toys. That was a *real* Christmas, he thought. Jerry said the most expensive Christmas gift he recalled was a toy cap gun and holster—Jerry thought they were having a rich Christmas. Despite Jerry's memories of modest Christmas mornings, for Eddie Lee, Christmas at his cousins' house was extravagant.

Outside of school and church, Ivery's childhood was work and play. The work was hard. With no indoor plumbing, they drew water from Naomi and Nether's well next door and carried the buckets to the house for cooking, cleaning, and drinking. When the well was dry, they had to walk to a neighbor's house farther away—and make the long, painful walk back with two full buckets of water. Without pipes for wastewater, they poured it outside. Mornings, they carried the chamber pot—"piss pot"—from the house and dumped it in the backyard outhouse, which the two families shared. (Many Cherokee households shared outhouses.) The children were assigned the nasty piss pot chore. "Every day!" Jerry stressed. "*No* exceptions." Eddie Lee lived on a corner lot, and once while carrying the piss pot, a bus passed, passengers staring out the window. Embarrassed, he quickly put the pot on the ground and pretended to be picking vegetables from the garden.

The two families planted, weeded, and picked collard greens, tomatoes, turnip greens, peas, corn, and peppers. They gathered pecans from beneath nearby trees. In summers, Eddie Lee, Jerry, and other kids climbed aboard a "pea truck" and rode to a farmer's field, where, for a dollar and a half, a baloney sandwich, and a cold drink, from seven in the morning to six at night, they picked peas in the heat. Sometimes Eddie Lee distributed flyers for a furniture store. They survived primarily on Thelma's welfare checks and Katie Bell's low-paying work. She picked cotton, cooked, and cleaned for White families—whatever she could to provide for her family. He would always appreciate his grandmother's toughness, a poor Black woman who kept her family afloat in rural Georgia.

When Nether brought home discarded wood from his job at Thomson Oak Flooring, the boys helped him unload and stack it behind his house. He sold the wood as firewood for extra income—a side gig to his main job. The money supported not only his own household but also his mother's (which included other relatives) and Eddie Lee's.

When Jerry turned 10, Nether taught him to drive the truck so he could make deliveries when Nether was busy. On delivery days, the boys would load the truck, then ride along to help unload at the buyer's house—climbing atop the pile and kicking the firewood off the back. Eddie Lee later wondered if the leg strength that helped him crash through defenders and accelerate downfield had its roots in those early days kicking wood off the truck.

Jerry recalled one delivery day when they played sports for too long, and with the wood only partially loaded, an angry Nether whipped them. He punished Eddie Lee as though he were his own son.

"Lord, have mercy," Naomi moaned, recalling the boys' failure to have the truck ready.

"We *never* did that again," Jerry said. They learned early on to be responsible and reliable.

Eddie Lee's Cherokee friend Bernard Grant had a house with the luxury of plumbing but no hot water. Bernard did not, however, avoid water-carrying duty because his grandmother's house did not have plumbing, and he had to draw well water and take it to her house. Grant said Nether Ivery was imposing and intimidating.

"My brother and I," he said, "were treated like we were family. I got several whippings from Nether. He was a big, rugged man, a hard worker. That's where we got some of our toughness, being around him. He didn't take any excuses."

Eddie Lee, Bennie Mae, and their mother slept in one room, their grandmother and uncle in another. The third room, the kitchen, had a wood stove for cooking and for heating water and the house. They improvised "closets": cardboard boxes for folded clothes, a wire strung between nails in a corner to hang clothes. The hanging garments also helped keep the wintry wind from entering the house through the cracks in the wall. Their grandmother crafted quilts. They bought ice in large blocks and kept it in the ice compartment of their refrigerator. They chipped off pieces for cool drinks in the hot summer. Each block lasted a few days. "I didn't see a real freezer until I was 17," Jerry said.

Using rainwater collected as it drained off the house, they cleaned clothes and bathed in a washtub behind the house. If it hadn't rained, someone had to fill it from the dreaded well and carry the heavy buckets. They heated bath water on the wood stove and used a small basin indoors for a quick wash-up. They boiled white laundry in a pot and scrubbed on a washboard. They rinsed the clothes in a separate tub. If they needed a phone, they used Naomi and Nether's.

"You could see light shining through holes in the walls," said Thomson assistant football coach Jerry Sellers, who gave Ivery rides home. While Ivery and his extended family knew they lived among the poorest of Thomson's poor (despite their hard work), they described Cherokee as fun and said that neighbors looked out for one another. Jerry said if he misbehaved, a neighbor might whip him—and his parents would whip him again when he got home.

"It was tough—but the best life," he said.

"You could sleep with your doors unlocked and not fear a break-in," Bennie Mae said. "Everybody knew everybody." They had little grass in their yard, but Jerry said they raked the dirt to create neat lines.

"We raked dirt. I shake my head thinking about that now," he said, expressing pride and bemusement.

In their desire to keep an eye on their children, Jerry's parents were strict. Once, he and his siblings decided to surprise their parents with money, so, without telling anyone where they were going, they helped another family with their chickens. They made just under a dollar each. "We got one of the worst whippings ever," Jerry recalled. "We were trying to help, but they didn't know where we were, so they beat us down."

Jerry's grandfather leased one of Hawes's fields and paid Eddie Lee, Jerry, and Grant $1.25 a day to plant, weed, and water a potato crop. The field was about a quarter-mile long and 40 yards across. It took them weeks in the blazing heat to plant all the potatoes. They weeded them by hand and watered them with buckets they had to carry—again, the heavy buckets—from a faucet at one end of the field. To make the time pass faster, the boys competed to see who could work the fastest. They also helped sell the potatoes at Hawes's gas station.

"You couldn't pay me enough to do that now," Jerry said, shaking his head as he recalled the hot, grueling work. Grant said when he told college friends about the potato planting, most didn't believe him. "Aw, you're exaggerating!" they scoffed. They were not exaggerating; they had even made a game of it.

What little money they had, they earned in the oppressive east Georgia heat—carrying water, picking peas, loading and unloading wood, digging, planting, harvesting, sweating. While Eddie Lee worked, his muscles strengthened, his stamina deepened, and perseverance settled into his bones. He called himself "country strong," a strength that came from daily testing of stamina and determination, using one's whole body, and pushing physical limits—laboring, sweltering, no air-conditioned home for relief. Before he ever lifted weights, he was a fine athlete, due to his daily life and natural gifts. He grew up accustomed to earning every penny. He expected life to be demanding and rewarding. If you're tired, keep going. If someone is counting on you, deliver.

When not working, Ivery and his cousins played sports with their neighbors. Ivery dashed through chores so he could play ball. He gulped down his meals and ran outside. Their dirt yard, packed hard by their relentless play, was their football field; the "football" might be a cloth-stuffed shirt tied in a ball. They played marbles in the dirt. Nailed to a tree, their basketball goal was an old bottomless washtub or a discarded bicycle tire rim missing its spokes. The basketball also might have been a stuffed shirt or an empty oil can their grandfather brought home from a gas station where he worked. The "ball" was "dribbled" by bobbing it up and down in one hand. Their "baseball" was an old tennis ball they found, their bat a stick from the woods. Teams were often determined by family—the Iverys versus the Robertsons or Grants. They would tease a vanquished opponent: "You're a cheap suit!" Jerry recalled the time as "some of the best days we ever had." Every free moment, Eddie Lee was outside, throwing, batting, catching, tackling, running, evading. As he grew, he surpassed his friends in speed and strength. When he ran with the football, it took two or three to stop him.

Looking out the window as she washed dishes, Aunt Naomi would say, "Hmm, look at that boy. When he gets hit, he gets right up and keeps going."

"Even at 10," Jerry said, "you could see a natural ability. Nobody could tackle him alone. Everybody wanted him on their team." Some of Eddie Lee's uncles were excellent athletes, and as a youngster, he would don their too-big shoulder pads and helmets and dream of playing for a crowd.

Sometimes, they illicitly played at the Thomson High football field, where Ivery would later become a legend. They sneaked onto that field because the stadium's tall brick wall hid them from view. The risks were high—Black boys on the White team's football field in the 1960s—but this field provided a luxury beneath their feet that their Cherokee yards lacked: grass.

They sometimes crossed a fence and sneaked onto a White farmer's land and swam in his pond, which they called Blue Pond. One time, the owner caught them and sicced his dog on them. The boys ran, but they kept returning, and if spied, sped off. Eddie Lee always escaped over the fence first. "That's when I found out how fast I was," he said.

He played hardest in an informal youth league when the opponents were from either Strawberry Hill, a neighborhood of Black homeowners, or "the projects," an all-Black public housing neighborhood.

Homes in both places put Cherokee houses to shame. The public housing residences were simple, but they were brick and had indoor plumbing. Strawberry Hill homes, many of them brick split levels, seemed magnificent, with garages, large yards, living rooms, and dens. School teachers sometimes had to step between Cherokee and Strawberry Hill kids who taunted one another. Jerry recalled a Strawberry Hill mother telling her children, "Don't hang around with those Cherokee kids. You can't learn anything from them." Bennie Mae remembered that Strawberry Hill residents didn't want to associate with those "country Cherokee kids." Eddie Lee and his Cherokee playmates, though they fiercely opposed each other in neighborhood games, saved their most intense blocking, tackling, defending, and fielding for games against boys from those two neighborhoods.

"We tried to break their arms and legs," Eddie Lee said. "We thought we were as good as anybody out there."

"We couldn't *be* them, so we wanted to *beat* them," Jerry added. "We were so geeked up, we *had* to beat them."

"They all wanted to beat us because Cherokee was the tough guys," Grant recalled. "You would beat the tough guys if you beat Cherokee." Already competitive, Eddie Lee, defending his neighborhood of ramshackle houses, nurtured a hatred of losing. *I'll show you.*

Some days, while Eddie Lee was outside playing with friends, a woman walked by whose mismatched clothes were unkempt. Her unstable, unfocused gait revealed that something in her inner makeup was awry, and when she spoke, the boys could tell she was cognitively impaired. Eddie Lee's close friends knew who she was, but those who didn't snickered, pointed, and ridiculed: "Look at that dumb lady. Look how she's walking." Eddie Lee said nothing but burned with shame. The lady was his mother. He would think, as the insults and laughter rolled out, *I'll show you.*

Grant knew. He and the Ivery kids were often in each other's houses, sleeping in a pile of kids. Other people thought they were cousins, and the kids didn't correct them. Cherokee kids bonded tightly, family or not.

"That was a tough subject coming up, Eddie Lee's mom," Grant said. "We didn't really talk about it." They sweated together in the heat of the potato field, tackled one another in the dirt, and slept in cramped rooms, but this topic—Thelma Ivery—they didn't talk about much. To Eddie Lee and Bennie Mae, their grandmother, Katie Bell, was "Mom" and their mother was "Thelma," so others wouldn't know that the "dumb lady" was their mother.

As Eddie Lee got older, he learned that being a good athlete diverted attention from his mother: Keep talking about the game, and family might not come up.

Sometimes his mother pulled a wagon holding two tubs. When their well ran dry and the closer neighbor refused to let Eddie Lee's family use theirs, Thelma retrieved water from a well further away. Returning, the water sloshed and spilled from the tubs.

"About half of that water had spilled by the time she got home," Bennie Mae chuckled. She and Eddie Lee were especially hurt when fellow congregants insulted their mother at church, where she shouted and fell to the floor as she praised God, the Holy Spirit moving her to exuberance. She had vociferously praised God since childhood (her mother tried to tone her down) and never stopped.

"There was no shame in her game," Eddie Lee said. At church, everyone knew her children, so their embarrassment was not private.

"Look at that stupid lady," said the voices in the pews. "Why don't she sit herself down? Her crazy self."

"When she shouted in church," Bennie Mae said, "some people didn't want to sit beside her, and they let their kids laugh at her."

Their kids.

Throughout childhood, Bennie Mae and Eddie Lee faced ridicule aimed at their mother (and at them by association), so it helped to pretend their grandmother was their mother—and that they didn't know Thelma. When schoolmates brought a mother or father to sports games or parent meetings, they brought neither. Despite her disability, their mother could tell time, was good at counting money, and had a good memory, Bennie Mae said. But Thelma was illiterate and "couldn't talk well." Why add to the embarrassment by bringing her to school? They wanted their mother to be like their friends' and classmates' mothers, and because she couldn't be, they acted as if they had no mother. Maybe no one would catch on that Katie Bell was really their grandmother, or, more importantly—that Thelma was their mother.

Eddie Lee said that when he was a child, he didn't like or respect his mother and openly disobeyed her. She was taken out of school after first grade and put to work in the fields—the only job anyone thought she could handle. His grandmother, whose husband abandoned her and their five children, he minded. She would whip him or summon bigger and stronger Uncle Nether. During the last whipping from his grandmother that Eddie Lee recalled, he cowered under the bed while she, kneeling, flailed at him with an extension cord. She was known to mutter, "Eddie Lee should have been whipped more than he was."

She also whipped Bennie Mae, who recalled once coming home after sundown—a curfew earlier than Eddie Lee's because she was a girl—and her grandmother whipped her with an electric iron cord. She said she "grew up hard. There wasn't no easy way for me."

Their fearful friends warily visited their home, Eddie Lee said, because "they didn't want to mess with Katie Bell. She had a way of telling you what it was without any sugar coating on it."

At 14, Bennie Mae experienced her own social embarrassment. She got pregnant, was expelled from school, and was compelled to apologize in front of her church. While out of school, she worked as a housekeeper for a White woman who was a teacher. The teacher spoke to the school superintendent and eventually convinced him to allow Bennie Mae to return. She was forbidden, however, from participating in extracurricular activities. Bennie Mae recalled being nominated for the homecoming court, but a "mean English teacher" blocked the nomination. For the rest of her school years, she felt like an outcast.

Eddie Lee rarely saw his father, who lived in Thomson. Occasionally, someone would say, "Eddie Lee, I saw your father hanging out with the other drunks." *I'll show you.*

Before being incorporated as a town in 1854, Thomson was a small settlement called Hickory Level, also called Slashes or Frogpond (due to its swampy land). Before that, the area was nearly all part of the John Langston plantation. The largest businesses in Thomson in its early years were timber and sawmills. In the 1960s and 1970s, its nonagricultural economy depended heavily on two employers: Uniroyal's shoe plant, which made Keds sneakers, and the Thomson Company men's clothing manufacturer, which made pants for department stores until 1997. Uniroyal once employed nearly 1,200 people and paid well. "It was what everybody aspired to," said former Thomson mayor Robert Knox. When it closed in the early 1980s, unemployment rose to 22 percent almost overnight.

Today, in front of the McDuffie County Courthouse in downtown Thomson, rises an obelisk that honors the county's White Civil War dead. A smaller, easy-to-miss reminder of the Confederacy, an Italian marble statue honoring White Confederate women, stands across from the former telegraph office and railroad depot, where Confederate troops once slept.

This statue, designed by a woman and depicting a woman holding a Confederate battle flag, was erected in the 1910s by Civil War veterans, the United Daughters of the Confederacy, and the Woman's Club of Thomson. She wears a simple homespun dress, like those worn by farm women who toiled daily through hard times. She likely owned no slaves but supported the side that upheld the practice. The statue honors, as the inscription on the pedestal reads, the "Women of the Sixties"—those who managed the homestead while their men fought in the war.

Behind the Confederate woman, on the long brick wall of a nearby store, a mural depicts Thomson landmarks and notable residents. Before the 1996 Olympic Games in Atlanta, an artist traveled through small towns offering to paint murals that might catch the eye of tourists curious about Georgia beyond the capital—visitors who might stop to see a historic site, grab a meal, or do some shopping. Two panels show men on horseback, referencing the fox "hunts" once hosted by nearby Belle Meade Country Club and the local cross-country course where sanctioned equestrian events were held. The historic Hickory Hill mansion is featured as well, with a woman in antebellum dress—long printed skirt and matching bonnet—standing in front. The artist also included the old brick train depot, a locomotive passing by in a plume of gray smoke, and at the end of the track, a large camellia blossom. (In the 1920s, a man came through selling camellia shrubs. Many citizens bought them, and a trend began—and accelerated—so much so that the city later declared itself "the Official Camellia City of the South.")

The mural also prominently features the Brickyard, where the high school football team plays. Local football legend Ray Guy, in his Oakland Raiders uniform, angles his right leg upward after booming one of his magnificent punts. Years later, master blues guitarist Blind Willie McTell was added.

When the mural was commissioned, Ivery, another of Thomson's iconic sports sons—the young man for whom in 1979 the entire city celebrated "Eddie Lee Ivery Day"—was omitted. During mural discussions, his name was not mentioned.

To young Eddie Lee, Cherokee was a big playground, but as he experienced more of Thomson, he saw what people with money could do. His grandmother babysat and cleaned for a White family and sometimes brought him along. The large house had toys that astounded him: a firetruck, a whole *battalion* of army men, a cowboy outfit with vest, hat, and holstered six-shooter. So many toy cars. She worked for a family that ran a concession stand at ballgames and sometimes brought home day-old popcorn, a special treat in the Ivery household: *free* popcorn. His grandmother also worked in the all-White Thomson High cafeteria and sometimes brought home pizza, lasagna, or soup—luxuries to Eddie Lee and Bennie Mae, who were accustomed to collard greens and "dog bread" for lunch. Dog bread was hard cornbread made by frying a cornmeal and water batter—no milk or eggs. Some people tossed it outside for the dogs. Having meat at a meal was special. They could afford to buy chicken perhaps once a month.

Eddie Lee had an uncle, Bill, who had a small farm in Cherokee. Once a year, they killed one of his hogs, usually by gunshot to the head. Eddie Lee said one man could kill a hog by hitting it in the head with the back side of an axe blade. Eddie Lee's first job was building a fire below a large metal pot that he helped fill with water (more tiresome trips to the well), then he helped drag the pig carcass to the pot. Boiling made it easier to scrape off its hair. The youngsters couldn't cut and butcher the hog, Eddie Lee said, so they were assigned the most disliked job: cleaning out the intestines so they could be used for chitterlings ("chitlins") or sausage casings.

"We were too little to handle those big knives, but we could squeeze intestines," Grant said. They manually ground some of the meat for sausage, then stuffed the ground pork in sections of the intestines. Brains were scrambled with eggs. ("That was a delicacy," Grant said.) They fried the skin for a delicious, crispy snack—a favorite of Eddie Lee's. Meat was preserved by salt-curing in the smokehouse. They flavored their collard greens with a piece of salt-cured ham hanging in the smokehouse. They made a stew from liver and lungs with onions, peppers, and tomatoes. No part of the hog was wasted.

Cooking chitlins was labor intensive. The intestines had to be cleaned thoroughly of pig feces for safety and to eliminate the strong odor—but, according to Eddie Lee, not *all* the odor.

"If there was no smell, it didn't taste good. Chitlins stunk when they were cooked, but it was some of the best food, cooked with a lot of onions, hot sauce, vinegar, and black pepper. That was good eatin' right there," he said.

Jerry said chitlins are an acquired taste and that in Black neighborhoods, older residents like it; youngsters less so. "My oldest daughter will eat it," he said, "but not my youngest. Grandkids? Forget it."

The Iverys rarely left Cherokee. When they went to Thomson's modest downtown—to shop or, rarely, see a movie in the theater where Black patrons sat in the balcony—they boasted to neighbors, "Hey, I went to town today." Cherokee had a barbecue place and a juke joint, the Honey Pot, but Bennie Mae said they weren't allowed there.

They would sometimes watch Thomson High football games as outsiders in their own town.

"We were segregated back then," Ivery said, "so we used to get on top of a barn and watch them play."

During junior high, Eddie Lee's family moved from Cherokee to a tiny gray cinder-block home with a tin roof on Ellington Avenue, where Black families had lived since the 1920s. To Eddie Lee and Bennie Mae, it seemed like a mansion.

"When we got off that corner in Cherokee, we thought, *wow*. It was like heaven," Bennie Mae recalled. The house, owned by Ivery's uncle, Jimmy Lee Ivery, had an indoor bathroom, a phone, a kitchen with a sink, two bedrooms, and a living room with a couch left behind by their uncle. They finally had a place with enough room for visitors to sit—though Eddie Lee was still hesitant to have anyone over who didn't know him well.

Under its tin roof, the house sweltered in the summer. They had a box fan that Ivery said merely stirred the hot, stale air. In the winter, they heated the house with a wood stove in the living room. They no longer had to go outside to use the bathroom or take a bath. "I felt like a human being," Ivery said. They were still poor. Christmases, Ivery noted, still included few gifts that weren't daily necessities. His Uncle Nether remained a presence. If he or Bennie Mae acted up, their mother or grandmother would threaten to call him. Cherokee wasn't far away. His mother often walked the streets of Thomson, picking up discarded aluminum cans to trade for a few bucks. Even years later, after Ivery bought her a house, she still walked around Thomson picking up cans—the mother of a pro football player.

By most accounts in Thomson, public school integration went smoothly compared to many other Southern towns (although Jerry recalled White classmates had newer books than Black students in the same school). One private school quickly opened the year that the schools integrated, but Thomson schools missed no classes due to opposition to integration. Still, there were some slights. John Barnett, Ivery's former high school football teammate, said that in the first year of integrated high school football in 1970, head coach Fred Bowers chose only White players to pose for a pre-season picture for the newspaper. Black players were appropriately upset, and assistant coach George Drake, former coach at all-Black R. L. Norris High and the first Black coach at Thomson High, intervened. A picture that included the entire team appeared in the newspaper.

Former Thomson High assistant principal, Luther Wilson, who was Black, credited in part Thomson's White leadership. Hoping to avoid the disruptions experienced in other Southern towns where Black citizens boycotted White businesses, a large number of White parents did not pull their children from the public schools. Jerry also credited strong, driven Black teachers who were determined to ensure Black students were treated well in the integrated schools. The Thomson Board of Education—under pressure by the Thomson Progressive Civic Club, a civil rights organization that had a petition with around 1,000 names—appointed a Black insurance salesman, Joseph Greene, to the school board. At first, the board offered to name Greene an "advisory member," but as that position was non-voting, the Civic Club rejected the offer. A White member resigned so Greene could take his place.

"It was pure economics," Greene said. "They didn't want integration, but they didn't want boycotts, either, so they said, 'Tell the boys to hold it down.'" He said perhaps some White football fans were intrigued at the thought of Thomson High and Norris High—both successful football programs—combining to create a powerhouse.

When Wilson was named assistant principal, he knew that in many newly integrated Southern schools, Black administrators were "head knockers" mainly expected to enforce discipline (on Black students). Many White administrators, Wilson said, assumed Black students would need a Black male to control them. Wilson said he, however, was given the full range of responsibilities of an assistant principal.

When he was in seventh grade, John Barnett, who had played football only with other White boys, received a letter from his new football coach, Calvin Sampson, who had previously coached at Norris High. The letter explained that the White football players from Thomson Junior High would ride a bus to Norris High (which became integrated R. L. Norris Junior High) and join the Black junior high players for spring practices. Barnett had little prior contact with Black children in Thomson. He knew, vaguely, that the Norris Rams had gridiron success parallel to Thomson High's. Three times in the 1960s (on teams that featured Ivery's relatives), Norris had undefeated regular seasons, and four times fell one game short of playing for the state championship. Like nearly every Southern White boy, Barnett assumed Black programs were inferior and thought the Black players would be "fresh meat." Then in the fall, Eddie Lee joined the team.

"This cat is arriving late," Barnett thought, "and I've been playing all this time, so I'll show him."

But then reality smacked him.

"The first time I hit him," he said, "it was like hitting a brick wall."

Coach Sampson, whom Ivery feared and respected, nurtured Ivery's talents. Ivery said Sampson taught him character as well as football and was one of the first well-educated Black men he met. The long-armed, barrel-chested Sampson was a "hard-nosed disciplinarian," Ivery said.

"If you didn't do it right, you'd get slapped upside the head or get told off right in your face," Eddie Lee said. Still, he recalled, "We were one of the most well-conditioned junior high teams," no doubt due to the number of times Sampson made them sprint up a hill near the practice field. Jerry recalled Sampson having big, imposing knuckles. In class, Sampson was equally demanding.

"If we didn't pay attention, he'd throw a chair," Eddie Lee said. "You hated to cross his path. I concentrated on trying to do everything right in football *and* math." He said Sampson might be writing on the chalkboard, then whirl around, point at a shocked student, and demand, "*What's seven times five?*" If the student couldn't recall the answer, Ivery said, Sampson might throw an eraser or embarrass the student with a sharp remark. (Bennie Mae regretted that when she was expelled from school for being pregnant, she missed Sampson's famously fierce teaching style.)

Sampson said his toughness was forged over the five years he spent in the United States Marine Corps, stationed in Korea. The Marines taught him to never accept no for an answer, to never quit, and to be disciplined ("with a capital D"). He learned "to be committed to what you're doing. There was no quit in the Marine Corps." He taught his players the same lessons.

"Be proud of what you do, how you dress," he insisted. "My players' uniforms were always clean. I didn't let their shirt tails hang out."

He also practiced and enforced punctuality. Once, Eddie Lee didn't arrive on time for departure for a game, and Sampson said to the team, "Let's go." "We loaded the bus and left," Sampson said. "His reason might have been legitimate. I never did ask." They lost the game, but he never regretted the decision to keep his players accountable.

Sampson began teaching and coaching in Thomson in 1956, at the Black high school, then called McDuffie County Training School. The word "training" was a sure sign that it was a Black school. "The meaning was obvious," he said. White students were *educated*; Black students were *trained.*

Sampson claimed the tales of his throwing erasers and chairs were exaggerations, but he did pressure students who preferred to be ignored. He said,

> I didn't accept "I don't know." If I could get you to start thinking, at least give some answer, instead of going on to someone else, then maybe we could bridge the gap between "I don't know" and the answer. Some kids were ready with

> answers right away, and some were not. The one that wasn't, that kid always interested me. I wouldn't care if he was wrong; I wanted to know what he was thinking. Show me something. I found out the one who gave the wrong answer might be thinking more logically.

Eddie Lee needed a teacher like that. Though he had passed each grade, he admitted he was a poor student when he entered the integrated junior high. He qualified for free lunches, so the White students, who were well-dressed, drove nice cars, and seemed so smart, intimidated him. But, after being in Coach Sampson's class, he excelled in math, and his highest score on his college entrance exam was in math.

In junior high, Eddie Lee was a good football player, but he didn't blossom into a star until high school. In ninth grade, his last year of junior high football (eighth and ninth graders played on the same team), he still wasn't a starter. In the last game of the season, with his team losing in the rain, he didn't play until the game was nearly over. Embarrassed that other players on the field were muddy, he wanted the ball so he could get tackled. The first play went to another running back, so Ivery dove to the ground, pretending to block someone so at least his uniform would be soiled. After the game, following tradition, players exited the field between the goalposts while the band played the school fight song. As they left the field, Ivery, crying, promised himself that he'd do whatever it took to be a starter. *I'll show you.*

When Ivery did become a starter in high school, his talent and hard work under Sampson's guidance merged to create an exquisite athlete more exciting than Thomson fans had seen in a long time.

Chapter 2

Betwixt the Bricks

Tenth grade football players played an eight-game schedule on the junior varsity team, known as the Bullpups, and after the fourth game, the top players were promoted to the varsity team. Stronger, bigger, and faster than the other JV players, Ivery dominated the outmatched competition. In the first game, he scored three touchdowns (another nullified by a penalty) in a 20-0 victory. In two consecutive games, he returned kickoffs for touchdowns. Opponents stopped kicking to him altogether. The JV coach told varsity coach Fred Bowers, "You need to check this guy out."

However, Ivery's record-breaking career nearly ended before it started.

Ivery arrived at his first varsity practice—and quit. The linebackers were huge and menacing, and Bowers, notorious for brutal practices, used lowly tenth graders, no matter how skilled, as fodder for violent drills.

"New players were scrimmage meat," another former player remarked. "It was brutal. He was a mean son of a bitch. He was an asshole." Bowers insulted players with crude, misogynistic language. "He would fly across the huddle and slap the shit out of you. He ran drills you couldn't run now," the player added.

In one dreaded drill, "Butt 'Em Up," a defenseless player with his hands behind his back took hits from a player who slammed into him. The drill made you tough, they were told. Coach Bowers's son Mark said his father was "one of those old discipline coaches who loved to see how kids would hit. A lot of that wasn't necessary, but his mindset was 'If you want to play, I'm going to find out pretty quick if you like this sport.'" Regarding the Butt 'Em Up drill, he said, "Oh Lord, that's probably why I had two neck surgeries."

Terrified, Ivery and a few buddies left. Junior high practices were tough but not cruel. While they were walking home, a car pulled over, and Coach Sampson got out.

"You're not going to quit. Get in!" he barked.

Arthur Greene, a former high school football star at Norris High, called Sampson, who had grown up in public housing, and told him the boys had left. Greene worked part-time for the Thomson police on weekends and holidays and full-time at the Uniroyal plant. Greene, whom Sampson had coached in the early 1960s, was well known in Thomson for his volunteer work with Black boys, especially those from poor homes, who, Greene feared, might succumb to the downward drag of poverty and oppressive racism. Sampson called Greene a "guardian angel." He watched practices and games, encouraged the boys when they were down, provided rides, and cheered them as they played. He steered boys away from trouble, and if they got in trouble, he helped them get out. Jerry Ivery said Greene was part of the "educated minority," who "got their degrees and came back and made a difference." Eddie Lee said Greene was "like a big brother, a mentor, for Black kids."

Sampson plotted as he drove. The former Marine, with a rock-hard sense of honor, would tell the boys to lie. He hated dishonesty, but he didn't want Bowers to know they quit. "That shows a lack of something," he said. "That's a cop-out. Bowers might not have let them play." He especially thought of Ivery, Cherokee boy with no father and a mentally disabled mother. "However low he has been," Sampson said later, "it might have been the top of where he would have been without football. If that had been taken away from him—Oh, Lord."

Sampson marched the boys into the locker room, commanded them to put on their uniforms, and led them to practice, where he made up an excuse for their absence. Because of Greene's perceptive intervention and quick compassion—and Sampson's impeccable reputation—Ivery was allowed to rejoin the team. Ivery still feared Bowers, though. He had seen Bowers snatch a player by the facemask and yank, and he didn't want that to happen to him. "I did everything full speed and didn't want to do anything wrong because he was so rough," Ivery said.

Since 1941, the Thomson High School Bulldogs have played in The Brickyard, a stadium surrounded on three sides by dark red brick walls that exude a hardened toughness players hope to absorb. After the original high school burned in 1938, the salvaged bricks were used to construct the Brickyard wall. Ralph Starling, who played offensive tackle and linebacker for the Bulldogs in the 1960s, said that when he played, his cleats sometimes dug up black cinders from the fire, which were layered beneath the sod. The nearby University of Georgia Bulldogs compete at Sanford Stadium on a field surrounded by Chinese privet, leading their fans to say UGA competes "between the hedges," while Thomson's team plays, as locals say, "between the bricks" or "betwixt the bricks."

Thomson fans were accustomed to winning. They won state championships in 1967 (the defense posted 10 shutouts and surrendered a minuscule 2.2 points per game) and 1968 (the offense averaged 36 points per game). After Ivery's time, they won again in 1984, 1985, 2002, and 2022. They are 6-0 in state championship games and had a 36-game win streak between 1966 and 1969. Starting in September 1964, they won 41 consecutive home games. From 1965 to 1970, they compiled a 62-4 record. During Ivery's Brickyard career, from 1972 to 1974, Thomson did not near a championship, but the Bulldogs featured one of the most electrifying running backs the town had ever seen.

In Ivery's first varsity game, Bowers inserted him to return a punt. He returned it 87 yards for a touchdown. In another game, the opposing team kicked off to the right to avoid Grant, a dangerous kick returner and later a scholarship player at the University of South Carolina. As a receiver, he provided a potent passing option alongside Ivery's running. Folks in the stands would say, "Those two—they're from

Cherokee." Barnett said Grant "could fly. He was an excellent basketball player, too. Catcher in baseball. Ran track. A three-year starter in four sports." The opposition knew about Grant but not Ivery. Ivery cradled the ball. Grant made a block; Ivery faked out tacklers and headed to the end zone. Grant was so fast that, after he made the block, he caught up with Ivery and, according to Ivery, said, "Come on!" Ivery returned the kick 80 yards. For two games, he alternated at tailback, and in the third, as the sole tailback, he ran for two touchdowns (one for 33 yards) and gained over 100 yards.

The shy Cherokee kid became a town hero. Classmates beyond his circle of buddies befriended him. As a sophomore, he had his first girlfriend, a senior. "I started liking myself because everybody else liked me," Ivery said. Jerry bragged that his cousin would be a pro football player.

"Your name is in the paper, your picture," Grant said. "Students hear your name on the loudspeaker. They see you score. That popularity is really big in high school, particularly because we were in the early years of integration, being uncomfortable in certain situations, and then the notoriety came with athletics. That played a big part in all of our growth."

"Ivery was the idol for younger kids," Sampson said. "When we went to an away game, we often had more fans than the home team. He emptied the town; they went to see Eddie Lee run. When we played Cedar Shoals in Athens, there was a convoy of cars and buses. Eddie Lee was the man!" Sampson watched the player he had coached blossom into a magnificent runner. Sampson said once Ivery pierced an opening in the line, he instinctively eluded defenders with quick moves and swift strides.

"He had the unique ability to cut back, make just the right move at just the right time," Sampson marveled, "even if the defensive guy was faster. He could bob and weave. He was the best diagonal runner. When we needed the yards, he got it. He was the money man." For days after Friday night games, Thomson residents would shake their heads and say, "Can you *believe* that run Eddie Lee made?"

When Ivery began paying attention to teachers and studying diligently, he discovered he was a good student. He performed best in math; the foundation laid by Sampson paid off. He was inducted into the Beta Club, an academic honors organization, and was elected president of the junior class (at a predominantly White school).

"You worry about athletes in math," said Tommy Carmichael, an assistant coach and math teacher.

> You want them to make the grades so they can play, and the first test we had was on a Monday after a Friday game. I asked him if he wanted to wait a day because he had had a game. But he said he was ready. Eddie Lee turned it in first, and I thought, "Oh no." Usually, whoever turns theirs in quickly does poorly, but he made a 95. I thought, "I don't have to worry about him."

Ivery liked being one of the guys, even though he was a star. As lineman Mack Alley recalled, Ivery "could make something out of nothing." Alley described one such moment: "He's going to be tackled," he said, "and the next thing you know, he is past the line and gone."

Despite his standout talent, Ivery "was not a prima donna," Alley emphasized. "He was down to earth and friendly. Even when he scored, his attitude was 'I'm just doing what I'm supposed to do.' There was no showboating, no hoopla."

True to form, Ivery routinely credited his offensive line for his success. One coach later admitted that the line "was not very good," which meant Ivery was often stopped at the line of scrimmage. On many plays, he either broke free for a long run or was stuffed for no gain—but regardless of the result, he always made a point to praise his linemen.

He wasn't one for fiery speeches or attention-grabbing antics. At pep rallies, Ivery barely spoke. He would clap his hands hard and shout, "Let's go! Let's go!" But his real leadership came through action—by playing harder than anyone else and running as if every outcome depended on him.

Ivery respected his coaches, but sometimes he would lean in close to assistant Jerry Sellers, who was only a few years older than Ivery, and playfully whisper, as though they were peers, "Hey, Jerry." Sellers laughed it off. Ivery had become self-assured enough to tease an authority figure, albeit a young one, and learned to use humor to keep things comfortable. He developed an easy-going personality that pleased and entertained teammates and adults. Everybody wants proximity to a sports star who can kid around. Football stardom and congeniality made him popular.

Even after leaving Cherokee, the stigma of being a "Cherokee kid" clung to him. His new home was a step up from where he came from—but most of his classmates wouldn't have felt comfortable there. (And there was always the chance they'd meet his mother.) So many of the other students had nice houses, clothes, and cars. For Ivery, athletic stardom was the only path to respect. Every time he faked out a defender, sprinted into the end zone, or hustled for a rebound, he felt like he was outrunning his Cherokee roots. Ivery loved the rush of competition—the thrill of beating an opponent, the roar of the crowd. "With the football in my hand, running down the field," he said, "I'm at peace." In those moments, the weight of poverty and the shame tied to his mother faded away.

Many in his extended family came to watch his football games—but neither his mother nor his grandmother did. It was his Aunt Naomi who signed the permission form so he could play. His grandmother and mother (who couldn't sign the form herself because she was illiterate) were too afraid he'd get hurt.

"Why don't you quit football?" they would ask.

They stayed home, unaware that a local legend was taking shape right under their roof. Ivery became a Thomson hero—but he still felt a stab of shame whenever someone found out who his mother was, or worse, saw—or stepped inside—the tiny house he called home.

In his first varsity basketball games as a sophomore, Ivery put up 17 points, then 16, then 12, then 26. Coach Willie Williams had a baller on his hands for the next three years. Ivery was named most valuable player of the team each of those seasons.

By senior year, he was leading the team in rebounds—as a guard. He wasn't tall, but he was scrappy, strong, and relentless. "Once he got position, you weren't going to get around him," Grant said. "People know him for his football, but to see him play basketball, it was a thing of beauty."

A former coach recalled that Ivery wasn't a natural shooter, but he still averaged nearly 20 points a game. He was smart, unselfish, and never stopped hustling.

"He was one of those guys you want to get the ball to when the game is on the line," Mark Bowers said. "You knew he'd do something good with it."

He usually tallied multiple steals per game and scored easy putbacks by outworking opponents for offensive rebounds. Time and again, he delivered the winning basket, the perfect pass, or the clutch steal.

Ivery was the greatest sports star Thomson had seen since Ray Guy, the outstanding punter for the University of Southern Mississippi in the early 1970s and the Oakland Raiders. Guy is the only punter chosen in the first round of the National Football League draft and one of the few kickers (and the only punter) in the Pro Football Hall of Fame. At Thomson High, Guy led the football team as quarterback, punter, and field goal kicker to two state championships. In the first, he scored a touchdown with a broken wrist, and in the second, he blocked a point-after-touchdown attempt and a field goal attempt, securing a tight 7-6 victory. During his senior year, he averaged 49.7 yards per punt. On the baseball team, he once pitched 15 shutout innings (10-year-old Barnett was there chasing foul balls for money). Classmate Rick Hawes said that when he caught while Guy pitched in practice, he added extra padding to his mitt to protect his hand from the punishing smack of Guy's fastball. At USM, Guy also played defense in football (intercepting eight passes in his senior year, tied for first in the country) and pitched a no-hitter in baseball. In the NFL, not one of his punts was returned for a touchdown.

Ivery was also a multisport star. In addition to football and basketball, he ran the 100- and 220-yard sprints, the 440-yard relay, and the mile relay. He long-jumped and once made the state tournament in the high jump.

"His sophomore year, on the 440-relay team, he was the leadoff man," Grant recalled. "We were region champs and didn't lose a race and qualified for the state tournament. In the regular season, that relay team crushed everybody. By the time he handed off the baton, the race was over."

At a track meet, Coach Carmichael saw how competitive Ivery had become. He said Ivery had preferred not to run the 220, but Carmichael said they had no one else to run it and gave Ivery no choice.

"I'm just going to jog it," Ivery said.

Carmichael told him to do what was best for the team, and "after the first 30 yards of him acting like he didn't want to be there, he realized he would be embarrassed, so he picked up his pace and won the race." It was not in Ivery's makeup to lose. *I'll show you.*

In the first football game of Ivery's junior year, he ran for 110 yards (half the team's total rushing yards) on only 11 carries, averaging 10 yards per carry. He scored a touchdown, with two more nullified by penalties. He was named Player of the Week by the local paper, the *McDuffie Progress.* In the next game, he ran for 130 yards (out of 205 yards for the entire offense). In the following game, he achieved 112 yards and two touchdowns, plus he threw a halfback pass for a third. In the next game, he recorded 154 yards, including a 65-yard touchdown run. He was also the leading tackler on defense, playing either linebacker or safety. Next, in a 19-0 victory, he rushed for 112 yards, scored two touchdowns, and threw a 27-yard TD pass to Grant. After missing a game and a half due to an ankle injury, he ran for 133 yards. At the season's end (which was a disappointing 4-5-1), Ivery was named Best Offensive Back and Most Valuable Player (the Coca-Cola

Golden Helmet Award). He finished the season with 907 yards, averaging 6.8 yards per carry, and intercepted three passes.

When handed the ball by the quarterback, Ivery wasn't one to wait for a hole. He just ran. "If I made a mistake," he said, "I wanted to make it at full speed." With his explosive first step, he reached the line of scrimmage in a flash and let his instinct take over. Sometimes he slammed into his own blockers and gained little, but if they created any opening, he was often able to dart past defenders with a quick change of direction. He didn't waste a valuable split second with stutter-steps or side-to-side fakes. His shifts in direction were subtle yet powerful. When he was hit by a tackler, he thrilled spectators with his balance. He might switch the hand holding the ball, put one hand on the ground, spring back up, and, in a flash, dash downfield. He could plant a foot and change directions quickly to make tacklers miss, losing almost no speed. For high schoolers, it could seem unfair: You have him nailed, you lunge, and he's no longer there. "He was fluid, smooth," recalled Barnett. "Before you know it, he's in the end zone. Other runners might have been as fast but not as smooth."

He was so smooth that he didn't appear to be as fast as he was.

Ralph Starling, who spent years as the radio color commentator for Thomson High games, put it simply: "He had deceptive speed."

Barnett noted Ivery played at 185 pounds, large for a high school running back at the time. "He had amazing cutting ability, but he could run over you, too," Barnett said. A defender might hit Ivery square on and briefly knock him off his stride—until he regained his footing and quickly escaped the befuddled tackler. Ivery said that as the game progressed, as his cuts and shifts succeeded, his confidence grew; his timing improved.

In Ivery's junior basketball season, he opened the season with three straight double-doubles: 29 points/12 rebounds; 20/12; 28/12. The Bulldogs ended that season with a loss in the subregional playoffs, and at the spring sports banquet (with Ray Guy as guest speaker), Ivery was named MVP for the second straight year and the team's best rebounder.

Ivery sometimes puzzled people by sleeping before a contest—football, basketball, or track. Some mistook it for a lack of awareness, as if he didn't feel the pressure. Assistant principal Wilson, one of several Thomson men who felt a fatherly protectiveness toward Ivery, saw it differently. To him, it was a sign that Ivery needed the steadying influence of men like himself and Coach Williams, especially as college recruiters came calling.

"Other players would be joking around in the locker room," Wilson said, "but he would be sleeping on a clothes bag. They might be about to play for a tournament championship, but he'd be asleep. He divorced himself from that kind of pressure."

But Ivery had Wilson fooled. He wasn't immune to pressure—he felt it deeply. Inside, he was churning. He just didn't want anyone to see it.

"I was almost fearful every football game," he admitted. "The only thing I knew to do was sit back and relax."

Once he took that first hit, the nerves settled. After that, he was fine.

In the first game of Ivery's senior year, University of Georgia head coach Vince Dooley visited the locker room and spoke to the team at halftime. Officially, he addressed the entire squad, but everyone knew he was there to see Ivery—and for Ivery to see him.

That night, in a 29-0 mud-soaked victory, Ivery rushed for 133 yards and a touchdown. The following game, he piled on 155 more yards and another score. Opposing teams began crafting entire game plans to stop him. None succeeded.

He did it all—offense, defense, kickoff and punt returns, and sometimes even the kickoffs themselves. By the end of games, he was spent. His legend only grew.

"Can you imagine what he would have done if he had played only offense and ran with the ball 30 times a game?" Barnett mused.

Thomson fans watched in awe as he bounced off tacklers and tore down the field. In the next game, against Screven County, he racked up 189 rushing yards. But late in the game, with the score still tied 0-0, Ivery left the field with an injury.

Burton Kemp, a defensive lineman for Screven, watched him limp off and felt a flicker of hope—*Maybe we'll win without him on the field.*

He was disappointed. Twice.

First, Thomson scored without Ivery—but missed the extra point. That gave Screven a chance: If they could score a touchdown and make the kick, they'd win. But then Ivery jogged back onto the field to play defense. On the very next play, he intercepted a pass and returned it 40 yards for a touchdown. Game over.

Years later, when Ivery was playing in college and then the NFL, Burton Kemp never missed a chance to watch him on TV—just so he could say *I played against him.*

The next game, against Peach County, was a showdown of No. 44s and undefeated teams. Both Ivery and Peach County's tailback, Matthew Jackson, wore the number. Both were stars.

Peach County, ranked third in the state, rolled into Thomson in a chartered bus—unlike the ordinary school buses Thomson took to nearly every game. Jackson had racked up more total yards and more touchdowns than Ivery. Still, Ivery didn't give a speech, didn't rally the team. He just told himself, *I know I'm as good as he is.*

That would become a pattern for Ivery: quiet confidence, a steely inner monologue, and a fierce determination to prove it. *I'll show you.*

Throughout the game, the two backs traded highlight-reel plays. One would break off a long run, the other would answer. In the second quarter, Ivery scored twice. By the fourth, Thomson led 13-6—until Jackson returned a punt for a touchdown, tying the score.

With four minutes left, Thomson lined up to return a punt.

Sellers said they called a timeout. The coaches huddled to talk strategy—Peach County's defense had been tough all night. After some back-and-forth, offensive coordinator Johnny McCarty, a former player on Thomson's 1967 state championship team, turned to Ivery and said, "To win this game, you're going to have to run the punt back for a touchdown."

"I'll do it," Ivery replied.

Sellers wasn't so sure. It felt like they were betting the season on a longshot. *Oh my god,* he thought, *we're in trouble.*

In the huddle, P. D. Adams looked at Ivery and said, "We're running out of time. We got to do something."

When the punt came, Ivery caught it. "I tried to block for him," Adams said, "but he blew right past me. He could stop, change direction, and accelerate like nothing I'd ever seen."

Ivery returned the punt 55 yards for the game-winning touchdown. Thomson won, 20-13.

Sellers recalled, "I looked at Johnny and he looked at me. Eddie Lee made the damnedest run I've ever seen."

After the game, one of the Peach County coaches said Ivery was the best player he had ever seen. According to Barnett, in an interview for his book on the history of Thomson High football, that same coach spent years asking himself *Why did we punt to him?*

Ivery finished the night with 128 rushing yards and all three of Thomson's touchdowns. A fourth was called back on a penalty. In what had become a routine announcement, he was named Player of the Week.

At 4-0 and ranked among the state's top 20, the Bulldogs seemed poised to restore Thomson's championship tradition. Fans attended games to watch Ivery and see the team vie for their first title in six years. In the next game, however, they lost 26-7 to the highly ranked Statesboro. Ivery once again starred; he scored a touchdown and recorded a 60-yard run from scrimmage. Barnett noted that once victory was out of reach, Ivery cried as he played, "but he still ran over people" and smashed into defenders instead of safely running out of bounds. During that game, Charlie Winslette, the assistant coach for a different school, scouted the team but later stated in an interview that he was so bedazzled by Ivery's running that he hardly wrote anything down and confessed to his head coach that his scouting report was poor. He said,

"I got caught up in watching the great Eddie Lee Ivery run with the football to the point my scouting report was not very good."

They lost again—21-19 to Cedar Shoals, a team with three future UGA starters—but Ivery ran wild. He racked up 204 yards, averaging 12 per carry, and scored all three Thomson touchdowns: runs of 63 and 57 yards, plus a 20-yard reception. A potential game-winning field goal was blocked.

Then came another loss, dropping their record to 4-3. Championship hopes faded. Ivery still delivered—162 yards and both of Thomson's touchdowns—but it wasn't enough.

They bounced back to win the next two games, with Ivery once again leading the way. The regular season wrapped up at home against a tough Swainsboro squad.

Ivery's final game began as a disaster. At halftime, Thomson trailed 27-0. One Swainsboro touchdown had come off an Ivery fumble. Thomson fans sat in stunned silence while the Swainsboro crowd was confident, relaxed. Among them was junior Tommy Herrington—an anomaly in small-town Georgia. While most around him cheered for the Bulldogs, Herrington was a Georgia Tech fan, like his father and grandfather before him. In a few weeks, he'd be thrilled to hear where Ivery would play college football. But for now, he celebrated that Swainsboro had shut Ivery down and was cruising toward victory.

That would change quickly.

Ivery emerged from the locker room with a fire in his eyes. *I will not go out a loser*, he told himself.

He scored his first touchdown on an electrifying 55-yard run that showcased every bit of his extraordinary talent. He bulldozed through two tacklers, bounced outside into a swarm of defenders, then reversed field with fluid precision. He cut back to the middle, broke free, and sprinted to the end zone.

On drives that followed, Ivery gained tough first-down yardage on third- and fourth-down plays. When they seemed doomed to give the ball back to Swainsboro, Ivery muscled past the first-down marker.

Frenzied Thomson fans came alive, roaring with each play, fueled by the rising hope of every sports fan's dream: a dramatic comeback win.

In the stands, Herrington and the Swainsboro faithful began to squirm. *We shut him down in the first half*, Herrington thought. *Now we can't stop him.*

Late in the fourth quarter, Thomson mounted a 94-yard drive. Ivery converted one third down and two tense, possibly game-ending, fourth downs. A teammate punched in the touchdown. Ivery followed with a 2-point conversion. Suddenly, the score was 27-21. One more touchdown could win it.

Thomson's defense held. Swainsboro was forced to punt. Ivery and the offense took the field. They were driving—momentum on their side—when time ran out. One Ivery run away from a miracle finish.

Reflecting later, Barnett said, "He could get so determined." Jerry Ivery said that during that game, his cousin looked "possessed."

It was classic Eddie Lee. He played with heart and pride, mustering every ounce of his country strength and competitive fire—not just for himself, but for the fans who believed in him. He hated losing. He hated letting them down.

Herrington admitted that, over the years, whenever he remembered that game and Ivery's heroics, he had to remind himself: *Swainsboro won.* "I was so taken by how good he was," he said, "that I almost felt like we lost."

Ivery finished the season with 1,710 rushing yards on 181 carries—an astounding 9.5 yards per carry. He scored 19 touchdowns and nabbed five interceptions, two of which were returned for touchdowns. When reporters asked about his accomplishments, he always credited his offensive line. He piled up awards: once again named the team's Most Valuable Player and Best Offensive Back, selected for the All-Southern Georgia team, recognized as a Georgia All-State football player, High School All-American, and Player of the Year in the Central Savannah River Area (their region). He was also named to the *Atlanta Journal* Prep Honor Roll and named football team captain during his junior and senior years. He set the school record for most rushing yards in a season. In his senior year, he was the basketball team's top scorer, a regional winner in track, and senior class president. The school yearbook shows Ivery, muscular and sleek, beside his trophies, wearing his favorite multicolored plaid pants and wide, patterned tie. After the final football game, assistant coach Dale Ricks kept Ivery's jersey as a souvenir.

In the final stretch of his senior basketball season, Ivery lit up the scoreboard: 31 points in a double-overtime thriller, 34 in the next game, 23 in the regular season finale, and 28 in a regional playoff loss. At the spring sports banquet, he once again took home MVP and Best Rebounder honors for basketball—and was also named Most Outstanding in track and field.

He was selected to play in the North vs. South Georgia All-Star football game in Atlanta. Initially, coaches told Ivery he'd be playing fullback, with William Andrews—the state's top college prospect, who would go on to star at Auburn and with the Atlanta Falcons—slotted in at tailback. Ivery was disappointed. But he didn't complain. He figured he'd just do his job and block the best he could.

Then Andrews injured his ankle in practice, and Ivery was moved to tailback.

He didn't say anything, but he thought it: *I'll show you.*

In the first half, the North team held him in check. But in the second, he broke loose. His signature moment came on a dazzling 47-yard touchdown run. He broke two tackles, nearly went down, steadied himself with one hand on the turf, then sprang back to his feet and raced to the end zone.

A reporter later described it as a "twisting, bobbing 47-yard scamper."

That touchdown—and the extra point by future Georgia Tech teammate Don Bessillieu—gave the South the final margin in a 21-20 win.

Some Thomson fans in the Atlanta stands overheard a man in front of them turn in disbelief and say, "How did Thomson lose a game with that guy on the team?"

Also watching that run—up close, from the ground—was Ivery's future Georgia Tech teammate, Tom Daniel, who was playing defensive end for the opposing team. Daniel had beaten his man and thought he had Ivery nailed.

"I thought, 'I got him. I see him,'" Daniel recalled. "And the next thing I know, I'm sitting on the ground watching No. 44 scamper down the field. I came up with total air. I didn't touch him—and I thought I had him dead to rights."

Then, watching Ivery disappear into the distance, Daniel had one final thought: "I'm glad he's going to be on my team."

Ivery rushed for 110 of the South's 131 total yards on the ground and was named Most Valuable Player of the game. But when he received the MVP trophy, it bore the name of a quarterback—who ended up being named Best Offensive Player.

Ivery suspected that after his quiet first half, officials had decided on the award at halftime, then changed their decision after his explosive second half. He was told the engraving was an error, that he would receive the proper trophy later, but he never did.

One reporter described Ivery as "a streak from Thomson," and told Georgia Tech fans, "Smile, you Yellow Jackets, for he'll be running for you the next four years."

That Ivery wound up at Tech was no accident. It was the result of relentless, tactically savvy recruiting by one assistant coach—and, at the last minute, a bit of well-timed chicanery.

Chapter 3

Bulldog or Yellow Jacket?

East Carolina University, a mid-major football program, wrote Ivery first. He excitedly filled out their questionnaire and returned it. It didn't occur to him that other colleges would be interested. Then, a letter arrived from Albany State University, a predominantly African American school in South Georgia. He showed the letter to family and friends and began to think he might, unlike anyone else in his family, attend college. As he heard more praise and left more tacklers in his wake, he pictured himself on a college field and dared to dream of playing with the unfathomably rich athletes in the NFL. He watched pro players on television and wondered if he could join them: the Dallas Cowboys' Calvin Hill gliding downfield, smoothly hurdling a grasping tackler; dynamic Miami Dolphins' Mercury Morris speeding across the turf, legs churning; O. J. Simpson, almost untouchable, of the Buffalo Bills. *Could that be me?*

Inevitably, successful football programs took notice. Letters arrived. Recruiters showed up. The principal at Thomson High assured them that Ivery was "a gentleman," "100 percent cooperative," and well-regarded by his teachers.

Ivery narrowed his options to the two biggest schools in the state: the University of Georgia Bulldogs and the Georgia Tech Yellow Jackets.

In the early 1970s, coaches and boosters could make unlimited visits. Technically, recruits couldn't be paid or given gifts—but with so many people involved and so few restrictions, violations were easy to commit and hard to catch. The NCAA's oversight was limited, and everyone knew it.

In Ivery's sophomore year, his first year on the varsity football team, Thomson assistant coach Tommy Carmichael, a Georgia Tech graduate, called Tech assistant coach Dick Bestwick and told him Ivery "has size, balance, running ability. *Everything* you want in a running back." Bestwick said they didn't recruit sophomores at Tech, so he would look at Ivery the next year.

"Next year, you'll be too late," Carmichael chided him.

Bestwick insisted Tech didn't recruit sophomores. Three weeks later, Bestwick was in a small town nine miles from Thomson to watch film of a different player, and Ivery happened to be in the game. Stunned, Bestwick watched the sophomore bedevil defenders. He promptly called Carmichael and said, "I'll be there in 15 minutes." Bestwick drove to Thomson, Carmichael introduced him to Ivery, and a two-year courtship began.

Tech head coach Pepper Rodgers eventually made his pitch to Ivery, but Bestwick was assigned the long, stressful, intricate task of discerning what approach would win over this enormously talented, likeable, impressionable athlete—one with no real parental influence. Rodgers said the head coach "closes the sale" after the assistant coach sells the player on the school and the head coach. Bestwick's job was to convince Ivery that Tech was the best fit for him and that no one but Rodgers would do as his coach.

Two assistants from UGA began visiting Ivery, who was starstruck. He thought, "Wow, dang, Georgia wants *me!*" UGA really wanted him. Dooley recognized Ivery's gifts and grit, his versatility, his explosive acceleration. (He spoke UGA heresy by saying years later that while Herschel Walker was faster and stronger, overall, as a running back, Ivery had more skills. He said, "Eddie Lee could stop and start and do a lot more things than Herschel.") As in most small Georgia towns, Thomson's football fans almost all rooted for UGA. Tech fans were sparse. A favored UGA recruit carried immense prestige. Students and adults across Thomson began smiling at Ivery, slapping him on the back. Thomson had the same mascot as UGA, so many said, "I know you're going to UGA, and you'll still be a Bulldog!" All the town's prominent families were Georgia supporters, and no Thomson football player had ever gone to Tech. The idea of a top talent choosing Tech over UGA was considered ludicrous.

For an insecure boy, ashamed of his family's poverty and lifted by the confidence football had given him, the Georgia pressure was enormous—and effective. The adoration he felt would only multiply—amplified by tens of thousands of screaming fans at Sanford Stadium—if he starred for UGA, whose support stretched far beyond tiny Thomson. He was told that a Georgia star gained personal contacts that would benefit him for life. Tech could boast about the prestige of its degree, but it couldn't match Georgia's reach or its passionate loyalty. Ivery loved the attention, but his insecurity sat just beneath the surface. When someone smiled and mentioned his inevitable enrollment at UGA, he felt happy. But when he allowed himself to think seriously about Tech, he was gripped by the fear of letting down the people who had cheered him on. Bennie Mae said, "He told me the town loved him so much he didn't want to disappoint nobody."

One day, McDuffie County Sheriff William Swan pulled up in his cruiser and picked up Ivery at his house. He said he wanted to take him to meet Coach Dooley. They drove to the county courthouse, fronted by a monument to Confederate soldiers killed in combat. Inside, Ivery met Thomson mayor Robert E. Knox, Sr., Dooley, and district attorney Kenneth Goolsby. While Dooley talked up the University of Georgia, Ivery thought, "Look at these important White people wanting to spend time with me." That, of course, was the intended effect. Ivery committed to play for UGA, a decision that momentarily quieted his inner conflict. But later, as he reflected, something about it unsettled him. Given the long Southern history of White authority figures shaping the lives of Black youth—through coercion, overt or implied—he couldn't help but wonder if he had been subtly intimidated. A small-town White sheriff driving a Black teenager to a courthouse meeting with a White prosecutor sent a clear message: the law wants you to do something.

Ivery continued visiting other schools: the University of South Carolina, the University of Alabama, and Florida State. South Carolina appealed to him because his childhood friend Grant played there. Florida State went big—they sent a helicopter. It was Ivery's first ride.

"Have you piloted a helicopter?" the pilot asked.

"No, ma'am," he said.

"Just take hold of this," she replied. Ivery thought, "Wow, I'm a co-pilot the first time I fly in a helicopter."

When Ivery visited UGA, Grant—home for Thanksgiving—tagged along. They attended the UGA vs. Tech game. (On a cold, muddy field, David Sims scored twice and rushed for 113 yards, leading Tech to a 34-14 upset. Both teams finished a middling 6-5, but Tech fans were ecstatic.) Though Ivery was there as a UGA guest, Grant—who had spent years with him playing sports on Cherokee lawns, sweating through school days, and crashing overnight in each other's homes—noticed something. When Tech made a good play, Ivery reacted. It was subtle, but Grant caught it.

"Eddie Lee's going to Georgia Tech," he later told his brother. "He's cheering for Tech in the middle of all these Georgia fans." One factor pulling Ivery toward UGA was Dooley's promise he could also play varsity basketball. But Ivery later said he felt little personal connection with UGA's players or coaches during that visit. Still, the pull of Georgia was powerful.

Ivery said there was little cheating involved in securing a commitment from him—some of it more implied than offered. He mentioned that UGA assistant coaches handed him a business card for an Athens sports clothing store, suggesting he could take it to the store and get whatever he wanted. Ivery's buddies had told him that college players received cars and suitcases full of money, so he told them he wanted a car. He said later that he can assure everyone he wasn't offered a car or money because had he been, he would have accepted. He was *waiting* for someone to offer him something. He recalled that the UGA coaches "said something vague about a '72 Corvette," but they didn't say he would receive a car. They didn't deny it, either. His aunt Naomi said their former landlord, Sheik Hawes, dropped by her house and offered

$100 if he would attend UGA. Thomson assistant coach Ricks recounted seeing a South Carolina booster tell Ivery in the locker room, "We take care of our players" as he thumbed through a wad of $100 bills. "I had never seen one of *those* before," Ivery said. A rumor circulated (and still exists) that a UGA booster offered a fast-food franchise to Ivery's Uncle Nether if he chose UGA, but his family denied that the offer was made.

Classmates, coaches, even adults who had never spoken to Ivery—most of whom didn't know Georgia Tech was even in the running—passionately wanted him to take his remarkable skills to UGA. He loved the attention, but the pressure simmered just beneath the surface. He knew there was a real chance he might choose Tech. As signing day approached, it seemed like every day someone reminded him they were sure he'd be a Bulldog. The confidence in their voices carried an unspoken message: *We know you won't let us down.*

Over and over, Ivery heard the same questions: "Where are you going to college?" quickly followed by, "It's UGA, right?" Barnett recalled, "We just about couldn't go to PE class without a Georgia booster coming by." His coaches were constantly handed notes from people who wanted to speak with Ivery—boosters, fans, supporters. His reputation as a local hero exploded. Through the summer and fall of 1974, no one in Thomson drew more attention. The kid from Cherokee was suddenly the most talked-about figure in town. His neighbors were delighted by the steady stream of people making their way down their street hoping to influence the young star.

This should have been an exhilarating experience, as multitudes seemed to love him and clamored for him to be on their team, but years later Ivery sighed and recalled, "It was the worst time of my life." The only way he could let all these people down? Choose Georgia Tech.

Rodgers made his closing pitch after Bestwick's dogged efforts when he showed up to shoot baskets a week before signing day. They played a game of H-O-R-S-E, which Ivery won. (Rodgers was a very good high school basketball player, so who knows if he lost intentionally?) Ivery was impressed that Rodgers seemed like "a grown man acting like a kid. He was funny, told good stories. I fell in love with that. When the head man comes to visit, it makes you feel important, but he didn't act like a head man. I could tell he was a players' coach." Rodgers was gregarious, exuberant, hilarious, a natural salesman, and an expressive, arm-waving storyteller who won over Ivery. A few days later, Dooley visited, and he seemed like a distant authority figure. (Why pour on the charm? Ivery had already told him he was headed to UGA.)

Experienced recruiters know how to determine who most influences an athlete's choice. For many, it is their parents; for some, a trusted relative. UGA coaches were following this typically successful approach. Ivery, however, had no father around. His mother and grandmother were oblivious to the recruiting saga. His Aunt Naomi and Uncle Nether, who supported his family and disciplined him when necessary, would seem to be key, but they left the decision to him. Naomi later said she favored UGA only because it was closer and she could attend more games but kept that to herself. Bennie Mae said they didn't want her brother to feel pressured by family. Uncle Austin Ivery advised him to do what he truly wanted, not what others wanted: *If you let people influence you now, they'll do it all your life.* Wise advice, but Austin was in the Army and had little influence on Ivery. Jerry, by then also in the Army, said people asked where his cousin was going. Jerry had to tell them that he didn't know.

Once, Tech running back David Sims and another player drove to Thomson to recruit Ivery, and Ivery made sure he met them at the school so they wouldn't see his house.

Recruiting African American athletes to predominantly White colleges in the South was still a relatively new development, and many Black families remained wary. Were the educational promises real? Although Ivery noted that he saw more Black athletes at UGA than at Tech, many of the Black adults in Thomson who held influence over him remained skeptical of Georgia.

While UGA supporters—mostly White—grinned, slapped him

on the back, and assumed he was Athens-bound, Thomson's Black community viewed the situation differently. "UGA didn't rate too high among Blacks here," Sampson said. "No Black athlete had distinguished himself at UGA."

For many, the question lingered: Why should Ivery attend the state's flagship public university, which, in the minds of many Black Georgians, represented, *more than any other college*, the society that had yet to prove itself committed to equality? UGA, they felt, shouldn't just *admit* Black athletes. It should *lead* in demonstrating equal opportunity. So far, many saw little evidence of that.

The story of Charlayne Hunter (later Hunter-Gault) being denied admission to UGA because she was Black was still fresh in many minds. It had been only a little over a decade since she'd sued for the right to enroll. That legacy lingered. Bestwick said he was told that one of Ivery's uncles had heard Dooley say on television that African Americans would never play for Georgia. Whether the story was accurate or not, it reflected the kind of talk that circulated among skeptical Black Georgians.

Wilson believed that the prevailing mindset among coaches at major Southern programs was simple and unsettling: Black players were wanted because they could run—they're mean, agile, and hostile. But what would happen when a Black player got hurt? Had a bad year? Wilson feared coaches would discard him rather than support him through a full college education. He wanted Ivery at a school that was clearly committed to seeing him graduate. Bestwick repeatedly made that pledge to everyone in Ivery's orbit.

Ivery said his coaches didn't push him toward any particular school. They told him to choose the one where he'd be happy and get a good education. Of head football coach Red Bullock—widely known as a "Georgia guy"—Ivery said, "I sensed he favored Tech, but he didn't say." Ivery's hunch was right. Bestwick had convinced Bullock that Tech was the best fit, and Bullock quietly helped Williams, Wilson, and Bestwick steer him in that direction. These men decided which school was best for him—and then shaped the recruitment to make it happen. Bestwick cultivated relationships with Ivery's uncles and grew concerned when he heard about UGA supporters giving gifts to family members. But in the end, it wasn't gifts that swayed Ivery. It was his coaches, an assistant principal, a well-executed campus visit—and a little behind-the-scenes maneuvering.

While Georgia's recruiters focused on Ivery's extended family, only Bestwick recognized the two men who mattered most: Williams and Wilson. These were the men who saw him nearly every day, who cared deeply about Thomson's Black youth, and who felt a strong, paternal instinct to protect him. They'd seen kids from backgrounds like Ivery's take wrong turns. They wanted to make sure the good-natured, big-hearted Eddie Lee Ivery didn't become one of them.

Wilson's concern came from personal experience. He had grown up in a community much like Cherokee. After graduating from McDuffie County Training School, an anonymous donor paid for his tuition at nearby Paine College. To this day, he has never learned who that person was. "If not for that donor," he said, "I probably would not have finished college, so I always felt a connection with Thomson. I felt I owed something to other boys and girls." But he also knew the obstacles young Black men faced. When he graduated from college in 1952, the same bank that had funneled the donor's money to him wouldn't extend a small loan—even though he had a degree and a job.

Wilson was struck by Ivery's humility. "If he scored several touchdowns on Friday," he said, "he was on time for class on Monday, and you wouldn't know he had scored several touchdowns." To illustrate Ivery's character, Wilson recalled arranging a part-time job for him, along with access to a car to get to and from work. Ivery, he said, turned it down—he didn't want Wilson to sacrifice on his behalf. "Not many 17-year-olds would give that up," Wilson said. (Ivery didn't remember the offer and scoffed at the idea that he would've declined a car.)

Wilson also said he was never offered anything by anyone representing Tech in exchange for pushing Ivery that way. "People know I'm not that kind of person," he said. And even if he had been, Wilson added, reflecting a deep skepticism of UGA, "it would have been simple to go to the other side. I would have been on the easy, winning side."

Bestwick made a point of sharing his own background with Wilson—growing up in a lower working-class family, wearing hand-me-down clothes. His father, a seventh-grade dropout, worked in a mill. When Bestwick visited Ivery's small cinderblock house with the tin roof that baked in the summer heat, he said he felt at home. He considered himself a social activist, someone who helped the downtrodden. "I'm a coach you can come to with a problem," he told his players. Williams and Wilson believed that was exactly the kind of coach Ivery needed—someone who sincerely cared for him and didn't see him as just a football player to be used.

Bestwick didn't open his pitch by talking about Georgia Tech. He started by asking Ivery what he needed from a school. Meanwhile, Wilson heard rumors that UGA alumni were throwing parties for Ivery's relatives—though those involved denied it. Still, Wilson had made up his mind. Ivery should go, he said, "where I felt he'd get the best for him, knowing him as I did. I was looking out for him, not my own preferences." Of UGA, Wilson added, "I thought maybe they saw him only as a 200-pound piece of meat. They didn't seem concerned about him as a whole person. I don't think he would have made it four years at Georgia. If a piece of meat gets a little stale, you throw it out."

Bennie Mae also felt her brother had a more genuine connection with Tech. "Georgia guys would take us to dinner to impress us," she said. "They invited some of us in the family to a big dinner in Athens. But when Bestwick called me, he was so nice, more like family, caring. He was more relatable to how a family ought to be. He saw how we were a caring family. I didn't feel that with UGA." The town was filled with Georgia fans, she said; "but I thought if Eddie Lee gets hurt, would they throw him out to pasture? I didn't feel that way with Georgia Tech."

When Ivery visited Georgia Tech, his hosts—David Sims, Rudy Allen, and Lucius Sanford—were both compassionate and perceptive. They tailored their approach based on their own experiences and a clear understanding of Ivery's likely concerns. They knew Atlanta might feel overwhelming and that a predominantly White university could seem intimidating. They told him, "You're being taken out on a bigger budget than most recruits, and you're hosted by three players, not one, and we're starters. Pepper must really want you."

A highly recruited athlete, said Sanford—who would go on to play in the NFL for the Buffalo Bills and later serve as Tech's director of student athletic development—encounters many "firsts." For Sanford, a native of Atlanta, it was his first time traveling to the Midwest and experiencing frigid weather during a visit to the University of Nebraska. For Ivery, it was his first time in a big city and his first time eating in a nice restaurant.

Sims and Sanford had been instructed to treat Ivery to the best. "David and I knew we'd get a nice meal out of that visit," Sanford said. Food, he added, was crucial to the experience. "Every two hours you get food put in front of you," Sanford explained. "They serve you a nice breakfast, then later a snack, then lunch, then another snack, then a nice dinner." One dinner was at a seafood restaurant, a first for Ivery, who rarely ate out. "I always order chicken," he said. They encouraged him to try the lobster. When it arrived, he picked it up and bit into the shell. Without embarrassing him, they showed him how to use the shell crackers. "The last thing you want a recruit to feel," Sims said, "is like he doesn't belong." They corrected him gently, in a way that made him feel at ease.

Sanford understood Ivery's hesitation—because he'd once had the same concerns. When Tech recruited him, Sanford had come prepared with detailed questions he and his high school coach had developed, covering athletics, academics, and the environment for Black students. At first, he was only interested in northern schools, which he believed might be less racist. But he also reached out to Eddie McAshan, Tech's first Black football recruit, whose career had ended controversially.

"My ultimate question to him, and my decision hinged on this," Sanford said, "was, 'Would you do it again?' He thought hard about it and said he would. He said some mistakes were his and some were the school's."

Their honest, thoughtful approach worked. "They put it to me straight," Ivery said. "I could tell they were shooting me no crap. Their honesty jumped out at me." They acknowledged Tech's late start in recruiting Black players but emphasized that the school was a good fit for him—and that its tutoring program was strong. Sims told him his best friend had attended UGA but hadn't played. "They won't treat you like that here," Sims assured him.

They highlighted Tech's academic prestige and professional network. A degree from Georgia Tech, they said, carried weight. Rodgers had built connections with Atlanta's political and business leaders and introduced them to Black players. They described him as a disciplinarian, serious about returning Tech football to national prominence, but also someone who wanted his players to enjoy the experience. Sanford recalled Rodgers once telling an assistant coach that unless he taught Sanford how to do a forward roll—essentially a somersault—he wouldn't be allowed to play. Rodgers sometimes had players perform the stunt as they ran onto the field, just for laughs.

They also took Ivery to the "Black house," where the African American Association at Tech hosted parties. He saw Black students at ease, having fun, feeling at home—even at a predominantly White school. Tech offensive lineman Roy "Sugar Bear" Simmons later wrote, "Those parties used to rock!" They were "all-out blasts," packed with sharp-looking students from Tech and the nearby Black colleges. Rodgers, they said, had made Tech a welcoming place for Black athletes.

According to Atlanta sports columnist Furman Bisher, some Tech supporters weren't thrilled. "I heard those comments around town," Bisher said, referring to concerns that Rodgers was recruiting too many Black players. Bestwick remembered a turning point. "Once Pepper came, that whole dynamic changed," he said. "I went from never having recruited any Black youngsters to Tech to where I recruited virtually all Black youngsters."

Bestwick returned to Thomson again and again—more times than he could remember. He ate barbecue, played golf and gin rummy at Belle Meade Country Club, visited with Ivery and his family, watched practices and games, and spent time with anyone who might influence the decision. He even made trips to visit Ivery's uncles, one in Albany, Georgia, and another in Miami, Florida. When Wilson ran for mayor of Thomson in 1974—against none other than E. W. Hawes—Bestwick donated 25 dollars to his campaign. (He emphasized the money came from him, not from Georgia Tech.) Wilson pointed out to voters that many of the homes Hawes owned still lacked running water. Hawes won.

After one game, Bestwick was invited to a party at Coach Bullock's house. He was scheduled to be in Auburn, Alabama, the next morning but wouldn't miss the opportunity to spend time with Thomson's head coach. He stayed for the party, then drove through the night, arriving in Auburn at 5:00 a.m., exhausted. He'd been on the sideline—at the back of the end zone—when Ivery ran back a punt for a touchdown against Peach County. Ivery ran straight at him.

Two days before signing day, on a Thursday, the Thomson football team held its postseason banquet. Bullock—despite his UGA ties, quietly in Tech's corner—invited Bestwick to be the speaker. Bestwick would later call the invitation pivotal. Without it, he said, Ivery would have gone to Georgia.

After the banquet, Bestwick congratulated Ivery, put his arm around him, and said, "Son, we've spent a lot of time together over the last few years, and I know whatever decision you're going to make is going to be very difficult, but it's now time for you to decide."

Bestwick said Ivery tilted his head, looked down at the floor, and said, "Coach, I think I'm going to have to go up the road."

Bestwick froze. "Up the road" didn't mean west to Atlanta. "Up" meant north—to Athens. He realized then that Ivery had committed to UGA. Desperate, he responded quickly.

"Whatever you do, Eddie Lee," he said, "don't sign anything or agree to anything until I talk to you one more time."

"Yes sir," Ivery said.

Bestwick had a problem. Ivery had a home basketball game the next night—just one day before signing day—and an NCAA rule barred coaches from recruiting a student-athlete on the day of any athletic event in which that athlete participated, even if it wasn't the sport for which he was being recruited. Bestwick was out of time, and he knew it. How could he make one last appeal to Ivery when the rules said he couldn't say a word?

He turned to Williams. "Willie," he said, "Eddie Lee's going to Georgia."

Despite years of careful, relentless recruiting—despite Bestwick's connection with Ivery's real influencers, the memorable visit to Tech, the rapport with Coach Rodgers, and UGA's mediocre showing—he was losing him. The pressure to please Thomson, to join the state's powerhouse, to not disappoint anyone... it was winning.

Bestwick told the story to Williams, ending with, "And I don't think 'up the road' means Atlanta."

Williams disagreed. "I feel sure he's not going to UGA."

"He is right now," Bestwick replied.

But he wasn't leaving Thomson empty-handed. Not yet. He and Williams bought a six-pack of beer, went to Bestwick's hotel room, and called Wilson—at 11:00 p.m.

Bestwick laid it all out. Wilson told them to meet him at his office first thing the next morning. Bestwick was waiting by 7:45. He reminded Wilson of the NCAA restriction: he couldn't "really talk to him."

"But I need someone to talk to him," he said.

That morning, while Ivery was in class, a message arrived: report to Coach Williams's office. Ivery had already made his decision—he was going to UGA. A family cookout had been planned to celebrate. The weight of that decision, he thought, was behind him.

But when he stepped into the office, he saw Williams, Wilson, Bullock—and Bestwick.

According to Bestwick, Bullock left the room, not wanting to be associated with what would happen next. Williams, who would later die in a car crash in 1992, did not leave, and his comments were later relayed by Bestwick.

According to Bestwick, Wilson asked Ivery if he remembered that he had run for mayor.

"Yes sir."

"Do you know I was offered $10,000 to get out of that mayor's race?"

"No sir."

Bestwick remembered Ivery's eyes going wide with disbelief. Wilson said he could have paid off his mortgage—but he hadn't taken the deal.

"They quit buying and selling us over a hundred years ago," he told Ivery. "And that's one thing you ought to remember. Don't ever let anybody buy you. We're not to be bought and sold."

(Wilson later said he had indeed told Ivery not to let himself be bought or sold but denied ever being offered money to drop out of the race—and said he never claimed he was.)

Bestwick, overwhelmed, began to cry. Wilson left the room.

What could Bestwick say now? The NCAA rule still stood: no recruiting on the day of an athletic event involving the athlete. But he wasn't walking away without trying something, rule or not. Later, he admitted that what he did may have been a secondary violation, but at that moment, he wasn't thinking about violations. He was thinking about losing Ivery.

The two remembered the conversation differently. Bestwick's version was more restrained; Ivery's was more pointed—and raw.

Bestwick said he simply asked, "Let me ask you one question, son. Where do you really want to go to school?"

Ivery remembered more.

He remembered Bestwick, tears in his eyes, saying, "Those rednecks at Georgia don't care about you, except for your ability to play football. After that's over, they won't care about you. But at Tech, we care about you as a person. We want you to graduate at Tech."

That line stunned him, not because of the words, but because of who said them.

A White man.

(Bestwick later denied using the word "rednecks." "Nah," he said. "I wouldn't have said that." He was working for UGA at the time of the denial.)

Ivery looked at Williams. Williams didn't tell him what to do. He simply said it was his decision to live with—and that he should go where he'd be happiest.

Ivery thought about why he'd chosen Georgia. Mostly, it was because it felt like everyone else had already chosen it for him. But the Tech visit—the honesty, the connection, the sense of being seen for more than just his talent—stuck with him.

Something shifted.

"Coach," he said, "I always wanted to go to Georgia Tech."

Bestwick grabbed his hand, shook it, and exclaimed, "Then you're a Yellow Jacket!"

He turned to Williams. "Willie, Eddie Lee's handshake is his bond, isn't it?"

Williams nodded. "When Eddie Lee tells you something, that's what he's going to do."

Bestwick turned back to Ivery. "Then Eddie Lee, you're a Yellow Jacket!"

"Yes sir," Ivery said. They embraced—both crying.

"Great," Bestwick said. "You need to get back to class."

Bestwick left the room relieved, thinking the matter was settled, but Williams wasn't so sure.

"Where are you going to hide him?" he asked.

"Hide him?"

"If you don't," Williams warned, "they're going to get to him—

and take him away from you."

It wouldn't take much. One more conversation. One more appeal from the wrong person. In this kind of recruiting war, the last team to score wins. Time to run out the clock. Bestwick knew he couldn't hide Ivery, but Williams had an idea: He'd take Ivery home with him that night after the game.

Wilson said later that they thought if word got out that Ivery had chosen Tech, he might be bombarded with UGA appeals so they should "make him unavailable." Bestwick gave Williams the national letter of intent so Ivery could sign it the next day.

After the game, Williams told Ivery that football recruiters were in the stands and he didn't want them to bother him, so Ivery was coming with him. Williams opened a window in his office, and Ivery—still wearing his sweaty basketball uniform—grabbed his street clothes. They climbed out, hopped in Williams's car, and drove to his house.

The next day, Vince Dooley and an assistant drove to Thomson, letter of intent on the seat. UGA alumni and fans had fulfilled their roles, and Ivery was destined to wear UGA red and black.

"Eddie Lee liked UGA," Dooley recalled. "Of course, he liked everybody. You didn't have to do much selling with him. He was happy to be wherever you saw him. Happy as could be. He committed to me a couple of times."

During Ivery's visit to campus, he told Dooley everything was great. Georgia was where he wanted to go. They had even planned to meet at a restaurant—but Ivery never appeared.

Dooley drove around Thomson—to the school, to Ivery's house, to a basketball court where Ivery liked to play—but could not find him.

It sank in. They'd lost him.

Dooley and his assistant drove back to Athens with the unsigned letter.

Years later, Dooley still didn't know exactly what happened. He figured Bestwick had a stronger influence over Ivery's relatives, but he couldn't be sure.

"It's one of the unpleasant parts of recruiting," he said. "It's pleasant when they change their mind to come to you, but it's not a fun thing when you go there and you can't find him. But you take it as part of the business."

The signing took place that evening in a banquet room at Sophie's Restaurant, a place Ivery believed few Black people ever visited. (According to Barnett, however, Sophie's was one of the rare White-owned restaurants in the 1970s that welcomed Black customers. Barnett said UGA had also reserved a room there—but it, of course, was empty.)

According to Helen Williams, Coach Williams's widow, Ivery spent that Saturday at their home. She said her husband had called Ivery his "adopted son," and that Ivery often came to him for advice. "They were like two peas in a pod," she said. She remembered the Tech representatives as "not overbearing," especially in contrast to others. One school—clearly UGA, though she declined to name it—had taken Ivery for granted. "You're our boy," they implied. Bestwick, she said, took a different approach. He focused on what Ivery wanted from a school. She said his attitude was that of a parent who wanted what was best for the child—not for himself.

On Monday morning, in his 8:00 a.m. class, Ivery sat down and put his head on his desk. Barnett, though an avid UGA fan, greeted him and said he thought Ivery had made a good decision. Word had gotten out. But, Barnett recalled, Ivery looked like the unhappiest person he had ever seen. Emotionally drained and dreading a full day of facing classmates, Ivery replied, "You're the only one who thinks so." Some classmates turned on him. Whispers spread: "Eddie Lee won't make it at Tech. He's not smart enough." Some said it to his face. "You'll flunk," a few sneered.

I'll show you.

After Ivery's sudden decision, there were angry people around town who believed their beloved Georgia Bulldogs had him locked in. Years later, most accounts of that reaction were retold vaguely. "It was messy," Starling said, but he declined to name names or repeat what he'd heard.

One former high school teammate recalled, "Some of the older guys at the golf course went from saying Eddie Lee was a fine young Black man to, once he chose Tech, calling him a (n-word)." A former coach, nearly ready to share stories of harsh words from jilted Georgia fans, stopped short. "Don't put that in the book," he said. "I got to live with these people."

According to a former employee of Hawes—who had UGA season tickets and donated to the athletic department—Hawes said Ivery "totally broke his heart." The Iverys' former landlord, reluctantly, told Ivery he wished him well, then added with a pointed reference to Tech's fight song and its most famous major, "You better become a hell of an engineer."

Later, Ivery couldn't point to one clear reason why he chose Georgia Tech. It certainly wasn't for recent football glory. Tech had gone undefeated in 1928 to win a national title and had been a national power through the 1940s, playing in all four major bowls. Under Coach Bobby Dodd, they went 11-0-1 in 1951 and finished ranked fifth nationally. The next year they were 12-0 with six All-Americans, finishing second. In 1956, they went 10-1 and were ranked fifth again. But all that was long past.

Did Rodgers convince him he could still be a star, even in a wishbone offense that divided carries among four backs? Ivery said he hadn't really thought about that. What he did remember was the way he was treated on his visit. His hosts made him feel cared for. They were warm, attentive, and stuck by his side at gatherings. At other schools, he said, he often felt abandoned.

At Tech, he said, "I felt special."

Chapter 4

The Pepper Rodgers Show

Everyone called him "Pepper." Even his grandkids: "I don't want you calling me 'Grandpa.'"

In Rodgers's apartment near Washington, DC, when he was vice president of football operations for the city's NFL team, he displayed gleaming helmets of teams he coached in college and the United States Football League (USFL), including a University of Florida helmet signed by Steve Spurrier, who won a Heisman Trophy with Rodgers as quarterbacks coach. Spurrier was once Rodgers's assistant coach at Tech and had recently been hired as the Washington head coach. Rodgers, it was reported, was instrumental in bringing Spurrier to the team. "I like to think so," he confirmed, unexpectedly modest. On display on his wall were tap shoes and a tiny outfit he wore when, between the ages of three to five, he danced in the *Kiddie Review*, a popular Atlanta live variety show, at the downtown Lowe's Grand Theater (where *Gone with the Wind* premiered), and a framed picture of young Rodgers dancing. Above them, a picture of a young woman, her blonde hair blown straight back by a stream of air. "That's my wife," he said, "when she was the number one model in America." That's more like Pepper Rodgers.

He was a high school star in Atlanta in football (1949 state champs), basketball, and baseball. He played on some of Georgia Tech's best football teams, which went 32-2-2 over the three years he played. In 1951, he kicked the game-winning field goal to defeat Baylor University in the Orange Bowl. Before the ball reached the goalposts, he raised his arms to signal "Good." In 1952, he led Tech to an unbeaten 12-0 season and a share of the national championship. He threw a touchdown pass and kicked a field goal in a 24-7 Sugar Bowl victory over the University of Mississippi. The next year, he was Sugar

Bowl MVP after throwing three touchdown passes in a rout of West Virginia. In 2018, he was named to the Sugar Bowl Hall of Fame—the only player to throw for a touchdown, kick a field goal, and kick an extra point in Sugar Bowl games.

Drafted in the NFL's 25th round in 1954, he instead served five years in the Air Force, flying F-105 jets. After several assistant coaching stints, he became head coach at the University of Kansas, then the University of California at Los Angeles, and finally at Tech. At Kansas, he coached in the school's first major bowl in 20 years, was named conference Coach of the Year in 1967 and 1968, and in 1968 barely lost to No. 3 Penn State in the Orange Bowl, finishing the season ranked sixth.

UCLA enticed him from Lawrence to glitzy Los Angeles, where in his second year, the Bruins upset top-ranked, two-time defending champion Nebraska in the season opener, ending the Cornhuskers' 32-game winning streak. They finished 8-3, ranked 15th. In 1973, they were 9-2, had the nation's highest-scoring offense, and ended the season ranked 12th. They rushed for a school-record 400.3 yards per game, including 621 in a rout of Stanford. Rodgers flourished, charming stars with his smile, wit, and rollicking stories. UCLA was ideal for Rodgers—the Hollywood scene, media attention, recruiting pitches about luminaries and sunny beaches. He likely could have built a winning tradition, with his offense regularly leading the nation in yardage. His son Rick said years later, "It may have been his favorite place to coach."

With Tech's former star player now a star coach, his offense gobbling up yards and piling up points, his alma mater called him home. He loved Tech too much to say no. His son Kelly said, "He liked L.A. and the life, but he was a Tech man, and I don't see him turning down his dream job." He had grown up listening to Tech football on Saturday afternoons on the radio and sold peanuts at Tech home games. (For decades after his tenure at Tech, he tried to attend at least one Tech football game every season. Once, in his eighties, Rodgers attended a game in Virginia and afterwards met with Tech fans at a restaurant, where he enthusiastically led them in the Tech fight song—still the entertaining center of attention.)

Tech boosters envisioned national championship contention returning to Bobby Dodd Stadium. "Everybody was excited," Jim Bell said. "He had won at Kansas, and he killed other teams at UCLA" (59-13 over Stanford, 61-21 over Cal). Tech football had slogged through several down years, so, Bell said, "We were waiting for a savior," a coach who could lead a college with high academic standards back to greatness. They could brag about their smarts—and their football.

"He was creative," said Leo Benatar, a 1951 Tech graduate, longtime football fan, and booster. He became a fan at 15, when he sold Tech pins outside the stadium for fans to wear as they rooted for the home team. At halftime, he could go in for free and cheer with the crowd. Of Rodgers, he said, "He made football fun. He had some unusual, crazy plays. Sometimes they worked and sometimes they didn't, but it was fun."

Some players said Rodgers had a gift for seeing a player's potential and moving him to a new position. Offensive lineman Tom Daniel said he had been a lightweight defensive end but became a starting center. Ben Utt started as a linebacker but was converted to offensive guard and played eight years in the NFL in a position he had never imagined for himself. Players also said Rodgers knew how to motivate each player differently. Linebacker Reggie Wilkes said he had been a starter, but his junior year, Rodgers put him on the second team. Wilkes had planned to attend medical school after Tech, but Rodgers's tactic pushed him to work harder—and he went on to play 10 seasons in the NFL.

Daniel said Rodgers could casually plant a thought that would later bloom into a pep talk. "He was a gifted leader. He would say stuff like, 'We're going to run the ball. Let's see how many yards we can get today, see if we can break a record.' He knew how to motivate people in ways unique to the person he was talking to. But you didn't know you were getting motivated. You'd walk away thinking that's cool, then later think, 'Wait a minute; I think he's doing that on purpose.'" In that game, Tech rushed for 561 yards.

Utt also appreciated that Rodgers taught his players perspective. After a loss, Rodgers would say, "You're young, enjoy yourself—just as long as you don't embarrass Georgia Tech. No one will remember this game a hundred years from now anyway." Student trainer Tommy Herrington said that during one halftime, Rodgers—as usual—propped one elbow in the other palm, spun his glasses, and said, "Men, win or lose, Janet and I are going out for a nice dinner tonight." No rousing rhetoric. No tirades about effort, mistakes, or halftime adjustments.

Offensive lineman Kent Hill liked that Rodgers believed in team discipline through autonomy, not rigid control. "He didn't have a curfew," Hill said. "He wasn't on you every minute."

"He was not going to babysit you," Defensive back Lawrence Lowe added. "He expected you to learn the playbook and come back knowing it."

"We thought he was cool. He gave us the freedom to be good players, to be your own man," tight end Donnie Sewell said. "He created an image that players at other schools wished they had. A friend of mine went to Florida, and they had a curfew that kept them inside all night. Not Pepper."

"Pepper said we were old enough to do what is right," recalled quarterback Gary Lanier, "when to come in at night, what not to do, as long as we give 110 percent on the field." Running back Rodney Lee said Rodgers would sometimes tell players that if they were going to do something that might embarrass Tech, they shouldn't get caught.

"He didn't encourage it," Lee said, "but he said if you can't control yourself, don't get caught. So, he wouldn't have to take some action."

Some former players wondered whether the fun-loving Rodgers should have been stricter. "I was fortunate to have a coach as creative and flexible and forgiving as Pepper Rodgers," Daniel said. "I'm lucky I didn't have a tough coach who would squeeze all the fun out of it, but we might have won another game or two with that approach. I had an unbelievably good experience, but the lingering thought is we could have been better with more discipline."

Ivery had the same thought: "With all those NFL players, we should have competed for championships." His four-year backfield mate Bucky Shamburger said bluntly, "I totally regret not playing for a hard-ass, traditional coach and program."

Rodgers brought to Atlanta his magnetic personality and L.A. cool. Zipping around the city—sometimes even onto the practice field—in a convertible or on a motorcycle, he was criticized for drawing too much attention to himself. He once wrote that when a high school basketball teammate was injured, he (already a shoot-first guard) suggested a reporter ask how he would adjust. The reporter took the bait, and Rodgers replied, "I guess I'll have to shoot more."

Atlanta sports reporter I. J. Rosenberg wrote that if coaching were based on personality, Rodgers would never have lost. Rodgers admitted he couldn't sell Tech football—the program's last great season was 12 years in the past—and the facilities hadn't been updated since 1950. So, he sold himself. It came naturally.

"Pepper loved to talk about Pepper," Utt said. Raised in rural Vidalia, Georgia, Utt remembered Rodgers as one of the first celebrities he ever met. "He had *The Pepper Rodgers Show.* He had been in Hollywood." Celebrity was exactly the image Rodgers cultivated. The message was clear: *Come play for Pepper! You'll play for a fun, famous coach!* "Pepper Power" bumper stickers, billboards, T-shirts (some with his picture), and buttons soon appeared across Atlanta.

Rodgers loved to spread his mirth around. John Kramer, engineer and producer for Tech's radio broadcasts, said, "He was a free spirit—on top of the free spirit pile. He threw great parties. You'd see famous and infamous people there. He never stayed in a corner. He moved around the room visiting with everybody. I was just a radio guy with no real status, and he was up with the hoity-toity, but he made me feel like somebody."

Rodgers's autobiography, co-written with sports journalist Al Thomy, is breezy—full of funny anecdotes, snappy quips, folksy life lessons, and a healthy dose of self-deprecation. He didn't take himself too seriously, even when boasting. It wasn't *"Look how great I am."* It was more like, *"Look at what I did—can you believe I pulled this off?"*

He described himself as an innovator. "What I did in the seventies," he said, "would be no big deal now. On my TV show, I interviewed the opposing coach; I wired myself on the sidelines." He once coached an entire USFL season with nearly every offensive play called without a huddle, the quarterback making decisions at the line. That's routine now. He claimed to have invented the "Genghis Khan offense," in which all 11 offensive players were substituted at once.

Once, he brought comedian Nipsey Russell to practice for a motivational talk. He included women among the students who, during games, brought players water and towels. Tech fans had never seen that. Ivery chuckled at Rodgers's round, floppy bucket hat—what he called a "Gilligan's Island hat." "John McKay became known for wearing that kind of hat, and I wore it before he did," Rodgers insisted. "I was wearing a visor before Steve Spurrier."

Rodgers's son Kelly said that when he was a youngster, he would ask his father why he didn't go for a first down more often on fourth down. Rodgers explained that it wasn't always the right time to take the risk. When he was coaching in a college all-star game, he called a timeout on fourth down and asked little Kelly what he thought they should do. Kelly told him to go for it. According to Kelly, "It didn't work. They got hammered." After the game, a reporter asked Rodgers why he went for it, and, chuckling, he said, "You'll have to ask my son."

Before a game against Stanford, Rodgers told his players, "Men, the rest of your life, the Stanford man is going to have the best job, make the most money, and marry the most beautiful women. This is your last chance to knock him on his ass!"

While head coach at Kansas, Rodgers once disguised himself as a hippie during a player gathering. He pretended to be a singer, strummed a guitar, and sang a goofy song he had written. When the players finally realized who he was, they booed. Rodgers loved it. Decades later, when asked about the story, he sang the entire song spontaneously—and laughed heartily.

Rodgers sometimes brought recruits into his office and said, "Do you want me to go on about how great Georgia Tech is, or would you rather listen to Gladys Knight and the Pips?" As part of his recruiting routine, he occasionally referenced the 1974 movie *The Trial of Billy Jack*, in which he had a small role—thanks to his Hollywood friend Tom Laughlin, who played the lead. Rodgers portrayed a trooper who shoots the title character. He would reenact the scene, assigning roles to the recruit's family.

Rodgers brought a level of self-promotion that conservative Tech had never seen in a football coach. Longtime Tech booster Allen Potter had become a fan as a boy, when his Boy Scouts troop ushered at Tech football games for three years. In one 23-year stretch, he didn't miss a single home game. (He was late to one game, thanks to his brother's wedding.) "From a conservative Georgia viewpoint," Potter said, "he was over the top."

Rodgers wore loafers without socks. He wore no tie. He wore his hair in a perm (which some said looked too much like an Afro). After an upset victory over a highly ranked team, Rodgers's mother overheard someone in the stands say it had been a good game—but that he still didn't like her son's hair. Rodgers slung a book bag over his shoulder. (Was it a purse?) He rode a motorcycle. He was criticized for the jersey colors the players wore and the music they played in the locker room.

Atlanta sportscaster Beau Bock said Rodgers once had the team rehearse carrying him off the field—just in case they were inclined to do so, so they'd get it right.

Rodgers wanted to win games—and have fun doing it. His son Rick said, "He didn't think that was a contradiction. Football is a game, and you should enjoy playing. There are big stakes, but he sometimes liked to be silly."

Although some thought he joked around too much, Steve Hammond, who played for Rodgers on the USFL Memphis Showboats, said, "He's no clown. He's a good coach who likes to have some fun."

Ivery said Rodgers might seem like he wasn't paying attention at practice—but then he'd bark, "You hit the wrong hole!" or "Accelerate through the block!" Ivery would wonder how Rodgers even saw it.

Kent Hill had the same impression. "He looked lackadaisical in practice if he was sitting in the stands," Hill said, "but he knew football and worked us hard. He could see everything that happened in practice. He'd come down and explain things to us."

He raised a few hackles by divorcing his high-school-sweetheart-Atlanta-native wife and marrying a model. Rick Rodgers said,

> He left my mom and moved in with Livingston, a California girl with blonde hair. They wouldn't have given a shit about that at UCLA, but they did at Georgia Tech. I talked to enough people to know that was a festering little issue. When he came back to Tech, at least one billboard said, "Welcome back Judy and Pepper," so my mom was part of the deal. It was a pretty ugly, messy scene and divorce.

Scott Woerner, who starred at UGA as a defensive back and punt returner and later played in the NFL and USFL, said, "Pepper was crazy as hell. He could have been a stand-up comedian. He recruited me in '77, and in his office, he says, 'Have a seat,' and every chair had a case of Cokes or Frescas in it. There was no empty chair. I thought, 'Frescas? Do they still make them?' Out of all the coaches I met and played for, he was about half a bubble out, and I thought there's no way I'm going there."

Woerner's teammate Ricky McBride wasn't charmed by Rodgers either. Laughing, he said Rodgers tried too hard to be "hip and cool" to draw Black players. "That didn't attract my attention," he said, "him not being himself. Some enjoyed what he brought to the table, but I was not one of them."

Rodgers was generous in allowing reporters to interview players, and he provided a steady supply of quips to keep their writing lively.

Often unusually straightforward with reporters, he was accessible at practices and kept them laughing. After Tech upset Notre Dame, Rodgers said an opportunity like that was like being in the same room as a beautiful model. "You never know when you're going to be in the same room with her again," he said, "so you might as well ask her for a date. What have you got to lose?" About former players, he said, "Ex-players are like ex-girlfriends. You don't call them, but if you happen to see them, you be happy to see them." Former *Constitution* reporter Kelly Dude said Rodgers liked to say playfully, "Kelly, if my name wasn't Pepper Rodgers, I'd want it to be Kelly Dude." Directing his wit at himself, he quipped, "I proved everything a man can prove in coaching. I proved I could win with good players. I proved I couldn't with bad ones." Even during games, Rodgers's personality emerged. Fullback Ray Friday said Rodgers once told assistant coach Bud Casey, "I'm going to call the first play, and you call the next two. If we don't make a first down, you're fired."

He broke the rules for a coach's television show, which usually featured game highlights and commentary. ("Here, we see a good fake and a great block.") Since most games were not televised, fans wanted to see an Ivery run that had been excitedly described on the radio the day before. In some shows, he aired highlights and had players help him describe the action, but some episodes featured no game clips. If a Hollywood buddy were in town, he'd invite them onto the show. He interviewed Bob Hope (Rodgers's first show), Charlton Heston, Al Hirt, Burt Reynolds, Ronald Reagan, Andy Williams, and Evel Knievel. Comedian David Brenner cracked, "Why don't you play more Jewish kids?" In 1976, Rodgers featured presidential candidate Jimmy Carter, along with the Allman Brothers Band. He opened one show by singing the Tech fight song while standing on his head. Once, he showed clips of himself interviewing cheerleaders and beer-drinking fraternity guys. He showed film clips of sideline action (mainly him talking) and his halftime talks. One booster noted that *The Pepper Rodgers Show* promoted Tech because it attracted non-football fans. But fans who wanted to see game highlights—and a coach in coat and tie—were not amused.

When Julia Child was a guest on the show, Rodgers wore a full chef's outfit—including the tall, pleated toque hat—and opened with, "Welcome to the Georgia Tech training table." He introduced himself as "the main chef here." The show was amateurish, but he was charming and funny.

When Child mentioned wine as an ingredient in a chicken dish, Rodgers joked about serving wine to football players. He took a bite and said, "Come to Georgia Tech. You'll have good food." He claimed that after a loss, they chopped raw onions so they would cry. Child demonstrated how to chop onions, and he gave it a try—awkwardly—joking with the studio audience, who laughed. He and Child laughed throughout the segment, and at the end, he kissed her on the cheek. There were no football highlights.

One generous booster recalled going home after church to watch the very first episode of *The Pepper Rodgers Show*. Rodgers appeared in loafers, no tie or socks, and a shirt open at the collar—looking, to some viewers, a little too *mod*, as the term went in the seventies. It was the opposite of the always proper Bobby Dodd.

The booster's phone rang. It was his father, also a Tech donor.

"Is that our football coach?" the elder asked.

"Yes, Dad, he is."

"He might be your coach, but he's not mine. None of my money is going to Tech as long as he is the football coach. You can give your money, but I won't give mine."

On some mornings before a home game, Rodgers, unlike coaches whose minds seized on football every minute on game day, would ride his motorcycle to the stadium, jog three miles around the field, shower, then ride to the Silver Skillet for a traditional Southern breakfast. Everyone welcomed him with cheers. Sometimes his wife visited his office before a game, and they danced the bump to pop music. "Does Bear Bryant do this?" he would say. But Bear won games—and championships. Could funster Rodgers win at Tech?

Rodgers shepherded Tech through the 1970s racial integration of college football. He hired the school's first two Black coaches and, according to Sewell, brought in "the biggest Black recruiting class Tech had ever had. We were all big, tough, and cocky. We were fired up and ready to whip older players' asses because we wanted starting positions."

Defensive back Bernard Stover said Rodgers "was cool. He was too cool for some of the Tech alumni, but his main thing was, let's win. Black and White didn't matter to him."

Like many previously all-White Southern colleges, Tech had boosters who disliked seeing "too many" Black athletes on the field. Safety and place-kicker Don Bessillieu said that one day at practice, Rodgers showed him an anonymous letter the athletic department had received. It said Bessillieu's next kickoff would be his last. "I had sat down a white player who had been the kicker," Bessillieu said. "Pepper brought in Black players who could play and stay in school, and he put Georgia Tech back on the map, but some boosters didn't like too many Blacks on the team. Pepper asked me what I wanted to do, and I said I was going to play."

Rodney Lee recalled a similar moment. He said Rodgers once read aloud a letter from an alum, complaining that he was recruiting too many Black players—which, the writer claimed, threatened the school's academic standing. Like Bessillieu, Lee had grown up in a military family and attended racially diverse schools. Arriving at Georgia Tech, he said, Atlanta's racial dynamics were a "culture shock."

Rodgers, booster Jim Bell said, generated excitement. But with mannerisms and actions that many older, conservative boosters found un–Georgia Tech–like, he also alienated a good number of them. "The older alumni didn't get it," Bell said. "But Pepper made it rough on himself. He gave his critics opportunities."

He listed the usual litany of sins: divorcing a popular first wife (an Atlantan), buying a red and black convertible (UGA's colors) for his second wife, the hair, the motorcycle. Bell, a businessman, added, "If I hire people that I count on, I don't want them doing something risky. When Pepper bought the motorcycle, it didn't look smart. He was too important to us. People were saying, 'If he'll ride a motorcycle, what other dumb things will he do?'"

Former director of sports medicine Bill McDonald said the team typically stayed in an Atlanta hotel the Friday night before home games. One evening, the players gathered for a meeting—when most head coaches would give motivational talks or final strategy reminders. Rodgers didn't show.

"Finally, we found him in the lobby visiting with folks," McDonald said.

McDonald mentioned the meeting, and Rodgers, still enjoying the conversation, said they'd taught the team everything they needed during the week. Nothing more was necessary. McDonald relayed the message: "Go to your rooms. See you in the morning."

Bell said he and other boosters were told not to approach Rodgers before games unless he summoned them. "He was concentrating on remembering recruits' names," Bell said, "and he didn't want us to introduce family and risk confusing names." That was a reasonable concern—but it rankled boosters used to VIP treatment. *I give you money, and you won't speak to me?*

According to trainer Herrington, Rodgers baffled some Tech people when he approached Eastern Airlines about sponsoring *The Pepper Rodgers Show*, hoping to get more than what he received from Delta Airlines. In Atlanta, you didn't mess with Delta. No deal was made, but the overture made him again seem out of step with the Tech way.

When asked about troubles with alumni, Rodgers was known to reply dismissively, "Alums don't get you fired. They just drive you crazy. The players get you fired." Innovative, fun, charming, gregarious, lenient, entertaining, attentive, ambitious—whatever labels a coach attracts, what matters is winning. In Rodgers's case: Can a coach have this much fun and succeed? Eventually, like nearly all coaches, he was fired for not winning enough. Potter said, "His *act*—he was a flamboyant show-off—wore thin. Of course, if he were winning, it would have been fine. We had some big wins—and some disappointing losses."

John Hunsinger, who owned a real estate business in Atlanta, played for Dodd in the 1950s and was named a 1954 First Team Academic All-American. He and Rodgers were on the 1952 team that won the Orange Bowl—back when, he said, players *complained* that they had to play a game during the holiday break. His conference room was generously decorated with football memorabilia, art books, charity awards, and pictures of political figures. One large check reproduction indicated his company donated $545,000 to a children's hospital. He played junior high, high school, and college football with Rodgers. They played in the high school band together. He referred to the athletic department as "we" and was once asked to introduce a new head football coach at an alumni meeting. "The Tech man," Hunsinger said, "on game day might work in the morning, go to brunch, then the game, then go back to work. In Athens, they start getting ready for the game on Friday afternoon, socialize that night, go to breakfast and lunch with other fans, go to the game, then go to the country club." He said some alumni have outsize expectations for sports, that "*anyone* will want to come to Tech, but academics is number one, not sports. There's no place to hide, academically."

"Pepper was always controversial," Hunsinger said. He recalled Rodgers signaling "good" before the Orange Bowl game-winner even split the uprights. "You didn't do that kind of thing back then."

Of Georgia Tech, Hunsinger said, "We're crewcut people, conservative Democrats. We build bridges that don't fall. We're the only engineering school with a Division I-A sports program. He divorced at a young age. He came here with a perm in his hair and a book bag over his shoulder. That was OK in Los Angeles, but you didn't do that in Atlanta if you were heterosexual."

At first, Rodgers seemed to bring big-time football back to Atlanta. In his first season, Tech dominated rival UGA, 34-14. The next year, they finished 7-4, and the offense piled up massive yardage. But in six seasons, Rodgers lost to UGA four times. He posted four winning seasons—more than his two predecessors—but fell short of Pepper-

Rodgers-hype expectations. Blame the facilities or Tech's academic demands, but he didn't win enough. In 1979, Tech went 4-6-1, and Rodgers's middling overall record (34-31-2), combined with strained relations with alumni, cost him the job.

Rick Rodgers said his father realized soon after returning to Tech that it was a mistake—that he'd had a romanticized view of the school. Rick continued,

> It dawned on him early on that there was a significant number of that old-line Southern group that didn't like anything beyond the Bobby Dodd type. They never liked him, and he knew it. Though he loved Tech. It's one thing if he had been fired at UCLA, but at Tech he was still so emotionally invested. He was a Georgia Tech guy, and to be fired by Tech—he felt pretty embarrassed and humiliated.

Maybe he should have stayed in Los Angeles, but it's hard to imagine his life feeling complete without giving Tech a try, regardless of how it ended.

Let go with two years left on his contract, Rodgers sued his alma mater—the school he had left glittery Hollywood for—arguing that he was owed more than the base salary Tech paid through the remainder of the term. He claimed he was also owed benefits like profits from his radio and television shows, use of a car, and country-club memberships—items he said were agreed upon but not included in his written contract. The suit was settled in 1983 and may have contributed to the emergence of more favorable contracts for coaches in the future.

Rodgers was replaced by former Tech assistant coach Bill Curry. A story circulated, according to Tech fan Jackie Copeland, that Rodgers liked to say being replaced by Curry, who had no head coaching experience, is like you're the sheriff and you're replaced by Barney Fife. Is that story true? Would he say that about his longtime friend and former colleague who speaks well of him? It sounds like something Rodgers would say—*definitely* like something someone would attribute to him. Son Rick said, "I never know what stories about Dad are all true, mostly true, or not true at all."

In an interview for this book, Rodgers shook his head and scoffed at the stories told about him. "Everything about me is exaggerated," he said.

About the story that he and his players did forward rolls as they entered the field: "It was *fun*!"

About the UGA-color car: "It was *her* car, that she brought from California, and it was *red*, not red and black."

About dressing as a hippie at a team party: He huffed, "I put on my ex-wife's wig and sang a song I made up about myself."

He shook his head, pointed, and said, "I've enjoyed my fuckin' life. You can write that down. I've enjoyed my fuckin' life."

Ivery arrived at Tech during Rodgers's second season, a time when Tech fans still hoped he would coach them back to prominence. Ivery would play in an offense that was new to him, one that produced huge rushing numbers and that Rodgers had mastered: the wishbone—a topic that brought Rodgers to his feet and elicited quick, animated bursts of illustration, energetically acting out a wishbone player's actions. "The greatest offense ever devised!" he roared. "The wishbone takes an average player, and he can gain as many yards as an Eddie Lee Ivery. You don't need a pro-style quarterback with a great arm. Gary Lanier was a little peanut, and he did great in the wishbone." He gleefully ticked off his accomplishments running the wishbone at UCLA: defeated two-time defending national champion Nebraska, won an Orange Bowl, achieved an 8-3 record, then 9-2, was twice voted Pac-8 Coach of the Year, and in 1973 gained 612 yards against Stanford, leading the nation in total offense and scoring.

Jim Atkinson, in *Texas Monthly*, called the wishbone "a combination of simplicity and duplicity, brute strength and sleight of hand…a magnificent shell game." The wishbone required skills honed through repetition: speed, strength, ferocity, blocking, quick thinking, and dexterity. Once those skills were learned and executed well by good runners, the wishbone amassed yards. Unveiled at the University of Texas in 1968, it became nearly unstoppable. The Longhorns won 30 straight games and two national championships. Averaging 500 yards of offense and 40 points was common. Barry Switzer's University of Oklahoma wishbone teams claimed national championships in 1974, 1975, and 1985. In 1971, they rushed for an NCAA record of 768 yards in one game and set records for total yards per game, total rushing for a season, and rushing average per game—472.4 (still tops). Bryant's Alabama wishbone teams trampled their way to three national titles.

Three running backs line up behind the quarterback: the fullback directly behind him, and two tailbacks a couple of steps back and to each side of the fullback—forming, more or less, a wishbone shape. (It could just as easily have been called the Y formation.)

The wishbone's execution is built on the quarterback "reading" the defense and reacting. At the snap, in the formation's standard triple-option play, the offense explodes to the left or right. The quarterback, watching only the defense—not his running backs—moves parallel to the line of scrimmage and shoves the ball into the gut of the fullback charging toward the line. Then comes the first decision: leave the ball with the fullback, who plunges into the defense, or pull it back and keep it. That decision, like the ones that follow, depends entirely on how the defense responds.

Next decision: keep the ball and run downfield or pitch it to the trailing tailback (the front tailback blocks), who sweeps around the end and down the sideline.

Former Tech offensive line coach Bill Curry said the quarterback "rides and decides"—and when he makes those decisions quickly and correctly, the defense is already one step behind.

Former Tech running backs coach Bud Casey said that when the wishbone is executed properly, "you couldn't stop it. You could take an average running back and make him great. It divides the defense. The defense is always one man short. The wishbone attacks the defense with seven men going right or left, and that leaves five and a half defenders on each side. Plus, you need someone to cover deep, just in case there's a pass."

The wishbone is simple, and not. There are strong, powerful defenders moving and guessing, and one quarterback countering those guesses. The quarterback quickly deciphers the defense's anticipation and gets the ball elsewhere from where the defense is going. The offense lines up in the same formation virtually every play, so the defense has no idea which way the play will go. If the defensive end edges in to stop the fullback, the quarterback keeps the ball and moves down the line. No one has to block that defender. Some defenders are *intentionally* unblocked. In wishbone lingo, a defender "eliminates himself from the play" by targeting the back who ends up not having the ball. If the defense ignores the fullback, the ball stays in his gut, and he dashes through a hole as the defense pursues outside. If the QB keeps and the next defender (often the outside linebacker) moves to tackle him, he pitches to the tailback, who has a blocking tailback ahead of him. The fullback who didn't get the ball—he's another blocker. Going right or left, that side of the field swarms with blockers—the linemen and the backs who don't have the ball—and half the defense is on the other side of the field. Every player blocks, and Ivery, a quick learner of offenses, became tough and ferocious at it.

Repeatedly, the quarterback fakes a handoff to the fullback, then suddenly doesn't fake, the defense doesn't expect it, and the fullback gains 8 yards. Since the tailbacks are usually the best rushers, a defender might—thinking he is anticipating smartly—head that way, and the quarterback zips behind him in the space he vacated. Smack the quarterback instead and he has flipped the ball to the streaking tailback a split second before he is hit. That tailback is already at full speed, and he has the lead tailback blocking for him, and he's heading toward defensive backs who are better at guarding lithe receivers than grasping strong, fast running backs. If the offensive tackle, trained to sprint across the field, blocks the safety, the tailback runs free.

There were variations besides the basic triple option. If the assistant coaches, looking down from their perch above in the coach's box, noticed the defense overplaying the outside, they let Rodgers know, and he would call a tailback handoff up the middle. If a receiver is getting little attention, he might call a rare passing play.

Rodgers's younger son, Kelly, said that when he was six years old in California, his father, at night under the streetlights, taught him the wishbone quarterback's technique for pitching the football to the tailback. When Kelly became a father, he taught his daughters how to throw a spiral and how to flip the wishbone quarterback pitch. It's in the Rodgers DNA.

In 2008, Georgia State University in Atlanta hired Bill Curry to build a football program from scratch. For his first teams—undermanned and inexperienced—he wanted to run the wishbone, which thrives on deception. But he was told he couldn't. His bosses wanted butts in seats, and they believed fans wouldn't pay to watch the wishbone. Too many people saw it as monotonous and boring, especially compared to a high-flying passing game. The quarterback merely "pitched" the ball? That wasn't entertainment.

Still, Curry stood by it: "I still think it's the best offense."

There were two wishbone plays Ivery especially loved. The first was the classic option: the quarterback, having passed the line of scrimmage, pitched the ball at the last possible second to a streaking tailback. Ivery's primary adversary was often a smaller defensive back, someone he could beat with a sudden cut or simply run through, using strength and balance to break free.

His other favorite was the counter. The quarterback faked to the fullback, then spun and handed the ball to Ivery coming the other way. The wishbone had conditioned defenses to move fast—and if they committed, even for a split second, in the wrong direction, Ivery's explosive first step took him into open space. When overused, it became predictable. But used sparingly? It could be deadly.

Rodgers's wishbone teams rarely threw the ball. (His 1972 UCLA squad attempted just 70 passes all season.) Fewer completions, yes—but also fewer interceptions, sacks, and incompletions.

"You may play a whole game, and your team might pass only twice," tight end Sewell recalled, "and those passes are not going to the tight end." If a pass *was* thrown to him, he said, "I got my hands beat up so much from all the blocking, by then I might not catch it."

When Rodgers switched to a pass-friendlier offense Sewell's senior year, he said, "I caught more passes in one year than all the other three combined."

The wishbone had a weakness, though: if a team fell behind by two touchdowns late, it had little recourse. Passing offenses could control the clock and move quickly. The wishbone couldn't.

Rodgers's response? He roared, "I don't want to *be* behind!"

Eventually, most college teams—even those that had thrived with the wishbone—abandoned it. Only a handful still run it today. Defenses learned to counter it with discipline and pursuit. They stopped falling for its misdirection. Linebackers got faster. Defensive backs grew stronger.

But in 1975, when Ivery arrived at Tech, Rodgers still believed in what he called "the greatest offense ever devised." He remained all-in on the wishbone—until Ivery's senior year. That season, Rodgers made a sharp turn, ditching the offense he had long championed for one he had previously dismissed.

Rodgers later regretted that switch. But Ivery would have the greatest season by any Georgia Tech running back, ever.

Chapter 5

The Best All-Around Athlete on the Team

Kim King, former Tech football player (three-year starter at quarterback), booster, and radio game color analyst (1974 until his death of cancer in 2004), saw many great players. He said,

> Eddie Lee Ivery was the best running back I saw at Tech. He had everything you want. He was quick and deceptive. You wouldn't think when you first saw him run that he was that fast, but he had great acceleration. And great vision. Some backs lower their head and see a limited area around them, but not Eddie Lee. He could figure out the flow of the defense and choose the right place to run. He was big—for that time—and strong. He could take and give punishment. It was rare that one person tackled him. He had a good juke move; he could run over defenders; or he could outrun them. He had good hands; he caught the ball well. He was intelligent. He was a complete runner.

These glowing remarks—just hype from a Tech loyalist whose job was to promote the program, right? Maybe. But nearly everyone who saw Ivery play at Tech says the same thing.

When defensive back Lawrence Lowe first saw Ivery practice, he thought, "There is something special about him. He runs with grace." He put Ivery in elite company: "His style was very elusive, like Barry Sanders, but he had the strength of Walter Payton. He was a big running back, like Eric Dickerson. Once he broke the line of scrimmage, it was hard for a small defensive back to bring him down. They seldom did with an arm tackle, and they couldn't get a solid lick on him. He had good hands. In the wishbone, that pitch was like a knuckleball—no spiral like a forward pass—and he could catch it cleanly and turn up-field without breaking stride."

"If he hadn't been injured at Green Bay, he would have been a Hall of Fame running back," said All-American safety Don Bessillieu. "He had the whole package: strength, hands, everything." Running back David Allen said that while Ivery could take a solid hit, "he didn't take a lot of hard hits because he kept people off his body."

"The best thing was real good vision," Rodney Lee said. "His ability to cut, jab somebody, slice back—that was all based on his vision. Sometimes, dude, he was in some weird positions and still land on his feet."

"From a raw talent standpoint, he was one of the best I've ever seen," Sewell said. "He was a damn *athlete*. He was the best all-round athlete on the team."

Offensive lineman Ben Utt, eight-season NFL veteran for the Baltimore/Indianapolis Colts, said,

> Eddie Lee was a beautiful runner. He was the most complete running back I've ever blocked for, and I blocked for good running backs. He could run with the ball, catch the ball, block. Smooth but powerful. I remember him getting hit behind the line and he about did a cartwheel. He put his hand on the ground and ran for another 8 to 10 yards. Eric Dickerson was faster, but Eddie Lee was more fluid.

Linebacker Reggie Wilkes, a 10-year NFL veteran and starting linebacker for the Philadelphia Eagles in the 1981 Super Bowl, ranked Ivery

> among the top three all-purpose, all-around athletes that I've ever seen. Ever. And I played against some of the best. So talented, and he was tough. If you were on the other team, you had to know where he was at all times. Had to. His talent was so unbelievable. Watching him was almost magical. And when I saw him play basketball, I couldn't believe it. He could jump out of the gym and had incredible skills.

"He was deceptively powerful," said quarterback Mike Kelley. "He could take a shot, square someone up, and they would bounce off him. He could deflect their energy; they thought they had him, and then they didn't." Kelley once noticed skin worn off Ivery's wrist and knuckles from being drilled into the brutally unforgiving artificial turf of that era—wounds Ivery barely acknowledged. "He was one of the tougher fellows I ever met," Kelley said.

"Eddie Lee was one of the greatest blockers ever," said Pepper Rodgers. He continued,

> He was a great pass catcher. In the wishbone, running outside the quarterback on the option, he had to snatch that ball from the quarterback. Then he ran smooth, not herky-jerky like some backs. Those are the ones who fumble a lot. Someone once asked me if I coached Eddie Lee Ivery, and I said, "I didn't coach Eddie Lee Ivery. I recruited him." He would have been great anywhere.

Running back David Carter called Ivery "one of the greatest running backs I've ever been around. He was unbelievable. He would go all out on every play. He could dunk a basketball. In softball, he hit long home runs. He was one of the best athletes I had seen."

Gary Lanier, who became the starting quarterback during Ivery's sophomore year, loved being a wishbone quarterback—making split-second reads, diving for yardage, fooling defenders—but some of his most satisfying plays were simply pitches to Ivery and then watching him work.

"He was the greatest running back ever at Georgia Tech," Lanier said. "He had speed, agility; he was durable. Even if I thought he was too tired or hurt to carry the ball—he might look exhausted or get hit and grimace in the huddle—with his determination and toughness, he would always give you one more play. I'm thinking, 'I have to call his number again?' But I'd look in his eyes and see a chance for a big play in every situation."

Lanier used the word nearly everyone did when describing Ivery: *balance.* "He would get hit, put that hand down, and sometimes get three or four more yards."

"That was Eddie Lee's patented thing," said Don Bessillieu, referring to the hand-to-the-ground move.

Fullback Ray Friday added, "He would get hit in midair, put his hand down on the ground, and not miss a step."

"You had to hit him hard and put him down to tackle him," said All-American linebacker Lucius Sanford. "You couldn't arm tackle him. And he was determined. He was never a slouch, in a game or in practice."

Former Tech athletics administrator Jack Thompson praised Ivery's "natural instincts—speed, agility. He could find the hole and burst into the secondary. The best thing a runner can have is natural instinct, and he had it. He could feel the flow of the game. He had a kinesthetic sense and great peripheral vision."

"People don't know how good he really was," said former UGA defensive back Scott Woerner. "He had all the skills. Some guys can run over you, and some can run around you, but not everybody, like him, can run over you and around you."

Atlanta sportscaster Beau Bock compared him to one of the greats: "He was a classic runner, like O. J. Simpson. His feet were never high off the ground. He could change directions without losing speed. But when he collided, he could deliver a blow to the defender. He was a big, complete back."

Another word often used to describe his running style: *glide*. His legs didn't churn like pistons. There was power, but it was smooth—silken, even—until it struck.

"He not only made people miss," said Tech center Tom Daniel, "but made them look foolish doing so. People go, 'Wait a minute, I thought I had him.'" Daniel added that Ivery got tougher as the game wore on. "In the fourth quarter, when you get tired and hurt, he would get harder and harder to take down. He would run maybe not faster, but harder."

David Sims, who shared the backfield with Ivery for three years, said, "If his number was called on a second down and 6, he was thinking, 'I'm going to get the first down now, not in two plays.' If we reached inside the 10, he didn't think about getting closer to make it easier to score next play. He planned to take it in."

Ivery's competitiveness showed in everything—shooting pool, ping pong, basketball, even diving off the board at the swimming pool. "I hated to lose," he said.

Kent Hill, Ivery's freshman-year roommate (six inches taller and 40 pounds heavier than Ivery) said, "He beat me to 300 pounds on the bench press." When they wrestled, Hill couldn't believe how often the smaller Ivery pinned him.

Sports psychologist Luis Valdez described what separates the elite: "Intense desire to excel distinguishes great athletes. You can't teach that. It is instinct, and once you have that instinctual feel for things—and that happens early on—then you have to follow it up with practice and training. You have to keep refining it through repetition."

Valdez continued,

> Some can't maintain it because they don't want to do the hard work that gets you to master it. Instinct is a necessary ingredient, but it's not the be-all-end-all. Even Eddie Lee Ivery had to master and refine his craft to make it to the professional ranks. That separates the really good from the great—they're never truly satisfied. They always want to get an edge, improve themselves. They might know they can't be perfect, but they're driven to get as close to perfection as they can.

Like many great athletes, Ivery couldn't explain how his instincts worked. They came in a flash—a split-second rush of violence and adrenaline that took over mind and body.

"I tell running backs to run fast and react," he said, shaking his head. "That's how I played. I never knew what I was going to do. I knew the direction I was going, but I just hit it as fast as I could. I don't see how you can think the game. The play might not happen as it was drawn up. You have to trust the blockers and just go like the hole is going to be there, and if it's not, then react. I couldn't think the game."

He never thought, *I will now put my hand on the ground and bounce back up.* He just did it.

Sims, who had set the Tech single-season rushing record the year before Ivery broke it, described an offensive play as "organized chaos." A play might be diagrammed with precision, but the moment the ball is snapped, 11 large, aggressive men do their best to shred the design.

"When we're describing a play, it sounds like a long time," said Friday, "but it happens just like that. I call football the world's fastest chess game."

That's what made Ivery's instincts so valuable—those split-second decisions that can't be taught, that innate feel for chaos.

"They lose consciousness, in that they're no longer thinking," said sports psychologist Valdez, describing athletes like Ivery. "They're going with the flow; they're in the moment. Over time they get in a rhythm and are running on muscle memory, in a flow, not thinking about what they're doing. If they are thinking, it's a split-second decision."

He continued, "They're in what athletes call 'the zone,' and it's all about rhythm. Basketball players say they're shooting in rhythm; there's a smoothness to it. They almost shut their brain off. There's no more chatter, no more what we call internal dialogue. You're simply letting your body do what you practiced with all the repetition. If you're using your brain, not your body, it's not the same."

Ivery's teammates appreciated not just his talent, but his personality.

"Eddie Lee Ivery is gonna treat everybody the same," said linebacker Mackel Harris. "Lots of laughs and fun, liked to joke. He cared for all the guys on the team."

Student trainer Tommy Herrington, who had first seen Ivery play against his own high school, remembered his antics off the field: "He'd sing in the hot tub. Once, he sang 'He's Got the Whole World in His Hands,' and he added verses. 'He's got everybody in this hot tub in his hands.'" The two traded trash talk whenever their former schools were set to play each other.

Defensive player Marvin Dyett, who arrived at Tech for Ivery's senior year, didn't yet grasp how revered Ivery was. During one practice, Dyett leveled him.

"I played defense," he said, "so I tackled him. That's what defense does. But it looked like a SWAT team swooped in, the way everybody ran over to check on him. They said, 'You don't knock him down.'"

But Ivery, for his part, didn't act like a star. He never carried himself as better than anyone.

"I thought he was going to come across as all-world, the golden child," said defensive back Bernard Stover. "But he wasn't arrogant. He wasn't cocky to the freshmen."

Defensive back Henry Johnson agreed: "He was humble though he was the star. He didn't act like he was better than anybody."

At one spring practice, Ivery noticed another running back was getting more reps and wondered aloud if the coaches had ranked him behind the other player. He asked Rodgers, who smiled and replied, "Eddie Lee, I don't need to see what you can do."

Players who didn't know Ivery well saw a friendly, polite teammate who liked to joke around. He addressed elders as "Mister." But his toughness wasn't always visible—until one tutoring session made it unmistakable.

During an evening math session, the tutor announced the hour was up. Ivery stood and said, "Let's go." One teammate, bigger and stronger, insisted on 15 more minutes. Ivery left the room, and others followed. Outside, the angry teammate confronted him. The argument escalated, and the teammate struck first—smacking Ivery to the ground and continuing the assault.

"He tore my ass up," Ivery recalled.

Still bleeding and shaken, he knew he couldn't let it stand. "I was crying and bleeding, so I found a two-by-four and went after him. I couldn't find him, so I waited outside the dorm."

When the teammate finally returned, he brought the tutor along.

The tutor suggested they shake hands and settle it: "You're teammates." The teammate extended his hand.

Ivery punched him in the face, knocking him down.

Bessillieu quickly pulled Ivery inside and handed him a knife. Moments later, the tutor and teammate entered again. The tutor, still trying to restore peace, repeated, "Shake hands."

This time, Ivery extended one hand—knife concealed in the other. He didn't use it. The teammate shook his hand, and the incident ended.

"That was a big turning point," said Bessillieu. "That got everybody's respect."

"After that," Ivery said, "everybody knew I was a nice guy but not a pushover."

Despite his rising stardom, Ivery stayed humble—and hungry.

"He plays like a star but practices like he's trying to earn a scholarship," Rodgers said. "Everybody plays their best in the games, but football is a hard game to practice."

Daniel agreed: "Right, and for a guy who didn't really need to practice. A lot of guys with his talent try to get out of the work during the week because they think they don't need it until the weekend. Not Eddie Lee."

Offensive linemen, Daniel explained, take note of who earns their blocks. "We're very critical of the backs behind us," he said. "We care about how serious the running backs and quarterbacks are—how hard they work, how willing they are to sacrifice. We sacrifice in obscurity, but our offensive line loved to block for Eddie Lee because he was always willing to do whatever it took to help us out."

"He was a workhorse who never quit working, which was unusual for someone so talented. We'd notice if a back slacked off and expected us to keep working—never taking it easy. If they did, hoping we'd make up for it with our blocking, that would be noticed quickly."

He was, Daniel said, "a player's player."

"He always cared about the linemen. Offensive linemen, in subtle ways, take stock in who they're blocking for, because we're doing what it takes to make them stars. And we don't want them to take it for granted. Eddie Lee Ivery never did."

His effort inspired others.

"Late in a game," Daniel said, "he'd be tired, hurt, and a little bit pissed off, and the next thing you know he's saying, 'Give me the ball!' That motivated us, because you knew if you gave him a little bit, he'd make a lot out of it."

"He ran hard and practiced hard," David Allen said. "He ran his gasses [very demanding, relentless sprints] hard. He never slacked on anything. Everything was full speed. He was the epitome of a first-class athlete."

Carter added that Ivery didn't "cheat the drill." While some guys coasted through practice when no one was looking, Ivery never let up.

Running backs coach Bud Casey praised both Ivery's natural gifts and his eagerness to master fundamentals.

"He could catch a pass—he could catch a *bad* pass," Casey said. "He had such great hand-eye coordination. He had great vision, great body tilt: leaning forward, bent legs, neck bowed. With that posture, he could explode through the tackler. He did all the fundamental things."

Casey noted how Ivery held the football. "The ball fit perfectly in his hand. We taught the eagle claw hold. The hold is important, or you'll fumble the ball too easily. You have to secure the front of the ball and the rear."

He turned his palm upward and demonstrated the grip. "Then you have to run with your arm pumping straight forward and back. That's not natural. It's natural to reach across your body at an angle—but that leaves the rear vulnerable. Most fumbles come from the ball getting hit back there."

For the rest of his coaching career, Casey used Ivery's story to motivate young players.

"If a player whined about his background," he said, "I'd say, 'Shit, let me tell you about Eddie Lee Ivery. He had no daddy and no running water, and he never used that as an excuse. He always arrived on time and did what he was supposed to do.'"

Ivery was enthralled by the sights of Atlanta: tall buildings, one after another, stores and restaurants—so *many* of them—open until late at night. "It was exciting," he said. "I rode around and looked at the tall skyscrapers, in awe, thinking, 'Is this real?'" Across North Avenue from Tech was a large public housing complex where he saw, for the first time, men selling drugs, sex workers selling their bodies, and unhoused people begging for money and sleeping rough. During his first few weeks at Tech, he called his Thomson girlfriend every night. He saw few Black students and missed his Thomson friends. He missed his mother's and grandmother's meals.

Like most college students, Ivery matured during his time at Tech, but he remained shy about public speaking and interacting with the press. He appeared on *The Pepper Rodgers Show* only once.

"I wasn't a very good interview," he admitted. "I was too shy to talk. I was on there maybe once but didn't want to. I was camera shy."

Though he was a good student, Ivery felt self-conscious about his background and nervous about how his speech might be perceived. "My sentences didn't always come out right," he said, which led him to avoid reporters altogether. King noted that when he interviewed Ivery, he received thoughtful and intelligent answers, but some White reporters unfairly equated Ivery's rural Georgia Black accent with a lack of intelligence. *Atlanta Journal-Constitution* columnist Furman Bisher began a profile but abandoned it, later admitting that he struggled to understand Ivery's accent and assumed—wrongly—that Ivery had been academically pushed through school just to play football.

In the classroom, Ivery had to adjust quickly. He wasn't used to lecture halls with 50 or 60 students. At first, he was shocked that students could walk out in the middle of class—but eventually, he did the same. After a tough first quarter, he made the Dean's List the next.

Like many athletes, Ivery majored in Industrial Management.

"It was hard," said Bessillieu. "I cried my freshman year. I was convinced my sociology teacher hated me. Every test was essay. I failed. I cried."

Jim Bell, a Tech alum and longtime booster, graduated in 1953. His office walls were lined with campus sketches and a framed newspaper profile of his support for Tech athletics. He was the kind of booster who once sent a coach an 11-page letter—and expected a reply.

"Every Tech degree requires calculus," Bell said. "Everyone with a Tech degree commands respect in the marketplace. We play against guys who take courses with no meaning in the marketplace. There is no analytical work in some schools—not ours."

Sewell recalled his own academic adjustment: "My college experience was good, but classroom was hard as hell. I came from a small Florida school and was not well prepared for college. We didn't have physics and those high-level classes. Some of the guys went through smoothly, and some didn't."

"We all tried to learn the system," Sanford added. "How to put a schedule together, how to pick a professor, how to ask what I need to do to get a good grade, how to graduate."

"It was hard for me, too," said King. "When you go to Tech, you have to work hard. They didn't have a PE major."

Sims, who graduated from Tech just one quarter after his four years of football eligibility ended, said the pressure on Black athletes was intense.

"I knew I couldn't miss a day in class," he said.

Any misstep by a Black student, he explained, risked reinforcing racist stereotypes among those who resented the integration of Southern universities.

"Failure was not an option for me," he explained. "I had been told I couldn't graduate from Tech, and I was determined to prove them wrong."

Tech lost the 1975 opener to South Carolina. (Rodgers would be dogged by season-opening losses.) Ivery didn't play. The next week, they defeated Miami, and Ivery, an 18-year-old first-year player, threw a halfback pass for a touchdown just before getting hit by a defender, putting Tech up 21-0 in the second quarter. "I was told just to get it out there the best I could," he said. "I chunked it out there." But no one expected it in the wishbone, so it worked. This was one of the wishbone's masterful deceptions. It is pounded into the defense's head: run, run, run. They chase the rusher, then he throws a pass they in no way expect. Rushing, Ivery was 10 for 71 yards (7.1 average), his longest 25. Sims, still the star, rushed for 132. Ivery returned a kickoff for 55 yards until the kicker tackled him at the 45. His total yards for the game—rushing, passing, returns: 172. If Tech fans did not already know they had a budding star, they certainly did now.

The next week, they defeated Clemson, and Ivery rushed 8 times for 66 yards. On his first carry, he ran for 22; on the next, 18—"dodging and staggering, sprawling to the 6," as one reporter put it—setting up a Tech touchdown.

Fans were noticing not just that he could run, but *how* he ran: with flair, with determination, never down until he was on the ground. Just when defenders—and spectators—thought the play was over, he'd spin, feint, or plant a hand and keep going. It wasn't just effort. It was instinct. And fans came to anticipate the moment Ivery got the ball.

At that point in the season, Ivery had carried the ball 24 times for 172 yards—7.1 per carry, second only to Sims. He had caught 8 passes for 66 yards—and thrown a touchdown pass of his own.

Rodgers gave him the start in the next game, against Florida State. "He can be as good as any back in the country," Rodgers told the press.

With his star rising, reporters asked Ivery whether he dreamed of the NFL. He said his priority was to get his degree, and if he was good enough to play professionally, "that's a long way off."

In a 30-0 thrashing of Florida State, he carried the ball three times for 18 yards and added a 13-yard kickoff return. But after the return, he took a hit. He felt no pain at first, but on the sideline, he noticed a sharp pinch in his left leg. Something was wrong. X-rays confirmed a hairline fracture in his tibia.

He missed the next five games.

In a win over Virginia Military Institute, the wishbone churned out a school-record 555 rushing yards. But momentum stalled in a loss to a struggling 1-3-1 Auburn team, where two costly fumbles led to Tiger touchdowns.

Rodgers, trying to stay upbeat, offered a wry take on the disappointing loss: "It shows how far we've come. Auburn upset *us* and carried their coach off the field."

The following week, the team traveled to New Orleans to play Tulane. The players loved playing there. It was typically an easy win, and as long as they won, which they did, 23-0, Rodgers let them have a good time.

"Pepper would give us 50 or 75 dollars, and we'd party on Bourbon Street," Sewell said. "Before the game, Pepper would say, 'You better win, or I'm taking you back home tonight, right after the game.'"

"I remember no curfew and a hotel bathtub full of ice and cans of beer," Stover said.

Out with a broken tibia, Ivery didn't travel with the team. But that didn't mean he wasn't in New Orleans.

Bestwick—who had once seen Ivery walking to class in worn clothes and quietly given him some of his own—left a French Quarter restaurant after lunch with another coach. Spotting a tour group near a historical site, he paused. "Isn't that Eddie Lee?" he asked. "And good God almighty, where did he get that suit?"

Ivery was wearing a stunning cream-colored suit—far nicer than anything he could have afforded. "Ask him about that suit," Bestwick later said in an interview for this book, "and how he got to New Orleans."

By then, Ivery had met Robert Gilbert, whom he referred to as "my sugar daddy."

Only star players were introduced to Gilbert. Roommate Kent Hill recalled that now and then, someone would knock on their door and say Mr. Gilbert wanted to see Ivery. Off he'd go—for dinner, usually. Packages showed up for Ivery.

"He walked with a cane," Ivery said. "He lived in this old wooden house you couldn't really see from the road. It had scraggly shrubs out front, but inside it looked like a cathedral. There was a white bear rug, beautiful wood floors. A chauffeur drove him around."

Gilbert bought Ivery's school-issued home game tickets for $500 apiece. Ivery used the money from one sale to make a down payment on a 1972 Oldsmobile Cutlass, and the next sale paid it off. Gilbert took him to New Orleans and showed him the town. At dinner, Ivery gawked at the biggest steak he had ever seen. Gilbert ordered a screwdriver. Ivery, who had never heard of it, ordered one, too.

Sims said he introduced Ivery to Gilbert. "He took care of me, too," Sims said. "If he was in town, he'd call and take me out for a nice steak. He'd give me some spending money—maybe $100 or $200. That helped a lot for a college student. I'd have a drink with my meal, usually a sloe gin fizz."

Other players sold their tickets, too. "A guy would call and say, 'Meet me at The Little Mug,'" said Stover. "I'd go there and get a couple thousand or so for all my tickets." He added that some restaurants let players eat for free and that "a couple of the better players got free tires for their cars."

Years later, Rodgers didn't pretend to be unaware of what was happening. He didn't say outright that he knew about the ticket-selling, but he waved a hand and said, "Of *course* they sold their tickets. It was the only way they could make any money!"

Sims admitted he sold his, sometimes all at once, walking away with as much as $4,000. There were other angles, too. Athletes who lived off campus received a housing allowance. If two or three of them shared a place, they could pocket the leftover money. The same went for food stipends. Technically, off-campus athletes weren't supposed to eat in the school cafeteria, but Sims said their status helped. They could get in without paying—sometimes someone at the door waved them through, or someone already inside would bring them a plate. Ivery learned quickly how to take advantage of those perks.

Recruit visits were another money-making opportunity. Sims said coaches gave him cash to entertain visiting prospects. The recruits usually stayed at the Royal Coach hotel, and Sims would take them to the hotel's restaurant. The maître d', a Tech fan, would charge the meal to the room, saving the cash. "He'd put the flair on," Sims said. "He'd help recruits with their table manners in a way that made them feel classy, not awkward."

After dinner, Sims would throw a party in the recruit's hotel room—buying some refreshments, inviting other players and a few Spelman students. Whatever money was left over, he kept. "You had to produce receipts to show you spent money on the recruit," said Stover. "So, you'd be asking for extras at the restaurant—'You got an extra one of those?'"

"We'd look for a party that was serving food," Ivery said, "so we wouldn't have to spend any of the money they gave us. Or we'd send the recruit to the 'famous Varsity.'" Across the highway from Tech, the Varsity—billed as the world's largest drive-in—was known for its hot dogs and dirt-cheap meals.

"Being broke in college was your worst nightmare," Sewell said. "My parents couldn't send me 20 dollars every two weeks. We'd work together to find out ways to stretch a dollar. We knew who had the key to the dining room, and we'd get free food." He said Rodgers once caught players using the athletic department's WATS line, a long-distance phone service, called the team together, and asked whoever had used it to stand up. "About the whole damn team stood up. Everybody did it."

After defeating Tulane, Tech's wishbone offense boasted the top rushing yardage in the nation, averaging 376 yards per game. They followed up with a 21-6 win over Duke, bringing their record to 6-2 and fueling hopes for a strong bowl bid. During that era, there were far fewer bowl games and limited contractual ties with conferences compared to now.

Bowls invited teams they believed would attract television viewers and fans in the stands. Teams relied on bowls for revenue, prestige, and recruiting. For players, bowls meant travel, excitement, and the experience of a new city. Next, Tech traveled to No. 12 Notre Dame, where they lost decisively, 24-3. Ivery was still unable to play.

"It hurt me all over. It's hard standing on the sidelines," he told a reporter. "I want to be out there so bad."

He returned for the Navy game, which Tech narrowly won, 14-13, thanks to a dramatic 68-yard, 20-play, 9½-minute drive that converted twice on fourth down and ended with a touchdown with a minute and a half left. It was a classic, clock-consuming wishbone drive that left Navy little time to score. Ivery carried the ball for 66 yards (with a longest run of 20) and appeared strong after his injury.

In the season finale, UGA stomped Tech on national television, 42-26. Although it was predicted to be a close game, the wishbone was contained by UGA's "Junkyard Dogs" defense. Ivery scored Tech's first touchdown and rushed for 45 yards. Tech's first pass of the game was intercepted and returned for a touchdown. They didn't pass again until they were down 42-0.

Tech ended the season 7-4 and received no bowl bid.

Rodgers lost a few supporters when *The Pepper Rodgers Show* aired clips of him on the sidelines during the game. Unsurprisingly, don't-take-yourself-too-seriously Rodgers wisecracked about getting their butts whipped. He wanted to win, but win or lose, he had fun. Still, some Tech fans grumbled, thinking he was flippant after getting clobbered by their hated rival.

Despite the disappointment, Tech fans got a glimpse of the greatness to come over the next three years. When Ivery touched the ball, something dramatic might happen. He could turn almost any play into a big gain. A defender drawing near only heightened the anticipation. Fans had become accustomed to seeing tacklers seemingly have him *nailed*—then, with a perfectly timed spin, a sharp-angled collision, a deflection, or even just a hand to the ground, Ivery would break free and dash away. His spin was so fast and powerful that defenders rarely had time to adjust their grasp.

In the wishbone offense, he might carry the ball only a dozen times or fewer, which made each touch feel like an event. If the play went Ivery's direction and the fullback didn't get the handoff, it was either the quarterback or Ivery—and fans always hoped it was Ivery. "It was beautiful to watch," said Al Ciraldo, Jr., son of longtime Tech broadcaster Al Ciraldo and spotter for the broadcast team since 1975.

Jerry Ivery, stationed at Fort Benning (just 100 miles from Atlanta), attended most home games. "Tech fans were crazy about him," he said. "They stood up whenever he had the ball." Eddie Lee's mother and grandmother never attended any of his games. Bennie Mae and other relatives made it to a few. Bennie Mae, though, sometimes missed plays—she closed her eyes, praying Eddie Lee wouldn't get hurt.

Booster Bell shook his head at the memory of those moments—Tech with the ball, third and five, the stadium on edge. "When he got that pitch on the outside, your motor started racing," Bell said. "He ran hard; he threw tacklers off him. He could either run over a linebacker or outrun him. He had a peculiar, deceptive gait, but he was flat running."

Bestwick announced he was leaving to become the head coach at the University of Virginia. He was the man who had guided Ivery to Tech, made him feel special, and even gave him clothes from his own closet. Now he was moving on. Ivery went to his office and said, "You're the closest thing to a father I've ever had." Bestwick embraced him and reassured him that others at Tech would look after him. "I'm gonna keep my eye on you," he told Ivery. "I'm not gonna forget you."

It was a promise he kept.

Ivery moved out of the dorm and into an apartment with Bessillieu. Having never been responsible for bills, he gave his share of money to Bessillieu, who handled everything. For personal expenses, Ivery paid in cash or with money orders. He wouldn't have a checking account until he turned professional.

While Ivery had grown up poor, Bessillieu came from a stable, middle-class family—his father was in the military. Confident and self-assured, Bessillieu was comfortable around White people and those with money. Ivery, during his first year at Tech, feared his country upbringing might betray him. Though he was polite to reporters and said the right things, he was nervous and reserved. Sewell said of Bessillieu, "He could teach a country boy things a city boy knew, the tricks and trades. Bessillieu taught a lot of guys."

Ivery had never had a friend like Bessillieu. Nicknamed "Elton John" for his flashy hats and suits, Bessillieu carried a worldliness that went far beyond football—he knew music, culture, and how to move through the world with style. Outspoken and gregarious, his laugh was loud and full, drawing attention and friendship wherever he went.

Later in life, he ran a hair salon in Columbus, Georgia, where he greeted customers with warmth and flair—hoop earrings dangling from each earlobe. "I'm sorry I missed you the other day," he told someone. "Can I take you to lunch to make up for it?"

"Dressing was my thing," he recalled. "Women noticed me. I wore three-piece suits. I was dead sharp after a game. I wanted to be the thing. I called myself 'Sweet Don.' If guys were around me a while, they started dressing sharp."

Ivery once wore Bessillieu's pinstripe suit to his future wife's graduation. Looking at a picture of it later, he laughed. "It looks like a pair of bell-bottoms because my thighs were bigger than Bessillieu's, but I thought I looked sharp."

When Marvin Dyett arrived at Tech, some nights he'd come home around 10:30 and see Bessillieu just heading out. Then, the next morning at practice, there was Bessillieu again—full of energy, revving up his teammates. Dyett asked, "Who is that guy with all the energy?" His teammates laughed and said, "That's Bessillieu. Don't pay any attention to him."

But Dyett did pay attention. Bessillieu took one look at how Dyett dressed and said, "I'm taking you clothes shopping and show you how to dress. You need some style! If you look good, you feel good."

"Two things Don taught me," Ivery recalled. "How to bake a cake and how to dress. I was from the country and dressed like it." Growing up, Ivery wore sneakers every day except Sundays at church. Bessillieu, by contrast, wore dress pants and dress shoes during the week and walked around campus with his shirt neatly tucked in. "Bessillieu was inventive," Ivery said. "He wore styles before they became popular."

He also put himself out there—with his big smile, bold wardrobe, and easy confidence. "If you were at a party," Ivery said, chuckling, "you knew Bessillieu was there. He'd let his presence be known."

Ivery continued,

> When we moved off campus, it was me, him, and his poodle, Fifi, and that's when I started loving pets. I wasn't used to "house dogs." He would talk to Fifi, hug her. "Hey Fifi, did you miss me?" The way he was loving on that dog, I was waiting for Fifi to answer. I saw his passion for that dog, and eventually I was saying, "Hey Fifi, how you doing?" In Thomson, all the dogs we had were outside dogs, and we didn't buy dog food. We threw a bone or scraps out there. He bought dog food and took it to the vet.

They hosted all-night parties—orchestrated by Bessillieu—after home games. Lawrence Lowe said the first time he appeared on *The Pepper Rodgers Show*, he went straight from a Bessillieu party to the studio—hungover.

"When Don said there was a party, that was *the party*," Lowe said.

"Those parties were legendary," Sewell said.

"I was the party man," Bessillieu boasted. "I started interracial parties at Tech. I did get upset at some White frat boys who came to my place and had fun but on campus acted like they didn't know me. But I was friends with everybody. I grew up on a military base in Oklahoma, so I had always been around White people." He said he dated White women in college and received criticism from Black friends. "But I didn't care," he said. "I was *Bessillieu*."

"We'd party from midnight till six in the morning," Bessillieu continued. "We'd be dancing and jamming. We'd have to blow a fan on the turntable to cool it off. I introduced friends to Wild Cherry's

'Play that Funky Music' and Peter Frampton. I liked having people over and showing them a good time."

Kent Hill said that if a home game reached the fourth quarter, Tech safely ahead, talk among the Black players turned to Bessillieu's party, where he'd serve kegs of beer and spiked Hawaiian Punch. "It was a sweatbox," Hill recalled. "If it was cold outside, we'd open the windows and doors because we'd be crammed in there dancing and sweating."

"I don't recall being outrageously drunk," Ivery said. "I was a control drinker then. Some players did drink too much, and some smoked pot and snorted cocaine, but all I ever had was Budweiser and gin and tonic. Then, you couldn't pay me to smoke a joint. I had gotten the message: Don't do drugs. Of course, I didn't realize alcohol was a drug."

That summer, Bessillieu was driving east along I-20 to see his father when he saw the exit for Thomson. He knew Ivery was home visiting family and decided to take it. The first place he stopped, he asked where the big football star lived.

At the Ivery home on Ellington Avenue, Ivery was asleep on the couch in the heat of the cinder block house with the metal roof. "He was lying on the couch, sweating like a pig," Bessillieu said.

That was the first time Bessillieu realized the depth of Ivery's poverty. "You never could tell he was poor," he said. "He never complained about being poor."

Before the 1976 season, Rodgers told a reporter, "Keep an eye on Eddie Lee Ivery. He had a terrific spring."

Chapter 6

Body Lean

Helen Williams, the wife of Ivery's high school basketball coach, invited him to speak at Career Day in her sixth-grade classroom in Thomson. A sign read "WELCOME EDDIE LEE." Another said "I AM SOMEBODY." Standing in front of a drawing of a yellow jacket, he spoke to the students about the importance of education, sports, and hard work. In a photo from the event, he's wearing a wide tie and a vest over a shirt with large, pointy collars and holding a certificate of gratitude.

Seven years later, Williams would think back on that day—and feel sad and hurt.

In one spring scrimmage, Ivery rushed for 193 yards and scored two touchdowns—one from 80 yards, the other from 47. In a newspaper profile, he said his biggest adjustment in Atlanta had been the traffic, which hardly existed in Thomson. He avoided it unless he had to. He said Atlanta had a lot to offer and that he might get a job there after graduating. Reporters referred to him as the star running back, but he deflected the attention: "I'm a team man, not an individual man."

Expectations were high for Tech's offense. The previous year, they had ranked third nationally in rushing, with Sims leading the nation in yards per carry. Their running back roster was deep. But they had no experienced wishbone quarterback.

Again, Tech lost its season opener—this time 27-17 to South Carolina—despite leading 17-7 at halftime. Ivery rushed only six times for 14 yards. Terrific spring or not, that can happen in the wishbone. After the game, the South Carolina coach said Tech would improve once they got consistent quarterback play. He added, "Sims is a good back, and Ivery is a great back. I don't want to play them again."

The next week, Tech was routed by Pittsburgh, 42-14. Tony

Dorsett—smooth, quick, graceful—rushed for 113 yards and scored three touchdowns. Ivery, who rushed for 41 yards, spent much of the game watching Dorsett from the sidelines.

"I wanted to be like him," he said. "I spent my entire time watching Dorsett. Normally, you're with your offense, but I wanted to watch this guy."

The following week, Tech tied Clemson 24-24 at home. Fans booed.

A few days later at practice, *Constitution* sports reporter Kelly Dude was mingling with the team when a player asked him, "Are we ditching the wishbone?" Dude said he didn't know and began asking around—but none of the other players knew either. Eventually, he hesitantly approached Rodgers.

Dude had interviewed coaches at other colleges, most of whom guarded their strategy tightly and didn't even allow reporters at practice. "They would have gone ballistic if I asked that question," he said, "then demand that I not write about it." He was amazed when Rodgers not only answered the question but explained the changes and why they were being made.

Tech was 0-2-1, and the offense was underperforming—partly due to inconsistent quarterback play. In the wishbone, without an accurate and quick read by the quarterback, the defense isn't fooled, and the scheme breaks down.

But Rodgers loved his wishbone. He wouldn't call the new formation anything else. Instead, he dubbed it the "open wishbone." The plays, he explained, were mostly the same—but run without the fullback. Grinning, he said they hadn't replaced the bone, they had "broken" it.

Grinned?

"If that happened with someone like Woody Hayes," Dude said, referring to the mercurial Ohio State head coach, "I might have suffered physical harm." He scribbled the quote down but hesitated—should he report it? Would he be helping the opposing team strategize? Unsure, he turned to *Constitution* columnist Lewis Grizzard for advice.

Grizzard didn't hesitate: "You're a reporter. Go ahead."

The "open wishbone" was supposed to allow for more passing, but in the game against Virginia—coached by Bestwick—Tech threw only six times. Still, they won 35-14. Ivery hadn't yet matched the expectations set by his first season (he had only 86 rushing yards at that point), but against Virginia, he broke out with 123 yards and a touchdown.

Some players, energized by the win and a seemingly productive offense, said they had a good chance of winning the rest of their games. But the next week, they were crushed by a mediocre Tennessee team, 42-7. Ivery was the lone bright spot, rushing for 107 yards. Players, Rodgers, and reporters alike were left scratching their heads: how was Tech just 1-3-1?

Then, in the following game, Tech suddenly looked like a complete team on both sides of the ball. They upset favored Auburn 28-10 on the road, holding Auburn's usually potent rushing attack to just 103 yards. The wishbone spread the carries among four backs, with Ivery rushing for 56 yards. On a crucial 16-yard touchdown run—with Tech up by 4—Ivery took the handoff up the middle, leapt over defenders at the line of scrimmage, and broke three tackles against a punishing Auburn defense as he scampered into the end zone.

In a mid-game move that changed the course of the season, Rodgers returned to the traditional wishbone and found his quarterback. Sophomore Gary Lanier, replacing the injured starter, rushed for 52 yards and two touchdowns.

Lanier, at five-foot-nine, was at Tech purely because of the wishbone. In high school in Savannah, he had quarterbacked the wishbone as a four-year starter, compiled a 33-7 record, and averaged five yards per carry. He was recruited by only two schools—Western Carolina and The Citadel—until Tech, searching for a quarterback familiar with Rodgers's favored offense, picked him up late.

"I was so low on the depth chart, I tripped over it," he joked.

His first role at Tech, like many players not expected to see the field, was on the scout team—mimicking the opponent in practice.

But as other quarterbacks moved to different positions or suffered injuries, he kept moving up. "Next thing you know," he said, "I'm at number two. Then finally, Pepper is like, 'You're all I have left.'"

Tech followed their Auburn win by beating Tulane 28-16. Ivery ran for 80 yards and a touchdown. On one 29-yard scamper, he deflected off a failed tackler, regained his balance, stumbled, regained speed, and broke another tackle. Lanier added a score from the 10-yard line—following a block by Ivery.

But inconsistency returned the next week. Tech was embarrassed by lowly Duke, 31-7. Ivery turned in several spectacular runs and finished with 99 yards, but the team committed too many turnovers.

In this uneven season, 11th-ranked Notre Dame—averaging 31 points per game—arrived for Tech's homecoming. Tech entered at 3-4-1, and expectations were low. Discouraged fans, including alumni in town for the festivities, braced for a beating.

Instead, they witnessed one of Rodgers's greatest coaching performances. His decision to start Lanier proved brilliant. Tech played standout defense against a team that would finish the season ranked 12th and go on to win the Gator Bowl. After the game, the Notre Dame athletic director told Rodgers it was the finest coaching job he had ever seen.

But over time, that impressive, unexpected, delirious triumph would come back to haunt Rodgers.

On Tech's first possession, Rodgers called for a pass—something many Tech fans had been desperate to see, despite the team's often gaudy rushing stats. The Notre Dame defense sacked Lanier for an 8-yard loss and celebrated with gyrating enthusiasm that irked Rodgers. He muttered, "We might not win, but they ain't gonna strut around no more." He didn't call another pass play the rest of the game.

The Jackets' offense committed no turnovers—after giving up 10 the previous week. The wishbone kept the Irish defense off balance, and Tech's own defense, which had underperformed so far that season, stepped up. Two Tech defenders logged nine solo tackles apiece, and Notre Dame managed only 34 yards of offense in the second half.

Tech rushed for 368 yards against a defense that had previously allowed just 195 per game and hadn't given up a touchdown in 20 quarters. On one run, already 10 yards past the line of scrimmage, Ivery slipped between two defenders and cut at just the right moment so that one tackler only grazed him. A second defender finally brought him down—but not before Ivery had picked up five more yards. On another 8-yard gain, it took three defenders to stop him. Tech fans chanted in rhythm, "Eddie LEE Iv-er-REE! Eddie LEE Iv-er-REE!"

Curry said Ivery ran with "body lean"—shoulder pads down in a slight crouch—which minimized the space a tackler had to strike. In that style, he explained, a runner keeps the bottom of the shoulder pads forward and can "hit them in the mouth. If you run too erect, you get hit under the chin."

Former Tech head trainer Bill McDonald said running with body lean—"nose over toes"—also helped a runner change directions quickly with a compact pivot, especially on contact. Ivery, he said, "was good-sized but not overpowering, fast but not the fastest in the world, but he had good body lean. He could see what was open and change directions quickly while at full speed."

"They don't run with that body lean now," Ivery said. "It would be like tackling a big ball. My shoulder pads would be down; I didn't run straight up like Eric Dickerson. They hit my shoulder pads before they hit my legs. And I had strong legs."

With 5:03 left in the game, Tech—clinging to a 16-14 lead—faced fourth down and 6 inches on Notre Dame's 23-yard line. A field goal would stretch the lead to five, but it would still give the Irish a chance to win with a touchdown drive. Ivery wanted the ball.

Sewell said that several times during the game, Ivery demanded in the huddle, "Give me the ball!" At times, he even looked toward the sideline and pointed to himself: *Give me the ball.* "A few times we even changed the play from what the coach sent in," Sewell added, "so Eddie Lee would get the ball."

When Tech needed a crucial short gain, Ivery's determination only deepened. "I'll get that yard," he would think. A first down here would let Tech burn more time off the clock—and possibly extend the lead—before Notre Dame's potent offense got another chance.

Ivery had rushed for just 81 yards on the day, but on this play, running with his signature body lean, he powered through a defender who had beaten his blocker and should have stopped him for a loss. Instead, Ivery pushed forward for four yards.

The crowd erupted, chanting, "Eddie LEE Iv-er-REE! Eddie LEE Iv-er-REE!"

Sims added a touchdown to seal the win, 23-14. Bessillieu intercepted a pass late in the game, and Tech ran out the clock.

Jubilation began.

Against Notre Dame's aggressive defense, the counterplay was particularly effective. The play appeared to go one way, but the tailback quickly changed directions, took the handoff, and dashed in the opposite direction. The Notre Dame defense, Curry said, started "creeping up and sliding over" to get a jump on the offense. In another deception, Drew Hill ran 46 yards on a reverse (with a late-hit penalty tacked on after he was shoved against a wooden bench).

Lanier—Rodgers's "little peanut"—scored on an 8-yard run through a huge hole, with blockers clearing space to his right and a defender closing in from the left. The defender had a clean shot at the slight quarterback but instead went straight for Ivery. The beauty of the wishbone.

One Notre Dame defender said afterward that they'd been a second slow all game, thrown off in part because they kept expecting Tech to pass.

Rodgers's impromptu, impetuous decision had worked.

Center Daniel, sidelined for the season with an injury, watched from the north end zone, where he had a clear view of the wishbone unfolding against Notre Dame's strong, fast defense—one that aggressively swarmed to the ball. He was struck by what he saw. "That's how the wishbone is supposed to be run," he thought.

Lanier, he said, was masterful. "He would turn upfield," Daniel recalled, "and even if he was five yards or so past the line of scrimmage, if he was about to be tackled, he'd toss the ball to Eddie Lee or David Sims, and they'd run another 10 yards. Notre Dame was completely frustrated because they were going after the ball, which would free up the running backs."

Lanier was small but quick and athletic. "Gary doesn't have to be the biggest guy or run faster than anybody," Daniel said, "but he has to be brave—an incredible warrior willing to go against guys twice his size and not blink—and be crafty and clever. He was perfect for the wishbone."

Tech athletic director Bobby Dodd called the game "one of the greatest Tech victories ever on Grant Field." Players triumphantly carried Rodgers off the field and into a delirious locker room, where they slapped hands, hugged, shouted, and danced. A beaming Rodgers climbed onto a table, basking in the moment, and shouted, "What can I say? If I live to be a thousand years old, nothing more exciting will ever happen."

When a reporter asked about beating No. 10 Notre Dame with a small, young quarterback, Rodgers offered a crack meant to compliment and tease Lanier—and to make a point about the wishbone. "I'll say this. He's the worst quarterback ever to beat Notre Dame."

Tech fans were thrilled by the upset, but many still grumbled that the team didn't pass enough. Winning that way came to be seen as gimmicky. Fans wanted both the victory and the spectacle—big throws, spiraling passes, and acrobatic catches. They envied other teams' aerial fireworks and longed to see speedster Drew Hill do more than run the occasional reverse. Some argued that a good running game was supposed to set up a dangerous passing game—not replace it.

Casey noted that Rodgers, always defiant, was apt to do the opposite of what people pressured him to do. The clamor to pass more may have only stiffened his resolve.

Rodgers loved telling the following story: "When I coached at UCLA, we beat Stanford 59-14. We had 621 yards rushing, and someone said, 'You didn't pass much.'" He rolled his eyes. "My reply: Before

6:00, two things are important to me: fast backs and big linemen. After 6:00, beautiful women and good music. Damn if it ain't past 6:00."

Another quip he relished: "I used to tell quarterback recruits who said we didn't pass much that we did pass a lot in the wishbone. I told them *this* [he mimed a quarterback pitching to the tailback] was a pass."

On his TV show, the "why-don't-you-pass-more?" question became a running gag. Whenever he had a celebrity guest, he'd prompt them to ask, "Pepper, why don't you pass more?"

The Notre Dame upset briefly tamped down the complaints. But the momentum didn't last.

Tech lost the next game to 2-7 Navy, 34-28. Ivery fumbled twice; both led to Navy touchdowns. He later said he and his teammates may not have fully recovered from the punishing Notre Dame game. He rushed for 64 yards and a touchdown.

The season ended against fourth-ranked Georgia. Tech hoped to avenge the previous year's blowout loss but fell on a last-second field goal. Tech fan Jackie Copeland watched from the end zone, hoping desperately the kick would miss. "It seemed to take forever," he said, "even though it was only 33 yards. I was hoping it goes left or right, and it didn't."

It was a respectable showing against a top team—but still a loss to their biggest rival. Ivery, who rushed for 63 yards and scored a 26-yard touchdown to tie the game at 10, fumbled inside the 10-yard line in the first quarter on a counter play when a helmet jarred his arm. Both of Lanier's pass attempts were intercepted. Tech's only completion came on a 9-yard touchdown pass thrown by receiver Drew Hill on a dizzying triple reverse.

Although the Jackets finished with a disappointing 4-6-1 record, Rodgers told the team in a tearful locker room, "I've never been prouder of a team."

Ivery finished the season with 754 rushing yards—an impressive number in a wishbone offense where carries are shared. He averaged 5 yards per carry, scored six touchdowns, and was named the team's Outstanding Offensive Player as a sophomore.

During spring practice of Ivery's junior year, Bessillieu experienced Ivery's deception firsthand. The first-team defense was scrimmaging against the first-team offense—a rare matchup. Ivery took a pitchout and zipped around the left end, where he came face-to-face with Bessillieu.

"He was the most aggressive hitter I've ever seen," Ivery said. "He wanted to hurt you."

Bessillieu had made the Freshman All-American team and, as a senior, was named First Team All-American. (He also booted kickoffs and sometimes kicked field goals.) He would go on to play six years in the NFL and two in the USFL. He fiercely defended his turf, even against a teammate—or, in this case, roommate.

"If you ran down that sideline," Bessillieu said, "you're mine. I didn't care who you were. So, I came at him with a full head of steam. It was he and I. I wasn't going to let him get past me. Then he gave me a leg and took it back. I hit nothing but air."

"I had seen guys get hit by Bessillieu and not get back up," Ivery recalled. "I made a move I don't think I ever did again in my life. I couldn't make that move again by thinking about it. It was instinctive. I wish I had that on film."

Trapped near the sideline, Ivery would normally cut back inside at the last second and hope the defender missed. But in a split-second decision he still can't fully explain, he faked to the inside. It was the logical move—the expected one. But something in his brain registered that Bessillieu was too smart, too fierce, to fall for the obvious.

He feinted right with his right leg—just a quick, almost imperceptible turn—and then pulled it back. Without losing speed, he darted along the sideline. Bessillieu lunged with full force—at empty space.

"It's the most embarrassed I've ever been," Bessillieu said.

Ivery shook his head, trying to explain the joy of running downfield, the thrill of eluding tacklers, the surge of crowd noise that followed. He felt it deeply—his moment, their moment.

"It was my safe haven," he said. "I loved the crowd noise. I felt comfortable there. Football gave me my identity. It's like no other feeling."

Linebacker Reggie Wilkes said making a great play in front of a crowd "is what you live for, to get the reaction from the fans. Coaches and teammates know it, but when *fans* recognize it, that's another level of satisfaction, what gets your juices going. If you're hurt and tired and *still* make a big play, you never forget that. Eddie Lee had so many of them. Watching him was almost magical."

For UGA quarterback Buck Belue, who played against Tech in Ivery's senior year, the thrill was in "the reaction of the fans, the 60,000-plus crowd, that you don't get any other place. You feel it; an enormous boost of adrenaline vibrates through you."

Sports psychologist Valdez said we start playing sports as youngsters simply because it's fun. "It stimulates the pleasure centers in our brain," he said,

> so it's rewarding even before you're an elite athlete: running, jumping, throwing, kicking. Even at a young age, we keep looking for that high, that first exhilarating moment when we were able to do something we didn't think we could do. It's not necessarily that we mastered something but that we did it. Even if we fall off a skateboard several times, but then the first time you get it and go a little way without falling down, it's exhilarating. Athletes are still looking for that first perfect high they got when they were little, so they keep trying to relive it, and it's really addicting.

Valdez says fans enjoy watching exciting replays again and again. "Well, an athlete does that in their head, over and over again," he says, "because it is such a rush, such a high, such a dopamine kick. I think that is the essence of sport, hitting that peak."

The thrill Ivery felt outrunning the Blue Pond farmer stayed with him.

He said he didn't necessarily feel exhilarated in the moment when he pulled off a spectacular move. He wasn't thinking through the decisions as a defender closed in. "It just came natural to me," he said. "It was just a reaction. Others may have thought it was spectacular, but to me it was an instinct thing. I didn't think about it; I would cut and fake and it just happened so fast. I felt the most exhilarated when I watched the film later. I'd think, 'Wow, that is a good play.'"

"I was not the fastest back," he added, "but I was always at full speed. I like to get the ball and go. If I'm already full speed with the ball, and a defensive back changes his direction to come at me, he's not going to catch me. That change slows him down. I would use the field, utilize my speed real well, and I had good peripheral vision."

Sims described great running as rhythm. "You get in a groove," he said. He continued,

> As the game goes along, you begin to pick up on tendencies for that game. Is a certain lineman beating the other one? How hard does that guy tackle me? Did I almost get by him last time? It all happens in a flash, but it registers in your mind. Some games, you're running better around the end, sometimes up the middle. Sometimes you might be a better receiver. It's instinctive, hard to describe. In a split second, you decide to take the right slant on someone; your peripheral vision sees something, and you react. It comes from practicing and practicing and practicing.

He said sometimes, the night before a game in which he made a long run, he dreamed it would happen.

"On a long run," he added, "you're motivated because a running back never wants a defender to walk you down—catch up to you. So, you just turn it loose."

Ivery agreed. "If somebody walks you down, you'll see it on film, and teammates will tease you in front of the group. I'd usually come up with some excuse. 'He had a better angle on me.' You never admit to being walked down."

For Lynn Dickey, Ivery's quarterback teammate later in Green Bay, the satisfaction lay in the team coming together with a plan more than in throwing a perfect pass. He enjoyed orchestrating a play to perfection, sometimes as part of barking signals before the ball was snapped—an "audible"—to change the originally called play.

"You work all week in practice," he said,

> and you find any little advantage in film, and, in the game, you recognize something the defense is doing, and you signal that to the team. You have seconds to relay it, the play clock is running, everybody gets it, they all do their job, you make a good throw, boom, you found a flaw in that defense. It took everybody doing their job in about two seconds. The team coming together—*that* was exhilarating, not really the throw. That was the easy part. It's getting everybody on the same page. Whenever it happened, I'd go to each lineman and say, "Good job." I wouldn't be able to do that without the other 10 guys doing their job.

Ivery knew the NFL was in his future and began taking the easiest—and fewest—courses necessary to stay eligible. "They told me which classes to take, and I said, 'OK,'" he recalled. "As long as I showed up to class and tutoring, I'd pass if I tried." He received a few failing grades, but not enough to lose eligibility.

He said he never received a grade change just for being a football player, but most professors were willing to give him a chance to make up work. "I'd realize I was in trouble," he said, "and ask the professor what I could do to pass. Some said there was nothing I could do, and I'd fail. Some assigned me a research paper, and I'd do it well enough to get a D."

Later, he admitted that once he realized he'd likely be rich in two years, his motivation shifted. He no longer cared whether he graduated. Publicly, he stuck to the script—"I want to win games and graduate," he repeated to reporters—but privately, he said, "I did only what I had to do to stay eligible."

He knew he was defying his grandmother's advice, but the dream of the NFL was too powerful. Seeing former teammates like Wilkes and Sanford driving nice cars after making it to the league turned his head. He recognized the value of a college degree when he visited the elegant brick home of Kent Hill's parents—both well educated—but that wasn't enough to make him change course.

The goal was simple: just stay eligible.

While academics faded into the background, football remained front and center. Ivery and his teammates entered the new season with high expectations.

There was optimism that with a very good backfield, an experienced wishbone quarterback in Lanier, and a solid offensive line, the Jackets would have a good season. But for the seventh straight season, they dropped their opener—this time to South Carolina, 17-0.

Still, Ivery was a bright spot. He romped through the Gamecocks defense, which included his childhood friend Bernard Grant, for 142 yards on 16 carries (8.9 per carry), including a 59-yard gain. A reporter noted that Ivery was the only part of the wishbone working well—though even he couldn't find the end zone.

In a 10-6 victory over Miami at home, Tech's defense was superb, but the offense managed just 163 rushing yards. For a passing team, that would be fine. But in the wishbone, it was anemic. Tech attempted just one pass, and though it fell incomplete, the crowd roared its (sarcastic) approval.

Next, Tech lost to Clemson at home, 31-14. They threw 19 passes and completed 8. Ivery rushed for 41 yards, added a 47-yard reception, and scored a touchdown. Rodgers snapped to reporters, "Write down we passed nineteen times. Everybody should be happy."

The Jackets then rebounded with a win over Air Force at home. The offense finally erupted for big gains on the ground and one long touchdown pass—their only attempt. Ivery rushed for 93 yards and two touchdowns, one a 2-yard plunge, the other a 49-yard breakaway. On the second, he powered through the line, cut left, and was gone. Ivery expressed relief that he'd finally gotten outside for a big run.

In a rainy Knoxville showdown, Tech defeated Tennessee 24-8 in another no-pass game. Rodgers, clearly speaking to a broader audience, pointed out that Tech had thrown just five passes in their last five victories—and 30 in their last five losses. Take that, critics.

After the game, a reporter mentioned to Ivery that a Tennessee defender had hit him on every play. He shrugged. In the wishbone, he said, he runs or blocks on every snap anyway.

The next week, Tech beat Auburn. Ivery rushed for 90 yards, scored two touchdowns, and, as one newspaper put it, exhibited "dazzling moves and quickness." He also threw a halfback pass to Drew Hill for a 5-yard score.

"Pepper was the only person in America who thought I could throw a football," Ivery said. "He said the receiver is going to be so wide open that it doesn't matter how you get the ball there. It can wobble like a duck; you can throw it like a shot put. Just get it down there."

Lanier also scored when a defensive back opted to chase Ivery, leaving a wide-open path.

Tech's first pass of the game fell incomplete. Afterward, Rodgers quipped, "I figured I'd get it over with then get on with the game."

At 4-2, confident Tech players said their defense, offensive line, and backs were all clicking.

Tech next easily defeated Tulane, 38-14. The wishbone ran all over Tulane for 561 yards. The first time he touched the ball, Ivery ran 64 yards for a touchdown—breaking tackles and faking out defenders and amazing the fans. He finished with 128 yards, averaging almost 10 per carry. In their four consecutive wins, Tech averaged 32.5 points and 394 yards. Usually beatable Duke was up next for homecoming, and Tech fans excitedly discussed bowl possibilities. Rodgers seemed, finally, to have things in place.

Representatives of five bowl games were in the stands. But Tech lost a heartbreaker, 25-24, even though they held what looked like a comfortable 24-9 lead at the start of the fourth quarter.

Ivery "pranced and broke tackles all day" for 102 yards, according to one reporter, including a 32-yard touchdown. But he also made a key error. The halfback pass that had worked against Auburn failed this time—he threw it after crossing the line of scrimmage, and Tech was penalized. It was a rare moment when his instinct let him down.

With 13 seconds left, Duke trailing 24-18, and facing fourth down at Tech's 6-yard line—one stop and the game was over—Duke scored a touchdown to tie it. Tech blocked the extra point but was flagged for offsides. Duke made the second attempt.

The wishbone has no plan for 13 seconds.

In a tearful locker room, Ivery said, "I'd rather gain 2 yards and win, than 200 and lose." Several weary players said they "need to bounce back."

Fans muttered on the way out, "You don't lose to Duke at homecoming."

Next up: fifth-ranked Notre Dame. Losing to them in their stadium wouldn't have been unexpected. But Tech didn't just lose—they were routed, 69-14.

Tech led 7-6, briefly, on a reverse kickoff return. Drew Hill, an outstanding return man and the perfect decoy, caught the ball at the 3-yard line, ran to the 10, then pitched it to Ivery. With the Irish chasing Hill, Ivery streaked the opposite direction—all the way to the end zone. (No one would return a kickoff for a touchdown against Notre Dame again for another 21 years.)

As Tech players celebrated taking a one-point lead on the nation's fifth-ranked team, Kent Hill overheard a Notre Dame player tell a teammate, "Let's kick their asses."

They did.

Years later, someone asked Sanford if he realized he'd made 16 tackles in the game. "When you're getting your butt kicked," he replied, "you don't notice your stats."

Notre Dame's rush defense, which had been allowing only 94 yards per game, stopped Tech's wishbone cold—holding them to 118 yards. Meanwhile, the Irish offense rushed for 349. There was no repeat of the previous year's baffling of the Notre Dame defense.

Sewell said Notre Dame anticipated the counter plays that had worked the year before. They fall flat, he said, if they're not unexpected. "They were looking for the cutbacks," he said, "and we fed right into them. Coach Rodgers thought his old tricks would work, and they didn't."

Ivery finished with just 22 yards on 12 carries. After the game, Irish coach Dan Devine explained that their defensive tackles keyed on the fullback—and if he didn't have the ball, they swarmed whoever did. That approach doesn't always work against the wishbone, but it worked that day.

Notre Dame quarterback Joe Montana was superb: 15 of 25 passing for 273 yards and three touchdowns—even though he played only three quarters.

Some Irish players claimed that during the previous season's upset loss, Tech players had mocked them as fat and slow. They came into the rematch angry. With 5:23 left, Notre Dame went for it on fourth and one and later scored on a pass play.

Once the game was out of reach, Ivery focused on self-motivation. "It becomes a matter of pride," he said. "I'm still blocking and running like it's tied. It's tough, but if you go out there and mess around, you can get hurt if you're not going full speed. You gotta keep playing the game."

Afterward, Rodgers shrugged about the blowout and said the players couldn't be blamed for wanting to score. That may be a healthy attitude toward life, but football fans want fiery motivation from their head coach, someone who *hates* to lose and reacts with more than a shrug after a 55-point loss. Rodgers even joked during the game. Lanier recalled Rodgers saying to running backs coach Casey, "If we don't score this drive, you're fired." Casey shouted, "Give the ball to Eddie Lee!"

The dreary feeling from the Notre Dame game carried into the next. Tech lost to Navy, 20-16, with President Jimmy Carter in attendance—he had attended both schools.

Almost nothing went right. Ivery was injured and rushed for only 26 yards. Tech's pass defense was porous. They reached the Navy 16-yard line with four seconds to play and a chance to win but threw an interception.

Just three weeks earlier, Tech had led Duke 24-9 in the fourth quarter and seemed on their way to a 6-2 record. Now, they were 5-5.

In an interview, Ivery said the stunning loss to Duke had continued to haunt the team mentally. The Jackets had one last chance to end the season on a high note, with 5-5 Georgia coming to town.

Ivery rushed for 112 yards and a touchdown, and Tech beat their rival 16-7. They led 16-0 at halftime but committed costly mistakes in the second half—two blocked punts and a muffed fair catch by Ivery.

He explained that his fingers were stiff from the cold, so he tried to trap the ball against his shoulder pads and dropped it.

Though Tech finished just 6-5, the win over Georgia was enough for celebration. Players carried Rodgers off the field in triumph.

Ivery became the first Tech back to rush for 900 yards in a season, delivering dazzling plays that left fans grateful he'd be returning for one more year.

And what a year it would be.

Chapter 7

He Breaks Tackles Like a Fullback

At the beginning of each season, Ivery set personal goals—but he never told anyone what they were. "They might think I'm selfish," he told a reporter. "If I keep it to myself, it's my challenge. If I don't reach them, I won't disappoint anybody but me."

Some goals, he said, depended on other players—like rushing yardage. And if he hoped to score a set number of touchdowns, "The coach might call someone else's number down at the goal line, and then I'd be PO'd at the coach." So instead, he focused on what he could control: not fumbling, not dropping passes.

That year, Ivery was voted team captain—and then came news that drastically changed his college career and launched him to national stardom.

Rodgers scrapped the wishbone.

The wishbone he'd brought to Tech. The one that had produced gaudy rushing stats at three different colleges. The one he loved for its ability to outfox even the best defenses. The one he called the greatest offense ever devised. He dumped it.

Rodgers told Ivery they would switch to the I formation—to better showcase Ivery's talent. (Within a few years, Oklahoma would do the same for Marcus Dupree; Auburn, for Bo Jackson.)

Ivery would now line up seven yards behind the line of scrimmage, rather than five, directly behind the quarterback, with a fullback between them. The fullback's job was mainly to block. Ivery would be the offense's centerpiece.

He hoped the time spent in the wishbone had limited the wear on his body and had prepared him well for the I. Always a selfless team player, he later admitted he enjoyed being "the man" in the offense—though, when asked by reporters, he stuck to the script: He was more concerned about winning and getting a degree.

Rodgers said there was no better back in the country than Ivery. He believed Tech had the potential for a strong passing game—Drew Hill, after all, would go on to have a superb NFL career—and he acknowledged that defenses were figuring out how to stop the wishbone. Too often, defenders would key on Ivery, forcing the quarterback to hand off to the fullback or keep the ball himself—leaving Tech's best runner without the ball.

Now, that would change.

Ivery would get the ball 30 to 35 times a game, instead of 10 to 20.

The more he ran and sensed defensive tendencies, his instinct sharpened and gave him an extra second's advantage. His deft cuts became more effective, and his confidence soared—as he did what he called "establishing a rhythm." He picked up on whether the defense pursued the ball carrier relentlessly and immediately or waited to see where the play was going. He noted how defensive linemen reacted to a certain blocking pattern, whether defenders were likely to arm tackle or bump him. As he ran better, the offensive line became more confident: "If we do our job right, he'll do his very well."

As Ray Friday put it, "That's a highlight of all great running backs. You've got to feed the beast, and the more you feed the beast, the better they get." Sewell said this in-game improvement also was due to competitiveness.

"If someone tackles you," Sewell said, "you say, 'I'm going to beat him next time.' Eddie Lee was that way in everything." And he was in no place more intensely competitive than on the football field. If he gained 900 yards sharing the load with three backs, how much would he gain as the featured runner?

No longer would Ivery crouch in a three-point stance, which had limited his vision. Now he would stand nearly upright, hands on knees, as the quarterback called the signals.

"In the wishbone," he said, "I didn't know what was going on over there until I got over there."

From this new vantage point, Ivery could see more of the field at a glance. He could use his exceptional peripheral vision and instinct to decide where to go. If a play called for him to run between the right tackle and tight end, but that lane was clogged with scrumming bodies, he could bounce outside or cut back to the left. The quarterback might call a sweep left, and Ivery could score on the right. When pitched the ball, he chose his hole and accelerated.

He would also use his excellent pass-catching skills more.

Lee, who had been recruited as a tailback, moved to fullback—primarily to block for Ivery. He had carried the ball 138 times in 1977 but would see just 82 carries in 1978.

The I formation also required a passing quarterback. As a result, Lanier, once a key figure in Rodgers's wishbone, hardly played during his senior season—except for pooch punts, short kicks designed to pin opponents deep. In 1976, Lanier had rushed for 268 yards; in 1977, 175. His regular-season total in 1978: zero yards on zero attempts. (He would reappear at quarterback in the bowl game.)

The shift opened opportunities for others.

"I became backup to Drew," receiver Matt Rank said. "It was the first year I lettered. If we hadn't switched, I might not have." A Pepper Rodgers team passing enough that a backup receiver could letter?

Jim Bell said the announcement brought relief—and excitement—to Tech fans. "There would be no more pressure about passing in the wishbone," he said.

A newspaper ad selling season tickets promoted the "wide open" I formation and highlighted Ivery's 900 yards from 1977.

Rodgers himself appeared to be evolving. A preseason profile referring to him as "Hollywood" Pepper and noting his trademark quips and hijinks also commented on changes in his appearance. His clothes had become more traditional—jacket and tie—and his hair was shorter. He wore a trim mustache, and the iconic "Gilligan's Island" hat had been replaced by a fedora.

Rodgers said his TV show would now resemble other coaches' shows, with more game film and less entertainment. Many speculated that he was trying to appease Tech boosters.

Some Black players suspected Rodgers had also bowed to pressure in other ways, specifically by playing some White legacy players more than their on-field performance warranted. One said, "Players know who the best players are. We play with them every day and know who should be starting."

Rodgers called this his most physical team yet—with the best defense he'd had and an experienced offensive line. Sixteen of 22 starters were returning.

And they had Ivery to run the ball.

Tech opened the season against Duke. The Jackets had lost seven consecutive season openers, and painfully recalling last year's embarrassing stumble against the Blue Devils, players confidently declared *It won't happen this time.*

Ivery did what everyone expected—he ran for 111 yards—but it wasn't enough. Tech lost 28-10 on a blistering 95-degree day in Durham, and Rodgers still hadn't found his quarterback.

Heading into the next game, against California, Rodgers said Cal was better physically and that the only thing favoring Tech was Ivery.

At Grant Field, with many empty seats, Tech lost again—34-22. Despite pulling a groin muscle on a 36-yard run, Ivery rushed for 71 yards and scored on a short pass that he turned into a 60-yard touchdown.

Tech was 0-2, and fans were disappointed that the I formation had not delivered on its promise. But, just as Rodgers had discovered Lanier two seasons before, he found his quarterback.

First-year player and third-stringer Mike Kelley, from Augusta, entered the game when both the starter and backup proved ineffective. Kelley threw two touchdown passes, with a third called back for pass interference. While he also threw an interception that was returned for a touchdown, he played well enough to give the team hope for the rest of the season.

"It was more out of desperation," Kelley said of his debut. "Our completion rate was terrible. Balls getting batted down. So, throw the freshman in there and see what happens."

Ivery was listed as questionable for the next game against Tulane, but he played—and rushed for what he called 75 "tough yards" in a 27-17 win. He was now just 62 yards short of breaking Tech's career rushing record. He also caught four passes, including a 35-yarder that set up a 1-yard touchdown.

He fumbled twice, but Rodgers brushed off the concern. In the I formation, he said, tailbacks take more hits and carry the ball more, so more fumbles happen.

"There are two kinds of backs," Rodgers said. "Those who fumble, and those who are gonna fumble." Plus, he said, *great* running backs fumble more because when they're hit, they go for an extra yard with second effort and get hit again. "I never fumbled," he said with a wink.

In the next game, against the Citadel, Ivery nearly broke the rushing record on a single play: a 51-yard run in which he broke tackles across the field, cut back, and dashed through the middle to the end zone. He finished with 91 rushing yards—"despite inept blocking by the line," according to a reporter—and returned a punt 71 yards for a touchdown. Tech won 28-0.

Ivery didn't hit the 100-yard mark, but he thrilled fans—and became Georgia Tech's new career rushing leader, with seven games still to play.

Despite several spectacular returns during his career, Ivery admitted he didn't enjoy returning punts.

"I was afraid," he said. "I had seen guys get hit right after they caught the ball. But I never told Pepper. I was a competitor; I did what I was told. But I was fearful. I prefer, let me see where I'm going and what the defense is doing. That's hard to do returning punts."

When he did return one, though, he relished the space and unpredictability. He especially liked when the coverage team followed the blocking to one side, and he could slip the other way.

"It was great," he said, "unless it didn't work. Then I'd hear about it in the film room."

In the next game, against favored South Carolina, Ivery was credited with carrying Tech to a 6-3 upset.

"Eddie Lee basically carried the team," Kelley said.

Despite entering the game with a hip pointer, pulled hamstring, and sprained toe, Ivery ran for 157 yards—nearly eight per carry. On the drive that began at Tech's own 30 and ended with the game-winning field goal with 57 seconds left, he gained 41 of the 53 yards.

Two of those gains—12 and 11 yards—were described in the paper as "two dramatically exceptional individual efforts," showcasing his full range of skills. The reporter wrote that throughout the game he "ran over and around defenders, dishing out punishment as well as enduring it."

On the final drive, Ivery demanded the ball. A newspaper photo showed him bowling over a South Carolina defender.

As usual, he credited his linemen. "They came off the ball and just blew them out," he said—still wincing from the three injuries he'd carried into the game.

Tech had started the season 0-2. Now, they were 3-2.

Next, at home, they faced Miami—fresh off an upset of No. 19 Auburn—and featuring running back Ottis Anderson (who would be drafted ahead of Ivery the following spring). With Dolly Parton sitting beside Rodgers's wife Janet, Tech jumped out to a 24-0 halftime lead, thanks largely to Ivery's 76 yards.

And the defense. Miami didn't cross midfield in the first half, managed only three first downs, and trailed in yardage 212-73.

Tech ultimately squeaked by, 24-19.

Ivery finished with 166 yards—his highest total to that point in his career. A frustrated Miami defender said, "You think he's down, and he keeps trying."

But Ivery was disappointed. He'd fumbled twice, including once just two yards from the end zone. A touchdown there would have sealed the game. After his first fumble, Miami drove for a touchdown that cut the lead to eight, and several Tech players couldn't help recalling last season's collapse against Duke—when they'd led 24-9 in the fourth quarter and lost by one.

"I'd say I had an even game," Ivery told reporters. He admitted he was pleading on the sideline, "Defense, please hold on," worried he'd let the team down.

He said the first fumble was caused by a lapse in concentration as he lunged for extra yards, and the second because he was still thinking about the first.

Rodgers, returning to his familiar quip about great backs fumbling more, joked to the press that without the fumbles, the game wouldn't have been exciting.

Ivery praised the offensive line for playing their best game, especially against a Miami defense that included an All-American tackle.

The Jackets were now 4-2.

In the stands was Green Bay Packers scout Dick Corrick, who said to himself, "When you think you have him down, he can explode out of there. He breaks tackles like a fullback!"

Next up was Auburn, at Auburn—a rivalry dating back to 1892 and, before 1963, one of the South's biggest. Each team had won 38 games in the series.

Ivery, with 127 rushing yards, and Hill, with a 97-yard kickoff return for a touchdown, were the stars in Tech's 24-10 win. By now, it was routine to chalk a victory up to Ivery's superb performance. He even threw a 17-yard touchdown pass to Bucky Shamburger just before the half—the first time Rodgers used that play all season. The pass wobbled and nearly carried Shamburger out of bounds, but he was so alone that even Ivery's clunky throw worked.

For his career, Ivery was 4-for-7 passing, with three touchdowns.

Tech had won five in a row. Ivery ranked 11th in the country in rushing, and the campus buzzed about football—especially his dazzling performances. Players confidently vowed there would be no repeat of last year, when they were also 5-2 but stumbled the rest of the way.

They made good on that promise.

In a homecoming heart-stopper, Tech defeated Florida 17-13 after trailing 10-0. Late in the game, Florida went for it on fourth-and-inches at the Tech 3-yard line, and the defense held. Tech then drove 97 yards until Ivery scored the game-winner from four yards out with 5:23 remaining. He was hit at the 3 and carried four defenders with him into the end zone. Four against one? No problem.

He had rushed for 29 yards in the first half and exploded for 117 in the second. Before the game-winner, he'd scored another touchdown to tie it—becoming Tech's all-time leader in touchdowns.

"He's the best back I've seen," said a Gator defender.

Representatives of four bowl games left impressed with both Tech and Ivery.

A *Constitution* sportswriter began speculating about Ivery's chances for the Heisman Trophy. Other running backs, however, had better stats and early publicity campaigns. Rodgers called it "a shame and a disgrace" that Ivery wasn't mentioned more often. The Tech sports information director admitted they hadn't promoted him well enough.

Ivery shrugged. He said he used the snub as motivation—to prove he was just as good as the others. *I'll show you.*

Pro scouts interviewed for the article said he'd be a first-round draft pick. One scout saw no negatives in Ivery's pro future, citing his size, quickness, balance, and desire.

"Plus, I understand he's a fine young man," the scout added.

Tech had a week off before traveling to Colorado Springs to face the Air Force Academy. Though unranked in the AP poll, they were ranked No. 19 in the UPI poll—the first time Tech had been ranked in six years.

Ivery's only appearance on *The Pepper Rodgers Show* came during his senior year. "I was camera-shy," he said. "So, I tried not to say too much."

But that brief appearance netted him something more valuable than airtime: a wife.

Watching the show was Spelman College student Anna Davis. Smitten by the respectful running back who kept saying "Yes sir" to Rodgers, she turned to a friend and said, "Who is that country boy? I want to meet him."

Stover's girlfriend passed the message along, but Ivery figured Davis was just another coed drawn to his growing fame.

Still, he invited her to his apartment.

When she pulled up in a new Thunderbird—and he was still driving his loud six-year-old Cutlass—he did a double-take. When she left, he thought, *Wow, I've met a real woman.*

On their next date, they went to church.

Davis came from a steady, middle-class family. Her mother worked as a beautician, her father drove a truck, and all three of their children would graduate from college.

Anna attended one of Bessillieu's parties, where she lay down in one of the bedrooms around 2 a.m. Ivery, after peeking and seeing her asleep, asked a former girlfriend to dance. Bessillieu put on a slow song, and Ivery made his move. They were dancing closely, Ivery kissing her softly, until he felt a strong tug on his shoulder. Anna, awake and alert, jerked him around and said, "Let's dance." Ivery said later that it was the first time a woman asserted herself around him. "She must really like me," he thought.

When Ivery proposed, he didn't know he had.

He bought Anna a $500 diamond ring as a romantic gift—not an engagement ring. Later, Anna showed the ring to her sister, and the next time the sister saw Ivery, she exclaimed, "Congratulations! When's the wedding?"

He replied, "I don't know. We haven't discussed it yet."

Soon, they did.

Once they agreed to marry, Ivery suggested they wait until he'd had a year in pro football. Anna, though, insisted they get married before he left Atlanta, so they did.

"I'd never been that close to a woman so educated, so aggressive," he said. "She apparently didn't mind me being a country boy. We hadn't known each other that long when we got married, so we grew to love each other more and more. She turned out to be the best woman I'd ever met, and I turned out to be something she didn't expect: a drug addict."

Bennie Mae was initially wary of Anna. Would she consider herself superior to the Cherokee Iverys?

"She was not uppity-uppity but embraced our family," Bennie Mae said. "She was not stuck up. She was set in her own ways but down to earth. She knew we were country but didn't make us feel bad."

Ivery needed just 57 yards to reach 1,000—considered the mark of a great season.

The Friday before Tech faced Air Force at Falcon Field was sunny and clear, in the 50s. Tech radio engineer and producer John Kramer toured the Air Force campus on that gorgeous day, the eastern edge of the Rocky Mountains in sight. He toured the fieldhouse and the beautiful Air Force cathedral, a popular tourist attraction. A former Air Force cadet, he strolled the campus with no thought of the weather.

Rodgers, an Air Force quarterbacks coach early in his career, warned players not to look past the 3-6 Falcons to season-ending contests against formidable foes Notre Dame and UGA. Military academy teams play hard and intelligent football, are disciplined, and won't give up. He said they will have plenty of oxygen on the sideline to cope with the thin-air altitude of 6,035 feet (compared to Atlanta's oxygen-rich 738). *Constitution* reporter David Davidson said when he walked from the press box down to the field, he had to pause to breathe deeply. Ivery felt it, too. "I couldn't get my breath," he said. (According to Air Force assistant coach Dick Ellis, that's what they wanted. When the visitors left their locker room, an ominous sign declared, "Welcome to Air Force, Altitude 6,035 Feet.") Tech was well prepared for the conditions, Rodgers assured them.

Radio announcer Kim King settled into his hotel room that Friday, then went for a jog, admiring the Rockies. "Tomorrow is going to be a beautiful football day," he thought.

Trainer Ken Smith recalled flying to Denver and switching to a smaller plane. The pilot told him not to worry about the Colorado Springs weather. A pilot would know, right?

During Friday's walk-through on the field, Rodgers chatted with Ellis and commented on the sparkling weather. Ellis warned that conditions in Colorado could change drastically from one day to the next.

Rodgers joked, "Don't you let any bad weather come in tomorrow."

However prepared Tech players thought they were, their reaction Saturday morning was disbelief that the game was even going to be played. Many—nearly all from the South—thought the game would be canceled.

Lowe said assistant coach Norm Van Brocklin assured players, "They won't play in this weather."

"I didn't think we would play either," Ivery agreed. "We looked down on the field from the hotel and saw sweepers scraping a foot of snow off the field, and I thought, 'There ain't no way we're going to play this game.'"

According to a media report, the field was cleared twice before the game and again at halftime.

When King woke up, he was stunned to see snow blowing sideways in a howling wind, with a foot of it already on the ground. He called Ciraldo and asked if he had brought anything warm enough. Neither had, so they drove to Kmart to buy gloves, hats, coats, sweatshirts, and thermal underwear.

A Tech equipment manager scrambled to find sideline heaters and thermal gear for the players.

Kent Hill recalled coaches telling the team, "The cold is all in your mind." But Hill noticed the coaches were bundled up in extra layers. Apparently, it wasn't all in *their* minds.

"It was so damn cold," Sewell remembered. "I'm from Florida, and I was out there on that frozen field."

Lanier said the rags hanging from players' belts froze when they got wet. Kelley said, with fingers stiff and the ball rock-hard, "It was painful to take the snap." Lee added, "Your hands were like stones, and the ball was like a brick. My feet were completely numb. I had no feeling in my toes."

Rodgers's 15-year-old son, Kelly, had traveled to the game. "That was the coldest I've ever been," he said. "The cold is all you thought about. That field was like cement. I kept thinking, *when they get hit and fall to the ground, that's gonna hurt.*"

When Air Force assistant coach Tom Backhus saw the weather, he figured the cadets would be fine—but not the visitors.

"No way these southern Georgia peaches are going to play well. No way," he said. "We thought we had an advantage and Ivery wouldn't run well. But he killed us."

Kelley's family had traveled from California. They may have wished they hadn't. "They stayed the whole game," he said. "They froze their patooties off. My grandpa was out there. They were covered in blankets. It was brutal."

Representatives of the Tangerine Bowl, held in Orlando, Florida, where the average afternoon temperature in November was 78 degrees, were also shivering in the stands.

Tech defensive end Lance Skelton said he couldn't feel his fingers or toes. When he came off the field, someone threw a big coat over him—but it didn't help.

"The coats were frozen," he said. "It was like covering yourself in ice. We were miserable."

Marvin Dyett recalled one player who was bleeding but didn't even know it—his fingers were too numb to feel it.

According to Lowe, assistant coach Norm Van Brocklin told players to keep their feet warm by putting on a sock, wrapping it in plastic, and then layering another sock on top. But for some, the strategy backfired. Their feet began to sweat, then freeze.

Air Force defensive back Charles Shugg said it was the coldest game he had ever played.

"It was freezing. It was a *penetrating* cold," he said. "We were used to being in cold weather, but it was so cold there weren't many fans in the stadium. We were wrapping our feet in Saran wrap inside our shoes, but the defensive backs coach was old school. He wouldn't let us use heaters or gloves. We wore extra T-shirts, but that's about it. It was brutal."

Non-football player cadets were required to attend games and wear coats and ties, regardless of the weather. They could wear an overcoat but not heavy-duty cold-weather gear that a day like that called for. In the stands, they were more exposed to the wind than the players below. To ease their misery, they rotated in and out of the heated bathrooms.

Air Force linebacker Bill Becker was injured and watched the game from the sidelines, almost wishing he were playing to generate some heat.

"It was cold to just sit," Becker said. Still, "For the guys on the field, it hurt even more to be hit or to hit somebody. The turf was unforgiving. It was like falling on concrete. We kept thinking, 'Can we have this over with now?'"

Air Force fullback Steve Drewnowski said it was the coldest game he'd ever played: "You'd put your hands down to the ground and your fingers almost get frostbite." He recalled only one experience that was colder: when he flew scientists to Antarctica. Offensive coordinator Ken Hatfield said he gave gloves to backs and receivers, but they removed them because they couldn't feel anything anyway.

Air Force's recruiting director, Jim Bowman, who had experienced 20 winters in Colorado Springs, watched the game from the press box. "It was terrible," he said, "the worst weather I remember, and we had some bad weather. I was thinking, 'Are you kidding? Are we playing in this?'"

King performed his usual pre-broadcast ritual: walking on the field to see the view from the ground and absorb the atmosphere—details that would help him convey the scene to the radio audience. The ground was frozen, and the fierce wind stung his eyes. He slid his feet gingerly to avoid slipping. He walked about 15 yards and thought, "This is ridiculous." He reported to Ciraldo back in the press box, "It's going to be hard to run or pass. I bet it's a 3-0 game. The first team to kick a field goal wins." He was unimaginably wrong, and footing turned out to be no problem. Ivery said the ground was slippery before the game, but after the snow was cleared, cleats were able to grip the turf just fine.

Reports on the amount of snowfall were inconsistent. Some media outlets claimed there was light snow, while at least one newspaper reported that the snow removal equipment could barely keep up with the snowfall. Herrington recalled snowplows clearing snow before the game and snow blowers removing snow from the line markers at halftime. Some players described conditions with lots of snow. (Not Drewnowski, who said, "I don't think it snowed that day. I'm from New England. That's not really snow.") Rodgers's son Kelly stated there was only "a remnant of snow." Matt Rank recalled only experiencing snow flurries. Media images and one brief video clip from the game show little snow on the field. Perhaps there was snow piled up off-field and out of camera view?

The National Weather Service archive indicates no snow all week and only a little more than a half-inch on gameday. Perhaps memories of a dreadfully cold day exaggerate the amount of snow. Whether due to snow removal or actual low accumulation, what made all the players miserable and sapped their motivation was the freezing temperature, rock-hard turf, and strong, vicious wind. When the game started, it was 20 degrees, and the whipping wind made the wind chill factor zero. Or thereabouts. One Denver reporter wrote that the wind chill factor was 20 below. Not true, but nobody there would fault him for exaggerating.

But Air Force had a bigger problem than the weather: Eddie Lee Ivery.

"We kept running the same damn play, and they couldn't stop him," Sewell said.

Air Force quarterback Dave Ziebart, who called it "the worst weather in my four years at Air Force," had high praise for Ivery.

"I knew a lot of tough guys there," he said, "but he played just as well in the fourth quarter as early in the game."

And he didn't even know about the throwing up.

Chapter 8

Like Something Not Happening

The Air Force head coach—for that one season—was future Super Bowl–winning New York Giants coach Bill Parcells.

According to Air Force players, preparation for Tech didn't include any special defensive scheme for Ivery. Still, Ziebart recalled Parcells telling the team, "Ivery's going to get the ball often, and we need to stop him."

Assistant coach Dick Ellis said that during the week leading up to the game, the junior varsity squad acted as the opposition in practice. They ran the I formation, and the JV tailback wore number 40, so the defense could get used to pursuing that jersey.

But while the defense may have prepared for Tech's offensive structure, the JV tailback wearing Ivery's number didn't come close to preparing them for the real thing—the tailback they had to chase on November 11, 1978.

Before the game started, Ivery was approached by Arden Zinn, an Atlanta fitness center owner who, for three years, led players in stretching exercises before practices and games. When Rodgers first proposed inviting Zinn to lead stretching, McDonald, director of sports medicine, thought the players wouldn't take it seriously and the staff would be ridiculed. Zinn and her assistant were young and attractive; they played popular music of the players' choosing. Would this become a joke? McDonald later realized the stretching was more extensive than what the players had been doing. Fullback Friday said the stretching loosened muscles tightened by weightlifting and reduced strains. "Sometimes, Pepper's unpredictability worked," McDonald said.

"The players had no clue," Zinn said. "They only knew strength and speed."

She had come to Rodgers's attention after repeatedly saying, "If football players would learn to release the tension in their muscles, they could take hits better." Rodgers heard this and hired her.

Like everyone else, Zinn was astounded by Ivery's talents.

"I was not knowledgeable about football," she said, "but I could see he had explosive speed. He had it all: balance, speed, peripheral vision." Even a football novice could tell.

Before the game, Zinn said to Ivery, "It's too cold to get warmed up outside, and you need to get loose." They went to a room where she helped him stretch.

Ivery later winkingly bragged to teammates, "I was by myself with Arden." It was exaggerated talk—they had only done stretching exercises—but he admitted, "I became very attracted to her. It was almost like a date."

They had a brief romantic relationship, and she gave him gifts, including a stereo. Bessillieu said she sometimes brought food to his parties.

At the end of Ivery's senior season, Zinn presented him with a carefully organized scrapbook of his press clippings—his name on the cover.

Before the game against Air Force, Ivery enacted his usual pre-game routine, visualizing each play. If Rodgers was giving a pre-game pep talk, he didn't notice.

"I was so focused on the game, and I was very nervous, so if Pepper was talking to motivate, I didn't hear it," he said. "I was in my own world."

"You almost didn't know he was there. He was concentrating on the game," Bessillieu said.

Then he vomited.

"I was scared every game," Ivery said. "There was no game when I was not nervous. Sometimes I threw up before the game. So, I would eat light at the pre-game meal." He threw up before every UGA game and every other big game.

"Eddie Lee better go throw up, so he'll have a good game," his teammates teased.

"At least one guy threw up before every game," Lowe said. "That let us know Eddie Lee was ready. It was his ritual, and after that, it was showtime." High school through the NFL, Ivery felt "healthy fear" before each game—but with his first hit of the game, the fear disappeared.

"That first hit gets rid of butterflies," David Sims said. "It doesn't matter who you're playing. You're anxious before the game starts, and you're glad after that first hit. Then you get it on."

"Athletes who have problems with performance think fear is something to eradicate, but some players realize it's part of the game," Valdez explained.

> Neural pathways of fear are the same as neural pathways for exhilaration. You can't tell the difference between fear and exhilaration. It's how we label or define that feeling that matters. If fear is thought of as preparation instead of something to get rid of, that's helpful, so those who embrace the fear and don't try to eradicate it are more likely to be successful. Some would say, "I threw up, so I'm not ready. I'm facing too much of a challenge. Something's wrong." But that's not the case at all.

This time, however, Ivery's vomiting was not pre-game nervousness. And it didn't stop after one hit.

Kramer said their small broadcast booth, perched atop the rim of the stadium, looked like a greenhouse—a box of glass and steel, with the strong frigid wind blowing against it and the Rockies towering in the background.

At least, he thought, they'd be inside.

But in those days, the radio broadcast was transmitted via phone lines, and Kramer couldn't find a phone jack in the booth. He ran a line to a jack outside the door—which meant the door had to stay ajar throughout the game—and the freezing wind howled into the booth. A small heater offered little defense against the cold.

Shivering play-by-play announcer Al Ciraldo began his radio coverage with an accidental mix-up. Probably linking the Atlanta Falcons with Falcon Stadium, he welcomed listeners to "Falcon Stadium in Atlanta."

But then he called a game he would never forget.

In the first quarter, Don Patterson intercepted an Air Force pass and returned it for a touchdown.

Early in the second quarter, Ivery was handed the ball on Tech's 27-yard line. He ran left but found no opening and was trapped behind the line of scrimmage. For a moment, it seemed the defense—playing with home-field (and weather) advantage—might contain him.

But Ivery reversed direction to the right, eluded defenders with quick fakes, and breaking tackles in a spectacular display, raced 73 yards for a touchdown.

One reporter called the run "a thing of beauty."

In a photo from the game published in the Air Force student newspaper, Ivery is shown sprinting, two defenders falling away—one on each side—futilely reaching to stop him.

Bowman thought, *That's a fluke.*

But it was just the beginning.

On the sidelines, Tech linebacker Mackel Harris said he and his teammates watched in frigid astonishment, asking, "How is he doing that?"

A stunned Bessillieu, who was injured and played little, said later, "It was so cold. What Eddie Lee did was like something not happening."

Ivery went to the sidelines, first to the oxygen. That reprieve didn't last. Breathing hard in the high altitude, he stepped from the oxygen and vomited again. This was not nervous vomiting. He didn't know if it was eggs he ate that morning or the altitude (nausea is a possible symptom) or the cold or the strenuous effort it took to play—or all of that—but he knew it wouldn't stop him.

A player told Rodgers that Ivery was throwing up, and the coach quipped, "If I was running out there, I'd be throwing up, too." Herrington now had a new and unexpected job: clean up after Ivery. He gave him towels to wipe his face, covered the vomit on the ground with snow, and, in the locker room, cleaned vomit off the floor.

According to Friday, Ivery didn't merely throw up.

"He was heaving," said Friday, who then saw even more proof of Ivery's toughness when he went right back into the game and continued to elude defenders.

"I don't know too many players heaving like that," Friday said, "who would get back out there and play. He would come off the field, heave, then go back. Some games, you didn't feel like he could go full speed, but at game time, it was like nothing had happened. He had the ability to block pain. Some players just could not take the hits he did and get back up and run the very next play."

Teammates and coaches would have understood if Ivery had asked not to go back in. But that wasn't Ivery's way.

Teammate Lance Skelton said he pulled a muscle and went to the locker room for treatment, where he saw Ivery, dehydrated from vomiting, lying on a table with his shoulder pads off, connected to an IV.

He assumed Ivery was done for the day.

"I have no idea how he got up off that table and went back in the game," Skelton said.

At halftime, the score 14-3, the team doctor gave Ivery an anti-emetic pill to ease the nausea, not sure if he would play in the second half. In the Air Force locker room, Parcells, who would normally speak with both the offense and defense, spent all his time with defensive coordinator Al Groh and the defense, trying to find a way to stop Ivery.

After halftime, Tech drove 80 yards for a touchdown. At 21-3, it looked like a blowout.

But despite the difficulty of holding, throwing, and catching the ball with rigid, numb fingers, the Air Force passing game rallied. Ziebart threw a 48-yard touchdown pass to receiver Cormac Carney, and Jim Sturch added another field goal, cutting the score to 21-13—and making Tech a tad nervous.

Until Ivery touched the ball 12 seconds later.

On Tech's first snap, Ivery dashed 80 yards for his second touchdown—surpassing Tech's single-game rushing record of 217 yards.

"It was one of my most beautiful runs," Ivery said. "I had great blocking."

The defenders—perhaps unwilling to use their throbbing hands any more than necessary—tried to tackle him by hitting him rather than wrapping him up. "That was right down my alley," he said.

He used his natural gifts and determination spectacularly. He cut completely across the field to the opposite side from where the play had started, leaped over both a teammate, Kent Hill, and the man Hill had blocked, kept his footing, and motored on.

Becker said, "There was conversation about his ability in the cold, if it helped or hurt. It might have helped him if the defense doesn't have as much motivation when it's miserable cold. But it was mainly a battle over desire, and he had more desire to run than we did to stop him."

Defensive lineman Kory Cornum recalled Parcells shouting that they better get their asses in gear.

But they could do almost nothing to slow Ivery.

Backhus remembered standing on the sidelines, thinking, "Holy mackerel, he is really good!"

Shugg was unaccustomed to encountering a running back so frequently so deep in the defensive backfield, but again and again, here Ivery came. He grew to dread each time.

"I'd run into him as hard as I could," he said, "and he'd just keep going. I never pushed him back; he pushed *me* back. When I did tackle him, I'm not sure if I really tackled him, or if I fell down in front of him, accidentally landed between his legs, and he tripped over me."

Because of his numb fingers, Ivery said he didn't change hands grasping the ball, as backs are taught to do to keep defenders from knocking it loose. He often reversed direction, switching the ball as he went, but not today, though it felt awkward. He was afraid he might fumble by moving it from one arm to the other. "My hands were never warm, and when I put them to the heater, they'd start aching," he recalled.

When a Tech player backed up too close to one of the kerosene-fueled heaters, his uniform caught on fire. At first, he didn't even feel the heat—he was too numb. Someone quickly knocked him down and put out the flames.

For student trainer Tommy Herrington, cleaning up vomit wasn't his only new task that day.

Occasionally, a player would get too close to the flame, and their shoelaces would catch fire—but it was so cold, players didn't notice. Herrington's job became kicking snow onto their shoes to extinguish the flames.

The cold had numbed everyone's lips, making it hard to understand each other. At one point, someone mumbled something Herrington couldn't make out.

"What?" he said.

Finally, he understood: "YOUR PANTS ARE ON FIRE!"

He looked down—and saw his polyester pants melting. Someone quickly kicked snow onto him to put out the fire.

"Roy Simmons had an icicle frozen on his helmet, hanging down," Lee recalled. "Roy said, 'Rodney, Rodney, look at this.' It was about two inches long."

By this point, according to Lowe, Ivery inspired Tech's defense to play harder.

"We stepped it up on defense because of what Eddie Lee brought to the game," Lowe said. "None of us wanted to play there, but he gave us more in Colorado than I've ever seen anyone give in a game. The way he was running, we couldn't help but play harder."

In Atlanta, Jim Bell listened to the untelevised game on the radio. Bell almost never missed a Tech game, home or away.

"I only miss for two reasons," he said. "Back when the Army had me, or if there was a death in the family. And my mother-in-law died that week."

"On every long run, Al Ciraldo would go crazy," Leo Benatar, another radio listener, said.

> Sometimes he'd call out the wrong yard line. "Eddie Lee's at the 50, the 40, the 20, the 20. He's going all the way!" On one long run, Eddie Lee ran around the left end. I could picture it as Ciraldo described it. He was skating along, right by everyone. I could just see him gliding along. He mentioned near the end that Eddie Lee was getting near the rushing record. It was just unbelievable."

"Al was going crazy," Kramer said.

Kramer usually paid little attention to games, not only because he wasn't a college football fan but also because he concentrated on directing the broadcast. When training someone for this work, he would say, "You're no longer a fan." If someone is a fan, he said, they couldn't focus on the work.

"If you have your hand on his fader, and you need to back him down if he goes crazy, you can't be a fan. Pay attention," Kramer said. But this time he peeked at the field. "Eddie Lee had these enormous runs," he said. "Nobody could touch him. Players would slide off him. It was amazing. He ran away from everyone, jumped over people."

John Barnett was listening, or trying to, in Thomson on his AM radio. He picked up the game on a small station 35 miles away. When the signal faded in and out, he fumed. "I had to get the dial in just the right spot," he said.

Near the end of the third quarter, Ziebart-to-Carney countered with a 5-yard touchdown pass, followed by a 2-point conversion, making the score 28-21. After Air Force fumbled with 10 minutes to go in the game and Tech recovered the ball, Ivery ran through a big hole, this time for a 57-yard touchdown ("ramming" his way downfield, per one reporter). Tech led 35-21.

Few fans remained in the stands. Military officers let cadets return to their rooms because they were miserable—something that almost never happened.

Groh, Hatfield, and Ellis shivered in the coach's box despite their heavy coats. Ellis said it seemed to an exasperated Hatfield that Tech only had to give the ball to Ivery and—boom—touchdown. After Ivery's third long touchdown run, a frustrated Hatfield threw his red felt-tip pen, splattering red ink on the window and on their white Falcon-emblazoned coats. Chuckling, Hatfield said, "It made a beautiful red splatter on the glass, and it froze to the window and made it hard to see."

Ivery's run gave him 309 yards—the most by any college back that season. Tech's sports information director looked up the record and discovered Ivery was just 41 yards short. The news was passed down to Rodgers, who declaimed, "I don't care about his yards. I care about winning." He was worried that Air Force, who had the ball, might somehow steal a victory. Tech had endured several agonizing upsets to lesser teams the last two years. A loss today would hurt.

Newspaper reporters watched from an unheated press box, shivering. Davidson said they had expected a dull game, with the ground frozen and the players miserable, and hoped it would end quickly. But as Ivery piled up the yards and made spectacular runs, someone tallied his total and said, "Hell, what's the record?" They looked it up and forgot their misery, now very interested in this unexpectedly exciting game.

When Air Force's next drive ended at the Tech 8, a relieved Rodgers said to put Ivery in and give him the ball until he broke the record. Ivery said later, "I had no idea about the record. Pepper comes over and says you have a chance to break it."

Ivery crashed over right tackle for 13 yards, leaving him 28 short. He dashed around the right end with 13:15 to go. But Ivery's stomach rebelled again—so excruciating that he left the game. Friday shocked everyone by bolting 67 yards for his second touchdown, making the score 41-21. (Cornum said of Friday's dash, "We must have been so focused on Eddie Lee that when they gave him the ball, away he went.")

Although Ivery was a team-above-individual player, he thought more about the record and wished he had another chance. A little over six minutes remained when Tech kicked off. How much time would the Air Force offense consume? Ivery assumed he was out of the game for good, so he stood with his back to a heater instead of trying to keep his hands warm.

But defensive back Henry Johnson intercepted a pass, and Ivery—nauseated, short on oxygen, tired, and with cold hands—reentered the game. Anyone who knew him knew he would play as hard as if he were fresh at the beginning of a game. According to teammates, he played harder.

On the first play, even though the defense and everyone in the sparsely filled stadium knew Ivery would get the ball, he rushed 21 yards to break the record at 356. As his teammates congratulated him, Johnson told him to go back in to reach 400, but Bessillieu, laughing, said not to do that—you might lose some yards. As they slapped him on the back to celebrate, he joked that they were just trying to keep their hands warm.

Ivery said later he had a hard time celebrating because he was too cold. He also said he had never been so tired during a game. By then, all that was on his mind was "getting the hell out of Colorado." A teammate shouted, "It's 72 degrees in Atlanta! Let's go home!"

All his greatness converged on that day. Determination, speed, strength, elusiveness. On a day when he was more tired than in any other game he had ever played, in the coldest weather and highest altitude he had ever experienced, on one of the sickest days of his life, he sped, faked, and powered his way for more yards than any college running back in history.

Perhaps the frigid weather made a difference, but that should have been a problem for the Southerners, not the cadets. Ziebart thought the conditions were irrelevant.

"Ivery would have been fine in any weather," he said.

Cornum recalled that the cleats gripped the grass turf well, so slipping wasn't a problem. Only once was Ivery tackled for a loss because *he* slipped. Even in those conditions, he was able to power through defenders. Footing was not mentioned by any player on either team as impacting the game.

"He was just a great player," Cornum said, "and we weren't very good, and he crushed us."

"You'll never forget it if you saw it," Bowman said. "When people mention the great backs who played here—and we've had some big-timers—he's as good as there's ever been."

Rodgers told Parcells he wouldn't have given Ivery the ball late in the game if he had not been close to the record. Ivery said the proper things to the press (some of it humble but not true): that he was more concerned about winning than the yards (the true part), that any back on the team could have done the same thing the way the line was blocking, and that it wasn't a matter of him breaking tackles but hitting the hole and outrunning the defense. A battered Shugg, not accustomed to attempting so many tackles that far behind the line of scrimmage, would disagree.

In an interview with Ciraldo, Ivery joked that if Friday hadn't run so well (115 yards on five carries), he would have gained more yards. McDonald asked Ivery how he pulled off the record, and he said the only way to keep warm was to keep running.

Other records fell. Tech's 510 yards rushing was the most ever against Air Force. Air Force ran a record 96 offensive plays and gained a record 508 total yards. The total yardage for both teams set a stadium record. Friday and Air Force running back Shelby Ball had career-high rushing games. Carney's touchdown gave him 8 for the season, an NCAA record for a freshman, and his 11 receptions brought him to 55, a new college record for receptions in a season.

Parcells said Ivery's 73-yard touchdown run "turned a 5-yard loss into a touchdown. He's everything they said he was, and more."

"He's the best I've played against," said Air Force linebacker Tom Foertsch, who added a familiar comment made by defenders going back to Ivery's tenth grade: "It seemed like every time we'd have him contained, he would get away."

Defensive tackle Ryan Williams said, "I haven't seen a back with the desire to win that he has."

For the second time this season, an opposing coach came to the Tech locker room to congratulate Ivery. "I just want to shake the hand of a great player," Groh said. "It's not his speed or his balance or his acceleration. It's just that he's so physically tough."

"We weren't big on offense or defense," Hatfield said. "Instead, we tried to use speed and mobility, but our linebackers and defensive backs hit him, and he bounced off and kept running with the dadgum ball. Eddie Lee just kept going. I've never been in a game like that, ever, as player or coach. Ever."

The game was not televised, and cameras from a Colorado Springs TV station and from Air Force froze and didn't work. Atlanta's WSB-TV sent a camera to get footage for *The Pepper Rodgers Show*, and it captured 335 of Ivery's 356 yards. (A WSB representative said that film footage is long gone.)

The camera was aimed at the field when Ivery set the record, but as he tore around the end, a fan stood and blocked the camera's view of the play. All those empty seats—and someone blocked the camera. All three major networks requested copies of the film for national sports shows, but no one was able to show Ivery's triumphant strides.

Kramer compiled Ciraldo's audio calls of every Ivery run on a reel and kept it in his desk at the radio station. "The guy who took over for me," Kramer said, "who knows what he did with it?"

A reporter asked Rodgers if he thought the Tangerine Bowl reps were impressed. "Ivery impresses everyone," Rodgers said. That was old hat by then.

Ivery finished the game with 26 carries for 356 yards (a 13.7-yard average, another team record), including touchdown runs of 73, 80, and 57 yards.

"It didn't dawn on me until the end of the season what an accomplishment that was," Ivery said later. "I wish I had gone for 400 yards" (which he could have done easily).

Tech, after winning convincingly and with Ivery setting a national record, expected a good bowl bid—perhaps the Cotton Bowl in Dallas. On the bus to the airport, Kramer said, Ivery—as usual—was in the back of the bus while the team chanted, "Eddie LEE! Eddie LEE!"

Rodgers led a cheer: "I love the Yellow Jackets, how about YOU? I love the Yellow Jackets, seven and TWO!" Kramer said they thought they would take the bus to the airport, board their chartered Delta flight, and fly home.

"Little did we know," he said. They were ready to get warm and celebrate. No one anticipated how they would celebrate at the airport, though.

They boarded the plane and began taxiing, only to return to the airport to fix a mechanical problem. They taxied again, but due to another issue, the plane returned once more.

"There was a problem with the engines that had to do with the high altitude and cold temperature, and they had to bring in a mechanic from Denver," Kramer said.

Trainer Ken Smith said they were cheering on the plane as it pulled from the dock, but when the pilot returned for the second time, the plane went silent. "There were some scared people on that plane," he said.

A nervous Friday recalled the 1970 plane crash that killed nearly the entire Marshall University football team. It would be several hours before the plane could be fixed, so Rodgers gathered everyone at the airport bar and said, "Enjoy yourselves."

They did.

"We were all so damn drunk by the time we left," Friday said.

"Pepper got loaded. He was smashed," Kramer said. "He sat down next to Al, Kim, and me and said, 'I can't wait to hear Al describing Eddie Lee breaking the record because until Al Ciraldo says it, it didn't happen.' He was shit-faced."

Utt said he and a teammate caught a ride with cadets they met in the airport and picked up four cases of Coors beer at a liquor store.

"Offensive line coach Larry Travis wasn't happy with us," Utt said. "But we were less drunk than those who stayed at the airport."

Coors was not yet distributed nationwide, which gave it a mystique among Eastern beer drinkers, especially college students.

"They took back as many as they could," Kramer said of the Coors haul.

Stories vary as to how the bar tab was paid. Kramer said he saw a Tech staff member pay it from "a wad of cash." One player said Rodgers pooled money among the coaches and announcers.

Smith said Rodgers announced the first round of drinks was on him, but soon the pilot spoke to Rodgers, who then announced, "Drink up. Delta's paying for everything."

With the plane finally repaired, the team sang the Tech fight song on the flight home and talked eagerly—confidently—about the next game against No. 10 Notre Dame and how they would avenge last season's 69-14 embarrassment.

They had six days to prepare for the Irish stout defense and their potent offense quarterbacked by Joe Montana.

Chapter 9

He Hurts You Emotionally

After Ivery's astonishing game, the Atlanta press again considered whether Ivery deserved the Heisman. He led the nation in all-purpose yards—rushing, pass receiving, and kick returns—and was third in rushing. Despite missing games his first year to injury, he broke several Tech career rushing records. But no one expected him to get the trophy for college's best player. A *Constitution* reporter called sportswriters and discovered some hadn't heard of Ivery before the Air Force game. One said Ivery might have a chance if he repeated the 356 yards against Notre Dame. Only one said, "Anybody who can gain 356 yards deserves it."

Tech fans were more excited about their football team than they had been in years: *We have college's best running back; our defense is finally playing well; we've won seven straight. We'll get revenge on defending national champion Notre Dame, beat hated UGA, and go to a top bowl.* All that seemed possible. Tech's sports information director said he received so many calls from the media asking about Ivery versus Notre Dame that he couldn't answer them all. A former Tech basketball star requested tickets, but all the SID had were end zone seats. *Sports Illustrated* sent staff to cover the showdown, and representatives from four bowls attended. Both teams were 7-2 after losing their first two. For the first time since 1966, Tech had won more than four straight. *Finally,* the hype and expectations over Rodgers's return to his alma mater would come true.

Ivery said he hoped he might be named All-American if he had a good game against the Irish, and that the team would be well prepared and have the biggest pep rally in Tech history. "We're going to play mad rather than being mad. Our team will be ready," he said.

Notre Dame, now ranked 10th, featured an imposing defensive

line, swift, strong linebackers, and an All-America candidate at safety. Bill Parcells, coach of their one common opponent, said Notre Dame had a stronger defense, but their offenses were about the same. Optimistic fans looked past that. *We've scored against good defenses before. And we have Ivery.*

The buildup to the Notre Dame game revealed years of resentment. Reporters claimed Rodgers and Irish coach Dan Devine despised each other. When Rodgers's Kansas team defeated Devine's team 70-0, Devine reportedly signaled his team's concession by waving a white towel at Rodgers across the field, but Kansas continued to score. Devine denied any rivalry between them but mentioned an alleged comment by Rodgers suggesting that Devine couldn't win big games. (So why bring it up?) Rodgers claimed he was misquoted, but, years later told an interviewer, "I might have said that; I don't remember."

Devine asserted that the previous year, Rodgers had told a Notre Dame player, "We're gonna whip your butt" (Rodgers denied saying it). There was no coaches' handshake at the end of last year's 69-14 humiliation, and emotions still simmered. Rodgers shared stories in speeches and elicited hearty laughs with this one: After Notre Dame took a decisive lead in the 1977 game, he gave Devine the peace sign. Devine responded with an obscene gesture. "He gave me half the peace sign back," Rodgers alleged. He remarked years later that Devine "had no sense of humor." Rodgers later recanted the flipped-bird story; he had made it up, preferring laughs over accuracy. "It was a *joke*," he said, still annoyed. "It didn't happen, but it was funny." Funny, but not to Devine.

Some Tech fans, including Rogers's wife, wore buttons that said, "Duck Notre Fame." The slogan was painted on a 40-foot sign at a fraternity house. Other signs reminded bitter passersby: "69-14." T-shirts proclaimed, "*Hell no, I ain't forgot.*" Rumors circulated that fans were stocking up on frozen fish to toss at Notre Dame players (an anti-Catholic gesture).

Tech fan Jim Bell said that after the 69-14 game, he was so angry he didn't stop for the night in Kentucky as planned but drove straight from South Bend to Atlanta.

Some players claimed that the year before, Irish coaches shook their fists in taunts as the score climbed. (Was that true? It didn't matter.)

They seethed as they recalled Notre Dame going for a first down on fourth and three at midfield with the score 62-7 and scoring their last touchdown on a *pass play*. And didn't they keep their starters in a long time?

Someone bitterly said they heard that Devine claimed Notre Dame was more of a national school than Tech. Tech fans wanted payback.

A sign in the Tech dressing room read, "Nov. 18, 1978—Day of Revenge." *Sports Illustrated* reported that as psyched-for-an-upset Tech players dressed before the game, they shouted last year's embarrassing score for motivation: "69-14! 69-14!"

"I'm 100% ready for this game," Ivery told a reporter.

On Friday night, around 5,000 Tech students paraded through the rain to the basketball arena for a pep rally. Some wore T-shirts with obscene language that the newspaper wouldn't publish (probably "Duck Notre Fame" and then some). They tossed damp toilet paper in the air, and when Rodgers pranced onstage leading the players, the students went wild.

He repeatedly led the crowd in the fight song, "Ramblin' Wreck from Georgia Tech," while shaking a yellow and white pompon. He held up a Lucky Charms cereal box (Irish leprechaun on the front) and screamed, "I love the Yellow Jackets. How 'bout you?"

Pure, uninhibited Pepper Rodgers—the exuberant showman.

"You give 'em hell in the stands, and we'll give 'em hell on the field," Ivery told the crowd. He was named an honorary citizen of Atlanta, and the state of Georgia declared it "Georgia Tech Day."

A letter from President Jimmy Carter was read, and student winners of a banner contest were awarded kegs of beer.

As they exited the arena, one student reportedly said, "Those (bleeps) better win tomorrow."

Just before Tech's first offensive play, the TV announcers mentioned Ivery's record-breaking game, and Kelley promptly pitched to him. He was hit by a swarm of Notre Dame players and gained a yard.

That is how the game would go. A great superstar running back faced a big, fierce, well-prepared defense. Emotions can rile up players and fans, but they can't outmuscle strong players.

A broadcaster said Notre Dame's plan was to gang tackle Ivery and "punish" him so that he "loses his desire."

Ivery was not punished, nor did he lose desire, but Notre Dame was ready—and good.

"Oooh, Lord, I remember that play," Ivery recalled later. "If I hadn't seen them coming, I might not be here now. Normally, I was good at breaking tackles, but those cats, once I got in their grasp, I wasn't going nowhere."

The series ended when Ivery was hit behind the line, still gained three yards, but fell short of a first down, and Tech punted.

On some plays, Ivery did exhibit his celebrated speed, deception, and power.

On one play, Kelley faked a handoff to Ivery, who cut across the middle. Kelley's pass to Ivery was off enough that Ivery had to reach and nearly stumbled, but he kept his balance and made a one-handed catch for 10 yards.

He received a handoff, was hit in the backfield, spun left, and gained 2 yards, downed by two tacklers. Again, he was hit in the backfield but broke past the would-be tackler for 3 yards.

An announcer noted they were getting to him in the backfield, but he was so strong the first tackler rarely stopped him—although they slowed him enough for others.

Kelley recalled one play when the Irish defense had a strong safety well placed for the play he had called.

"He was about to tear Eddie Lee up," Kelley said, "but Eddie Lee gave a dead leg and spun and gained six. I was blown away. A dead leg and shake, shift gears, gear down, and back up. Dude could take a shot. He was tougher than tough."

Meanwhile, Irish running back Vargas Ferguson had the game Tech fans wanted Ivery to have (and that they needed to win): breaking free for long runs, cleverly evading tacklers. He set Notre Dame records for rushing yards in a game and season.

On Notre Dame's second offensive play, Ferguson ran for 68 yards to Tech's 6. He cut completely across the field, eluding and breaking tackles, finally stopped by Bessillieu. Notre Dame settled for a field goal.

Toward the end of the first quarter, Ivery was popped ferociously for a loss of 2.

"He was waiting all season for that tackle," an announcer said. Decades later, Ivery said it was one of the hardest hits he ever received playing football.

"Someone clobbered me out of nowhere, only one of two times in my career that I didn't see a lick coming," he said. "That one and my second knee injury against the Bears. I staggered up and heard the guy taunting, 'You're not gonna get no 300 yards today, baby!' I barely made it back to the huddle."

Tech punted to end the first quarter.

Right after an announcer labeled the game a defensive standoff, Montana led an efficient drive for a touchdown. The drive featured elusive, powerful running by Ferguson, a 10-yard first-down run by Montana, and a 26-yard touchdown pass.

After a Tech punt, another great run by Ferguson, and a pass interference call on Tech, Ferguson leaped over the line, broke two tackles, and dashed to the end zone. It was 17-0, Irish.

Tech finally countered with a touchdown on a drive that featured a long pass to Drew Hill to the Notre Dame 16. Then on third and 4, Kelley tossed to Ivery, who stopped, jumped, and—just as he was hit in the air—tossed a touchdown pass to Bucky Shamburger, who made a nifty one-handed catch. (The pass actually had a nice clean spiral.) Tech drew to a manageable 17-7.

With two seconds left in the half, Notre Dame attempted a 39-yard field goal, but it hit the crossbar. Ivery had rushed for 63 yards and Ferguson for 188, but Tech players felt confident in the locker room, only 10 points down to the No. 10 team.

After a Tech punt in the third quarter, Montana passed Notre Dame to the 1 and sneaked in for a 24-7 lead. On a fourth-and-2½, the ball was pitched to Ivery, who was met by two defenders and made only a yard. Even the great ones get stopped.

Ivery said that once he played in the NFL, he realized how big and strong the Notre Dame defense was.

"Usually if it's two or less, I'll get you a first down," he said, "but they were the most physical team I played against in college."

Notre Dame took control of the game with a 5-yard touchdown pass on a drive featuring a Ferguson 27-yard run, tackles broken along the way. The score was 31-7, and Tech was running out of time.

Tech scored in the fourth quarter on a 65-yard touchdown pass to Drew Hill, who got past the Irish defensive backs and, even though the pass was a bit short, snagged it and outran everyone. (How many of those plays would Hill, a senior, have made without three years of the wishbone?) Tech lined up for a 2-point conversion, Ivery in the slot rather than the backfield. Wide open, he caught the 2-pointer to make it 31-15.

With five minutes left, Tech on their own 8, Kelley threw an interception (the pass was tipped), and Notre Dame scored one last touchdown. Then something happened that belied the academic-minded–Tech-people-are-above-all-those-sports-nuts attitude.

The bitterness over 69-14, the weeklong hunger for vengeance, the exuberant pep rally, this disappointing game, having to watch an opposing running back run like Ivery, Ivery being limited to "only" 102 yards—all that frustration exploded.

Debris, reportedly including liquor bottles (by now empty), ice cubes, eggs, and frozen fish (the rumors were true), rained down on the Irish team from the stands. Notre Dame players retreated to midfield, and Tech players signaled to the fans to stop.

Devine told his players to keep their cool.

"Act like Notre Dame," he said. "You have more class than that."

(A dig at Rodgers?)

When the throwing ceased and the Irish players returned to the sidelines, Notre Dame players and Tech fans shouted and vehemently gestured back and forth. After a 10-minute delay, Notre Dame accomplished the point after.

"That was embarrassing, poor sportsmanship," Lee said. "It was mostly drunks throwing liquor bottles. You should take it like a man if you're getting your butt kicked. Notre Dame didn't do anything wrong."

"That was pretty shameful," receiver Matt Rank said. "A trainer started laughing, and I told him it was not funny."

Devine, when asked about the ugly scene, gave a Pepper-Rodgers-like response: "The fish smelled like hell, the eggs were interesting, and the ice sort of stings when it hits your face. Let's talk about the game."

Tech scored one last touchdown, mainly via passing, with 50 seconds left. The 2-point conversion pass attempt failed: 38-21, Irish.

While Tech had wanted to avenge last year's huge loss, Ferguson said *they* had revenge on their minds, recalling the (no-pass) 1976 loss at Tech and wanting to win in front of the Tech crowd. Montana was masterful, completing 14 of 19 passes for 190 yards and two touchdowns. During one stretch, he completed 10 straight passes, tying a Notre Dame record.

"They were bigger and better and didn't make mistakes we needed them to make," Bessillieu said later.

"We had big boys, and they had bigger boys. They were huge," Kelley said.

Friday's assessment was simple: "They just wore us down."

Devine said their plan was to bounce Ivery outside and keep him from cutting inside.

"Once I have momentum, I'm a big threat, but when I cut back, ooh lord, they were waiting on me," Ivery recalled. "That was the hardest 102 yards I gained all season."

The Peach Bowl, played in Atlanta, invited Purdue University in mid-November, and they accepted. Now, they wanted a Southern team to attract fans who wouldn't need to travel far. A matchup of Purdue against Cal, Oregon, or Wyoming wouldn't do, so they extended an invitation to Tech after requesting Rodgers consult with the players. Rodgers reported that the players were enthusiastic.

"I'm thrilled to death," he said. "There's no such thing as a bad bowl game."

Bessillieu told a reporter, "We're honored to be asked."

Rodgers mentioned that Atlanta was a great place to be; players would stay in a downtown hotel, and their families could attend. Family members attended, yes, but hardly anyone else did. Moreover, Rodgers's and Bessillieu's enthusiasm was a mirage.

The season finale, against UGA, was next. By the end of the game, Ivery would be hobbled, and UGA defensive back Scott Woerner would never chew correctly again.

Media chatter compared Ivery and UGA's Willie McClendon, a big strong runner also having an outstanding season. A reporter interviewed mutual opponents of the teams, and one coach said, "If I could take only one of them, I'd take Ivery. He's more dangerous, tougher to hem in.... He gives you all kind of trouble in the open field."

"Ivery frustrates you," a South Carolina player said. "Just when you think you've got him stopped, he slips away, not with strength but with his moves. McClendon hurts you physically. Ivery hurts you emotionally."

Days before the game, Lowe pleaded with teammates not to let his former high school teammate, first-year quarterback Buck Belue, beat them.

"We can't let Buck Belue beat us," he said. "We can't let Buck end this game, fellows."

They scoffed: "Oh, Sweet, you're just bragging on your homeboy."

He warned them: He can throw the ball.

Belue said UGA coaches warned they needed to slow Ivery down to win.

"He was the most talented guy on the field," Belue said, so coaches told them, "We're gonna have to gang tackle him."

Woerner said there was no special game plan for containing Ivery, just *Don't let him beat you*. But he knew how tough that would be.

"When you take him on one-on-one and he's coming straight at you, you got a problem," Woerner said of Ivery. "If you have an angle on him, wrapping him up and taking him down was doable. But if you have to slow down his head of steam, it's going to be a long day."

Twenty-five years later, Ivery watched a recording of ABC coverage of the game. Still a competitor, he grimaced at some of his plays and snapped at teammates and coaches. He still hated to lose.

In an on-camera pregame interview, Ivery was wearing a wide-lapel leisure suit and said he expected Georgia's defense to show different fronts. ABC showed an Ivery highlight.

"That's from the Notre Dame game—," Ivery said, "my spin move. I'd get into the tackle, and he thinks he has me, then I spin away and keep going."

An announcer predicted the two tailbacks would neutralize each other, so the quarterbacks would be key. Another announcer called Rodgers an iconoclast who would "wear a Brooks Brothers suit with white socks," and said, "You got to dig that guy."

The team captains, including Ivery, lined up for the toss.

"Your adrenaline is flowing," Ivery said. "You see the opposing team out there; you're ready to get it on, get that first lick in so you can get the nervous stuff out of the way."

Ivery called "heads," and the coin came up tails.

UGA chose to receive.

On UGA's first possession, McClendon was hit hard and fumbled. Henry Johnson recovered it in the air. Ivery chuckled and said, "He's trying to run with the ball," when Johnson then fumbled. But Johnson recovered it back. On Tech's first play, Ivery received the handoff, was hit by several Bulldogs, and gained 1.

Later, Ivery gained 8 yards to the 4, on a run that took four defenders to tackle him. Ivery scored a touchdown from the 4 and became the first player ever to score in all four UGA-Tech games he played in. He was hit by two defenders as he reached the goal line, and he powered in.

"Eddie Lee Ivery makes it look easy," the announcer said and added that Rodgers had told them Ivery, like Chuck Foreman, can do everything.

Rodgers fooled everyone, even most Tech players, by calling for an onside kick, which was so well executed that some people thought the kicker, Bessillieu, mistakenly shanked the ball, which spun awkwardly until a Tech player pounced on it. Instead of changing the swing of his leg to kick softer, he swung straight on but glanced the ball on the side, so the spinning ball traveled 11 yards.

"Pepper Rodgers told us he would have a few tricks up his sleeve," an announcer observed. Ivery said that he wondered from the sidelines how Tech had gotten the ball.

On the ensuing drive, Ivery ran for 8, 16, and 4. On the 8-yard gain, he was brought down by a lone tackler, Ricky McBride, UGA's bruising linebacker from Savannah, one of the few who could tackle Ivery solo.

"You could *feel* it when *he* hit you," Ivery said. But Ivery dragged him forward for a few yards before going down.

"You couldn't be lazy with Eddie Lee Ivery," McBride said. "Don't let that man get started; don't let him get lathered up."

On the 16-yard gain, Tech ran a counter play that seemed to go left, but Kelley handed the ball to Ivery, running right. UGA was caught off-guard. On first and goal, Ivery ran into a wall of red for no gain, then fullback Lee ran 1 yard for Tech's second touchdown.

UGA's excellent kick returner Lindsey Scott fumbled the kickoff, and Tech recovered it. On third and 7, Kelley threw to Ivery on the right, and he gained 3 yards, once again brought down single-handedly by McBride. Ivery smacked his hands together in frustration. Watching, he said, "I turned up field too quick." Tech kicked a field goal and led 17-0 with 4:09 remaining in the first quarter. Ivery ended the quarter with 81 yards.

During Tech's next possession, Ivery spun around after gaining 2 yards and was speared in the back by a UGA helmet. The defender he spun away from held onto his foot, preventing him from spinning all the way, which left his back vulnerable. He stayed on the ground for a few moments before slowly walking off the field. After a long punt return by Woerner, Tech recovered a UGA fumble. Ivery carried the ball four times for 64 yards during the drive. Following a 7-yard gain, the announcer remarked that even when there's no room to run, Ivery finds some. After a 36-yard run, an announcer noted that he was a one-man show, although he didn't have much blocking.

He used a stiff-arm (a rare tactic for him) to get around the edge and, barely staying in bounds, used his patented cut inside to break free for more yards; the announcer said the move reminded him of Gale Sayers. With 117 yards so far in the first half and on second and goal from the 4, Ivery ran within inches of the goal line, again stopped primarily by McBride. Then Kelley faked to fullback Lee and ran an option play to the left, which likely would have included a pitch to Ivery, but Kelley slipped and fell at the 3.

The announcers questioned the play call. So did Ivery, watching: "Come on, Pepper, what the hell are you doing?" According to Lee, Rodgers called the dive play but privately told Kelley to fake the handoff and keep the ball. Lee fell into the end zone without the ball.

"I was so mad after that play," Lee said later. "We moved the ball to the one and had to kick a field goal? We didn't get the score because Kelley kept it. I was pissed. That was an easy touchdown. Get to the one and not score? Pepper got more creative than he needed to. That was completely unnecessary."

The field goal provided a 20-0 lead, instead of 24. But Tech was in control, leading in first downs 11-3 and total yards 172-54. Ivery was nearly unstoppable. The announcers marveled at his performance and wondered if he might break his own single-game record. They repeated Rodgers's comment that Ivery was the finest all-around football player he had ever coached. Kent Hill said he and other linemen sometimes told defenders where Ivery was going to run ("He's coming right at you!"), and they still couldn't stop him.

"When your secondary is making most of the tackles, you're in trouble," Woerner said of the first half. "I tackled Eddie Lee half dozen times in the first half, all the way across the field and back, and then some."

Whenever Ivery made a great play, UGA-Thomson-and-*especially*-Ivery fan Ralph Starling stood in the stands and cheered, surrounded by Georgia fans, who cursed him.

Tech later punted, and Woerner called for a fair catch but was blasted by Tech long snapper Lonnie Meredith, who tore downfield and smacked into Woerner as he caught the ball. Woerner was flattened, and Meredith ran past him, exuberantly throwing both hands in the air.

But a penalty was called for fair catch interference.

Woozy, Woerner lay on the ground, not knowing which sideline was his. As he walked off the field, his head wobbled, his chin bled. He said later that, for the rest of his life, when he chewed a steak, his jaw popped.

With the 15-yard penalty, UGA had great field position, and onto the field trotted Sweet-N-Lowe's buddy Belue, who had grown up watching this rivalry game on television, to replace the starter.

Belue said later there was no pep talk from the coaches about providing a spark for the team.

"They just tell you what to do, and you do it," he said. And he did. He led UGA to a touchdown.

At the half, Tech led 20-7, confident they would keep rolling with Ivery leading the way.

It wasn't easy being a Georgia Tech fan in rural Greene County. Growing up in the 1960s, Jackie Copeland had a relative who attended Tech, listened to Tech football games on the radio, and brought him Tech fan gear. Though teased by UGA fans, Copeland listened to Tech games and later bought season tickets, driving 80 miles each way. He attended as many away games as he could—including this game in Athens. Before he drove from college in Milledgeville, he boldly pronounced to a classmate that Tech would win; the classmate said they wouldn't, so they bet $50. With Tech leading at the half and Ivery running wild, Copeland found a pay phone in the stadium and called his classmate, collect, and suggested they raise the bet to $100. The classmate, having seen Ivery's first half on TV, declined.

In the UGA locker room, Dooley didn't say much more than they needed to eliminate their mistakes (four turnovers) and play better. McBride said UGA's fiery defensive coordinator Erskine "Erk" Russell told the defense they weren't doing what they were coached to do, so get out there and do it. Belue was ready to continue leading the team, but, again with no explanation, he was back on the bench for the third quarter. "Oh well," he thought, "I guess you have to do more than just help them score one touchdown to get back in."

After watching himself gain 1 yard when most backs would have gained none, Ivery commented, "There ain't a whole lot of fooling in the I formation, like in the wishbone." A few plays later, he blamed himself: "Damn, I missed that hole."

On an 8-yard gain, Ivery ran through a crowd with power, and the announcers noted that he was not only elusive but "punishing, slashing." All his gifts were on glorious display. He was not likely to surpass 300 yards, but hitting 200 was several handoffs away.

After a missed opportunity for a nice gain on a pass not thrown, Ivery complained, "Kelley, throw the ball! Godamighty! Drew had 5 yards on him!" Lee got the first down on a third and a foot as everyone was keying on Ivery.

Midway through the third quarter, the Tech defense missed a tackle, and Ivery exclaimed, "Damn!" UGA went for it on a fourth and 1½. The chains broke on the measurement, and UGA was granted the first down.

"Damn chain got shortened. Ain't no way he got that damn yardage," Ivery fumed. McClendon leaped over defenders and in for the score.

Ivery said, "I never did that. I didn't like to expose myself."

The score was an uncomfortable 20-14.

"I'm thinking we need to get something going offensively," Ivery said. "I'm saying, 'Guys, we still got the lead. Let's take the crowd out of the game.'" After a play that didn't work, Ivery said, "Stupid call, Pepper!"

"Patterson! Patterson! Dang, *Patterson*!" he shouted when Patterson dropped an easy interception with a clear shot to the end zone.

Near the end of the third quarter, after a long gain by Ivery, which gave him 162 yards, the announcers again raved that he was both fast and strong. As Russell had instructed, he was tackled by a swarm of Bulldogs. But he didn't get right up.

He was helped off the field, gingerly limping. ABC showed tape being cut from his right ankle.

"I was in pain," Ivery said, "hoping I could get retaped and get back in. I was crying at one time. I tried to run and couldn't. I told them I couldn't put any pressure on it." It was later determined ligaments were badly sprained on both sides of his ankle.

"The worst kind of sprain for a running back," said Tech trainer McDonald.

Reporter David Davidson wrote that Woerner was holding Ivery's ankle as other players made contact, and the ankle "twisted horribly as he went down."

"I didn't celebrate seeing him go down," Belue said later, "but it helped our chances. First day of the week they're saying he's the one we have to stop, and so far he's dominating. When you see him being helped off the field, you say that's going to hurt them."

In the stands, Copeland sensed momentum shifting—and his $50 slipping away. "I was sitting with Georgia fans," he said, "and you could see relief in their faces. I could hear whispering that Eddie Lee is out, so maybe we can win this game."

Tech alum Leo Benatar was at the game, and he felt sick. "We got this game," he had thought—but now thought the injury must have been intentional. He watched Ivery on the sideline more than he watched the game. He saw Ivery try to walk, then sit back down and hang his head. "He kept trying to run, bless his heart, but he couldn't go."

Ivery demanded his ankle be retaped so he could return to the game. The team doctor warned him of possible permanent damage, which could risk a lucrative pro career, but he insisted.

This was no fake bravado. Repeatedly, in tough situations, he snapped, "Give me the ball!" He was one of the toughest players on the team and ignored pain.

McDonald taped it and gently put on Ivery's shoe. Ivery stood, took a few painful steps, and sat down. The young man, who had run so strong, wept.

He said he didn't care who saw him cry; he was hurt and angry, disappointed that he couldn't help defeat their rival. His emotions poured out.

Thus began a controversy that persists.

As Ivery told it, while he was on the ground—after he was tackled—waiting for the pile to disentangle, a player grasped his foot and twisted it fiercely. Earlier in the game, a player had speared him in the back, and he shrugged it off—it happens—but this made him angry. But he didn't shout or curse, didn't fight back.

"I was in a zone in that game," he said later. "The weather was beautiful; the stands were packed; there was a whole quarter to go. I was devastated. He was turning my ankle like he was going to break it."

Tech fans still ask: Did someone grab and twist Ivery's ankle as (or after) he was tackled?

When Copeland met Ivery in 2021, he asked. Tech online message boards can still light up when the topic comes up.

"We felt like it was intentional but didn't want to just say that," Harris said. "You don't say that unless you're sure. You know they're thinking: 'If we can get him out, it's going to make it easier.' I'm pretty sure they were saying, 'Let's get him out of there,' whatever. But you never know."

"It looked to us like he was already down and there was some scruffing going on," Herrington said. "It will forever be argued."

"I remember those conversations," Daniel said, "and I said maybe or not. Probably, but who knows? It's part of the game."

"Usually, when you twist your ankle, you're up on your feet," Lee said. "If Eddie Lee knows he was down and then feels pain, that's unusual. It wouldn't surprise me if it was intentional. The only way they win is if Eddie Lee isn't there anymore."

He added that if he had done such a thing, "I wouldn't admit it either. I'd say it's just part of the game."

UGA players also still talk about it.

Woerner had an outstanding career at UGA. In the 1981 Sugar Bowl, he intercepted a pass near the end of the game, assuring UGA the national championship.

"When you play for Erk Russell," he said, "especially against Georgia Tech, it was 'Eliminate the guys, get 'em out of the game, pound 'em, and you won't have to worry about 'em.'"

Tech defensive back Henry Johnson said the Tech mindset was similar: "Take out their best player, take him down. We didn't want to injure him, but if he had the ball, we went after him."

Woerner said of Ivery's injury, "That's what everybody blamed me for, but that's—nobody ever, ever—I played years and years of football, and nobody ever intentionally tried to—unless maybe a cheap shot on a quarterback standing there, knocking him out after he had thrown the ball. Oh, no. You're running lickety-split trying to tackle somebody, and who knows how it happens?"

When asked if he thought Ivery had been intentionally injured, McBride said, "No, no, no, not that I'm aware of. I never heard anything from any teammates that it was something they set out to do."

"There's a legendary narrative that one of our guys twisted his ankle in the bottom of the pile," Belue said. "I never did believe that. I have no way of knowing." But he added: "My mother used to ask why I got up so fast [after being tackled], and I said, 'Mom, you wouldn't believe what goes on at the bottom of the pile.'"

With Ivery out of the game, Tech cheerleaders chanted, "Do it FOR Eddie LEE! Do it FOR Eddie LEE!"

The next time Tech punted, Woerner, his foggy brain now clear, deftly weaved through defenders, avoided six tacklers, and returned the kick 72 yards for a touchdown.

"Awful, awful tackling," Ivery said, watching. Then: "Come on, give me a flag! That's a tackle!" about a block during the return. Suddenly, Tech was behind 21-20. Then just as suddenly, Tech led 28-21 after Drew Hill returned the kickoff 101 yards with 4:42 to go in the third quarter, running nearly untouched, followed by a 2-point conversion.

At the start of the fourth quarter, Dooley again summoned Belue. Watching the game, Ivery became quiet, knowing what was about to happen.

"We got nothing at all," he commented on a crucial third-down play.

Late in the fourth quarter, after Belue ran for a fourth-and-3 first down to Tech's 43, UGA scored on a pass as Belue was hit by two defenders.

"Helluva throw," Ivery said softly. "He was right in his face. God almighty."

The replay showed Patterson left his man when it appeared Belue would be sacked by Harris, leaving the receiver open for the score. "Damn, Patterson! Damn, Patterson!" said a perturbed Ivery. Patterson may have thought Harris, who was fast and strong, had him.

"Mackel Harris had him sacked and he threw it off balance," Lowe said later. "I was on the ground, and I see the ball trickling away and he caught it." UGA trailed 28-27.

The 2-point attempt failed. Tech seemed to escape without Ivery, but Johnson was called for pass interference; the infraction was so blatant that three flags were thrown. Johnson later said that the penalty was intentional because the intended receiver was open. Thinking quickly, he grabbed him to stop a certain score, which gave Tech another chance to defend and possibly win. Agonizingly for Tech fans, the second attempt succeeded, making the score 29-28, which is how it ended.

"They convert two first downs," Ivery lamented. "Unbelievable. All we needed was one stop." On the broadcast, Ivery could be seen sitting dejectedly on the sideline. There were four plays in UGA's drive that, if Tech had stopped them, Tech likely would have won.

Ivery squirmed watching the last few plays and continued to react as if the game happened that day.

"Look at Dooley. Get your ass off the field.... Damn, Henry, all you got to do is... shit." Johnson made the interception that allowed Ivery to re-enter the Air Force game and break the single-game record, but now Ivery—these years later—still hates to lose.

Tech had one last chance to score without their greatest rusher and scorer.

"This is where I really wanted to be in the game," Ivery commented. "Dang, Drew," when he let a pass go through his hands. "He's not going to miss that too much." But UGA intercepted a pass when Tech was nearing field goal range, ending Tech's chance to win. "Damn!"

In a quiet locker room after the game, Ivery told reporters, "There I sat knowing they needed my help, and I couldn't be out there." In the hyped matchup against McClendon, Ivery outgained him 162-73, despite missing a little over a quarter of the game, and Ivery was voted the ABC Offensive Player of the game.

"Yards don't mean anything when you lose," said Ivery, who left the locker room on crutches.

"We all wanted that game so bad, and to lose it the way we did hurt," Lowe said. "I don't think I've ever seen Eddie Lee that crushed. He was the last one out of the locker room and onto the bus. The trip to Atlanta was the lowest I've ever seen him because that was the end of a huge relationship. A small-town boy from Thomson, Georgia.... They couldn't stop him."

Other Tech players reflected on their own play and how a miscue here or there could have made the difference.

"I made a couple mistakes," Sewell said later. "I was supposed to run an out route, and it was thrown that way, and I didn't run the route right."

Lee seethed over the missed opportunity to score a touchdown in the second quarter. Those four points would have won the game. He blamed the loss not on someone twisting Ivery's ankle but on the head coach: "We lost that game because of Pepper Rodgers."

Tech led the game in first downs, yards rushing, and total yards, but lost by a point. In his four games against UGA, Ivery rushed for 380 yards—6.7 per carry.

Copeland drove back to Milledgeville and forked over $50 to his jubilant classmate.

Years later, Dooley said, "We would have never beaten Tech if Eddie Lee hadn't been hurt. We couldn't stop him."

Woerner said, "If he doesn't leave the game, we never win. We couldn't stop him."

At the end of the regular season, Ivery was named Second Team All-American by AP and UPI. Although not a receiver, Ivery was Tech's second-leading pass receiver, behind Hill. He caught 20 for 238 yards, including a 60-yard touchdown. The Atlanta Touchdown Club named Ivery and McClendon co-winners of Southern Back of the Year. The Georgia State Hall of Fame chose Ivery as Amateur Athlete of the Year. At the Tech football awards banquet, Ivery was awarded the Coach Bobby Dodd Award, as the team's Most Valuable Player. Ivery finished eighth in the Heisman trophy voting (including 11 first-place votes), and as expected, he humbly said he was honored to receive the votes. Ivery said he would like the Atlanta Falcons to draft him, his pal Bessillieu, and UGA running back McClendon so they could play together.

Rodgers's contract was extended to 1981. The Tech Athletic Association statement praised the team's overall progress since his hiring in 1974, especially the current season. In 1981, however, he would no longer be Tech's head coach.

Rodgers said he thought Ivery would play in the Peach Bowl,

which gave Tech fans faint hope. As late as December 20, Ivery said he might play "a little," that his ankle felt OK when he *walked.* Rodgers said Ivery might play only in the flanker position, but soon it became clear he would not play at all.

Rodgers said he wouldn't risk Ivery's career, adding, "He's done too much for Georgia Tech." Ticket sales to the game were so low (who wants to go to a bowl game on Christmas Day without its marquee player?) that the Peach Bowl risked losing its NCAA accreditation, so Rodgers's wife organized a ticket-selling phone campaign. She called one doctor, who said he would buy tickets if Tech would send Ivery to him so he could fix his ankle.

The Peach Bowl, for many Tech players, was not a triumphant end of the season, even though playing in a bowl was a season-long goal.

Daniel summed up the Jackets' predicament:

> Eddie Lee was out. Bucky [Shamburger, tailback who replaced Ivery] was half speed with a thigh injury, and we were disappointed. Going into last two games we were 7-2 and hoping for a good bowl in a fun place we would travel to, and then we lost two games. We were talked about going to the Cotton Bowl. A game in Atlanta against Purdue was a letdown. We stayed in Atlanta, it was on Christmas Day, and they painted the field green for television. It was a baseball stadium, and there had been a season of Falcons games. You fall on the ground and instead of getting grass stains, you get green paint. The only people in the stands were family and folks with nothing else to do on Christmas. We didn't take it as seriously as we should have.

"I don't think the staff and everybody else did a good job of preparing," McDonald assessed. "It was hard to get motivated. Purdue came in with the right attitude, but we didn't."

"It was kind of a deflated feeling," Herrington agreed. "We were staying at a hotel three miles from campus, not in Dallas or Orlando or somewhere."

Even those glad to be in the Peach Bowl weren't so well prepared.

"We had an absolute blast, which probably cost us," Utt recalled. "The coaches had as much fun as we did. Everybody was out in Atlanta and had a lot of fun. I was out really late one night, then I went to Tech to the sauna, and I had to wait my turn because some coaches were in there. Pepper made that shit fun."

"We had access to things we probably shouldn't have," said Kent Hill. "I think being home, having that as a distraction, that played a part in it. It didn't seem to have the importance of a bowl game, as when you travel somewhere, and fans come along."

They received souvenir Peach Bowl watches and more meal money than usual, which helped them celebrate too much.

"Guys were looking at everything," Hill said. "Strip clubs. I went in one, but I couldn't stay because an older guy wearing a top hat said, 'What if your mom and dad saw you here?' That gave me a picture of my mom and dad being disappointed, so I left. But we were exploring parts of the city we hadn't been in before."

Tech fan Allen Potter, who rarely missed a game in Atlanta, bought tickets to the game but also had a tradition of spending Christmas Day at his parents' house. No Eddie Lee Ivery? Tickets in hand, he watched it on television.

On the other hand, this was Purdue's second bowl appearance in 92 years, and they had traveled to the big city, so while the Jackets wanted to be in Dallas, the Boilermakers were ready to rip and roar. They were a solid team, ranked 13th, with two losses and a tie, all against top-15 teams.

Rank, who caught his first pass of the season in the game, said, "Pepper saw it as a reward for us players. He wanted us to enjoy it, so he wasn't going to break our backs in practice." Rank said one day after practice, in the bus going back to the hotel, "We drove by while Purdue were out there in full pads busting their ass a lot longer than we were every day."

Predictably, Tech lost 42-21, in a stadium replete with empty seats, while Ivery, on the sidelines, "pawed the ground like a caged tiger," according to one reporter. A picture in the *Constitution* showed Ivery with his back to the field, his head buried in his hands after a Tech fumble. "Too painful to watch," the caption said.

Purdue took a 21-0 lead (thanks in part to Tech fumbling at its own 3) and led 34-7 at the half. Tech had -29 yds rushing and 29 passing: zero total yards. At halftime, Rodgers told the players to play like the score was 0-0. Johnson recalled they played better in the second half, but "We knew it was too late to come back without Eddie Lee."

When behind 28-0, Rodgers ditched the I formation (which, he said, "might as well stand for Ivery formation") for his beloved wishbone with Lanier back at quarterback. On one good run by Lanier, he kept the ball and dashed through a large gap. Another nice gain advanced to the 4 on a reverse to the right, when the wishbone seemed to be going left, and Purdue pursued. Tech scored a touchdown on a fullback dive three plays later. After that, Rodgers alternated the I and wishbone.

The wishbone scored another touchdown in the second half, but the game was over. They were out of sync in the wishbone, and the I was not the same without Ivery. Kelley was pressured and rushed for much of the game. All 95 Purdue players played, or the score would have been even worse. Late in the game, Purdue players danced on the sidelines.

Announcer Paul Hornung said Tech had practiced the wishbone only twice before the game, and it showed in the second half when a pitch from Lanier to Shamburger was mis-timed and Purdue recovered the fumble. Before this season, that pitch would have been practiced repeatedly until it was second nature to toss it right into the streaking tailback's hands. Still, Hornung noted the only time Tech moved the ball well was in the wishbone.

Rodgers tried to be upbeat about a desultory performance: "We won the second half 14-7." He joked that they "mixed it up" by making different kinds of mistakes. He never turned off the charm.

"We couldn't do the things we normally do without Eddie Lee," Rodgers concluded.

"You can substitute for Eddie Lee, but you can't replace him," Bessillieu said.

"It was very hard. Here you are wanting to help them win," said a dejected Ivery. "My first bowl game, and I wasn't able to play. Very disappointed."

Loyal fan Copeland—who had listened to all those games on the radio since childhood and had driven 80 miles to home games and more to many away games—watched at home but turned it off when the score reached 28-0 and there was no Ivery to lead a comeback.

It was the lowest-attended Peach Bowl in history—until January 1, 2021, when COVID-19 limited attendance. If not for a worldwide pandemic, 1978 would still be the lowest.

Ivery ended his Tech career as the all-time leader in career rushing, punt return yardage, and scoring. During his senior year, he rushed for 1,562 yards, averaging 5.9 yards per carry. He was the first Tech running back to rush for more than 1,000 yards in a season. He caught 20 passes for 238 yards, one of which was a touchdown. He scored 11 touchdowns and completed one 2-point conversion.

There was that magnificent 356 yards in the bitter cold. He had the most touchdowns in a Tech career, most rushes in a season, most rushes in a career, and the highest average gain per rush in a game (13.7 against Air Force).

Even after Ivery's phenomenal senior year, Rodgers said years later he regretted switching to the I formation:

> It was a mistake for Oklahoma to drop the wishbone for Marcus Dupree, and it was a mistake for me. We took a team recruited for the wishbone and changed it. We had to use a freshman quarterback. When you do that for one person and that one person gets hurt, it defeats the purpose. But people were excited about it. For Eddie Lee, it was great—except when he got hurt. Every running back wants to run in the I. Why do you think they called it the "I"? Because "*I* run with the ball."

Ivery now thought primarily about Anna and the NFL. He ignored his classes and asked Kent Hill to lie to professors about absences. "Tell them I'm at an NFL combine," he said. Hill covered for him at first but then had second thoughts: *They'll say I'm the one who's lying.*

Some had muttered Ivery wasn't smart enough for Tech, and he felt motivated to prove them wrong, but now the NFL allure dazzled. That decision would haunt him.

His grandmother, he said, was disappointed when she learned. "You better stay your butt in school and graduate," she said. But with NFL money months away, who needed a degree?

Ivery was invited to the Senior Bowl, the Hula Bowl, and the Japan Bowl—all for college all-stars. Injured, he declined them, except for the Japan Bowl, which paid his way though he didn't play. In Japan, he was awed by the swift trains and leery of the food, so he mostly ate at McDonald's. He was offered acupuncture for his injured ankle, but his agent advised against it. Teammate Drew Hill returned a kickoff 102 yards for a touchdown. In the fourth quarter, Montana threw three touchdown passes, and Ivery thought, "Man, this guy is good."

In February, the city of Thomson held "Eddie Lee Ivery Day." In the afternoon, Ivery spoke at Thomson High on academics and athletics. Next was a motorcade through town, followed by a reception in the high school gym, with a screen featuring Tech highlights. He said all the attention made him uncomfortable.

The Thomson Progressive City Club was started by Black teachers who had been required to sign a loyalty oath to teach in public schools. The oath listed organizations they were prohibited from joining, many of which, such as the NAACP, were important Black associations. By creating a local club, they could join a group not on the banned list that would support Black causes. They created a Wall of Fame in their building, and Ivery's picture was placed next to former Thomson football-player-turned-heart-surgeon Mack Bowman and prominent lawyer Evita Paschal.

In the evening, a standing-room-only banquet was held at Belle Meade Country Club (where a banquet for Ray Guy Day was held six years prior). John Barnett skipped a night class to attend. The banquet featured speakers and proclamations by elected officials. The crowd cheered loudly when a speaker said that "in spite of all of the honors he's had, he's still Eddie Lee." The local paper featured a picture of Ivery signing an autograph for a little White boy.

Bennie Mae said she was apprehensive entering Belle Meade but felt welcomed.

"I had never been there before," she said. "We had never been anywhere like that. They were like royalty to me. All the White people with status were there. I thought they would be snobbish, but they weren't. Everybody was the same, no Black or White. Everybody treated us so nice. That glory Eddie Lee received helped the Ivery name."

The banquet was a completely new experience for Ivery's mother, who had never been to a restaurant. She ate with her hands, and, as happened often in Ivery's life, he felt embarrassed. As speakers praised his athletic ability, hard work, engaging personality, and affable nature, and as they enumerated his accomplishments, she became so happy and proud that she wailed and fell on the floor—as she often did at church. This happened while a former principal was speaking, and he kindly remarked that she had done a fine job as a mother.

Trainer Ken Smith said Ivery mentioned he would always remember Thomson fondly, even on his deathbed. At the mention of "deathbed," Ivery's mother cried out, "Oh Lord!" It was the first time many in the room knew anything about Ivery's mother since he and Bennie Mae called their grandmother "Mom." As the crowd noticed where she sat and how Ivery's family responded to her, the realization sunk in: *She is his mother.* They looked at one another in astonishment.

A local reporter met Ivery for the first time and expressed hope that it wouldn't be the last. He noted Ivery "has what it takes to make a success out of life...character and class."

Rodgers repeated his Ivery mantra, which he never failed to express with enthusiasm: "I've never seen a back who does so many things so well. He's a complete player. He runs, blocks, catches passes, returns punts and kickoffs, and even passes the ball. He practices every day like he's trying to make the team."

Ivery's beloved basketball coach Willie Williams introduced him, and Ivery concluded the celebration with a short, gracious talk, in which he thanked many who helped him: family, friends, coaches, teachers, and community members. He thanked Bestwick for taking a personal interest in him and especially thanked Rodgers for switching to the I formation. He said he would always be from Thomson and would never forget this special day. He said no matter how successful he became, he would never change or "get the big head."

"I was nervous in front of all those people," he said later, "and I was eating at this exclusive club that rarely had events for Black people."

Thomson had the hero every small town wanted. He grew up in poverty, was a good student and person, worked extremely hard, and was about to be wealthy. He was humble, gave credit to everyone around him, and told children what adults wanted to hear: Stay in school and work hard. He loved his hometown. Surely, he would never let them down.

Anna Davis and Ivery wed on July 7, 1979, in Thomson because they believed most of his friends couldn't afford a trip to Tampa. Before the wedding, he felt nervous, so he shared a drink of cheap liquor with Jerry. When he saw Anna coming down the aisle, he thought she was the prettiest woman there was, and his heart fluttered. When they kissed at the end of the ceremony, it was not a quick peck but a long, sensuous kiss.

"I couldn't wait," he said.

After his first NFL season, they honeymooned on a cruise ship to Jamaica.

Years later, Ivery said, "If someone treated me as I treated her, I'd probably kill 'em. I was the worst husband and father."

Eddie Lee Ivery breaks free of one University of Georgia tackler and prepares for contact with another. He was able to use contact to his advantage by spinning or glancing free of the defender's grasp.

Courtesy Georgia Tech Athletics

Eddie Lee Ivery breaks into the clear against the University of Georgia. In 1978, he became the only player to score a touchdown in all four games he played in the Georgia Tech/UGA rivalry.

Courtesy Georgia Tech Athletics

Despite a pulled muscle, Eddie Lee Ivery gained 71 yards rushing and scored a touchdown on a 60-yard pass reception against the University of California, 1978.

Courtesy Georgia Tech Athletics

Once Eddie Lee Ivery made it to open field, he was elusive and fast.

Courtesy Georgia Tech Athletics

Eddie Lee Ivery used his great field vision to anticipate contact and avoid receiving a direct hit.

Courtesy Georgia Tech Athletics

Like many great runners, Eddie Lee Ivery could change directions and lose very little speed.

Courtesy Georgia Tech Athletics

Eddie Lee Ivery ran with "body lean," a compact style that was difficult to grasp and allowed a quick change of direction.

Courtesy Georgia Tech Athletics

Eddie Lee Ivery exhibiting his explosive acceleration against Tulane University.

Courtesy Georgia Tech Athletics

Chapter 10

A Fresh Start with Bart

Everyone called him "Bart."

It's almost impossible to exaggerate how Bart Starr was adored and admired in Green Bay. Not merely a Hall of Fame superstar and two-time Super Bowl Most Valuable Player who led the Packers to five championships, Starr—a devout, principled Christian deeply loyal to friends and supporter of many charities—engendered a mythology of greatness and saintliness. He had championship rings—and a halo. Players and colleagues over the decades frequently used a variation of one phrase to describe him: "A fine human being."

Scads of people in Green Bay had heartwarming Starr stories: words of encouragement, acts of kindness, patience with autograph-demanding fans. One fan rang the doorbell at Starr's home, where Starr was meeting with assistant coaches, wanting an autograph for his ailing father, who waited in the car. Over the man's objections, Starr interrupted the meeting and invited the enthralled elder into his house. He was *in Bart Starr's home!* According to Packers former assistant coach Bill Curry, Starr treated the man "like a dear old friend."

One fan said, "I met Bart in Milwaukee, and he said, 'Next time you're in Green Bay, drop by for a Coca-Cola.'" Another: "My brother was driving over the river bridge, and it was 20 below, and his car broke down, and the first one to stop to help was Bart." And on and on. And the thing is: They're probably all true.

Curry played with Starr at Green Bay in 1965 when they were NFL Champions, and the following season he was the starting Packers center in their 35-10 victory in Super Bowl I. Curry said he was "terrified" when he first arrived in Green Bay, and at a team dinner, not sure where to sit or how to act around veteran players and coaches, almost threw up. Starr sensed Curry's nervousness and invited him to church and Sunday dinner. That began a lifelong friendship. "He stayed by my side until he died," Curry said.

When Curry became an assistant coach in Green Bay, he asked Starr for an autographed photo. Starr agreed, but it took longer than expected because he didn't just pick one from a stack; he chose a special one: a shot of the two of them in the Super Bowl, with Starr poised for the snap from Curry. "It took him a while to wrangle it from *Sports Illustrated*," Curry said. It had been on the magazine's cover.

Starr comforted Curry when Curry was fired as head coach at the University of Kentucky in 1996, on his 54th birthday. He agreed to stay for the final four games, and the next morning he told his staff, "No visitors. No one but family. Don't knock on my door." There was, however, a knock, and in walked Starr, who had heard of Curry's dismissal.

"I'm going to spend the day with you," Starr told him. He had driven from his home in Birmingham to support his friend.

After Starr's playing days ended, he coached Packers quarterbacks for one year, then became a TV NFL analyst, ran his businesses, raised money for charities, and was a popular speaker. His future was set. Meanwhile, the team in "Titletown" came nowhere near a title. The tenure of the most recent coach, Dan Devine, ended in turmoil, with players despising him.

The hiring of Starr as head coach was an only-in-Green-Bay tale. The executive committee—a small group selected from the board of directors, all members of the Green Bay community—ran the team, along with the president, whom they chose. The Packers, a publicly owned nonprofit corporation, have no team owner. At the time, they had no general manager with the authority to take charge and use his acumen and experience to hire a coach. Hence, locals could influence the hiring of a head coach in a manner inconceivable at any other NFL team. Citizen by citizen, fans decided only Starr could restore the quaint town's tarnished image.

This movement became powerful. The slogan "Fresh Start with Bart" proliferated: bumper stickers, handmade signs in shop windows, and banners fluttering in the Lambeau Field stands. Starr had no head coaching experience and only one season as quarterbacks coach, but Packers fans hoped, dreamed, fantasized that he could translate on-the-field success to coaching success.

The board and executive committee routinely interacted with avid Starr endorsers. In line at the grocery store, one might get a nudge from behind: "You're going to hire Bart, right?" The executive committee, according to Packers former historian Lee Remmel, "felt they had no choice." Green Bay sportswriter—and later Packers historian—Cliff Christl said, "That was almost a case where the fans hired the coach." Corporate general manager Bob Harlan said, "The executive committee said the fans demand it and will have a fit if we don't hire Bart." No NFL team owner would care about fans having fits, but the executive committee did.

"Bart was smart, a take-charge guy. We assumed he was everything we needed in a head coach," recalled Packers fan and Lambeau Field tour guide Larry Francois. Fans had vivid memories of gleaming trophies, and Starr's mythical stature shaped their thinking.

"We were hoping that putting Bart in that position would call in the gods of football and we would be contenders again," fan Dave Raabe said. "He was a gentleman and a fine human being, the face of the Packers, closely connected to the championship years, and I thought that would carry over and his lack of experience would be overtaken by his status."

Surely, Starr absorbed coaching knowledge and motivational methods from the great Vince Lombardi, right? Starr, known for his cool precision (once throwing 294 consecutive passes without an interception) and steely leadership, would add "head coach" to his list of successes. He lacked experience, but the Starr golden glow was irresistible. After Devine's abysmal tenure, the Packers needed a sure-fire hire to redeem themselves. Starr seemed perfect.

Christl, in 1974, endorsed Starr in the *Press-Gazette*, but with reservations. He cited Starr's inexperience and named three great quarterbacks who had failed as head coaches. He listed Starr's strengths and called him the "logical candidate." Other NFL teams had tried to hire Starr, so the Packers' interest wasn't purely blind adoration. "Should Starr by chance fail, which I doubt would happen, that too might have a redeeming effect," Christl wrote. Packers fans would "realize even their heroes are fallible." Hardly anyone, however, at the time, found Starr fallible.

"That's the only time that happened," Harlan said years later. "The town didn't have much influence other than that one time. It was a very unusual situation. Believe me, it never happened again and would never happen today. We took the executive committee out of making that decision. They were extremely effective businesspeople, but none of them were football people."

Starr's friends advised him to decline the offer, given his inexperience, promising businesses, and the difficulty of the risky job. The scouting department needed updating; their early draft picks for the next two years had been traded away (more on that). But, deeply loyal to the team that let him rise from 17th-round pick to five championships, he said, "They could have cut me, and they didn't."

Later in life, Starr said he wasn't ready to be head coach and that his decision was clouded by emotion and loyalty. But briefly, to others also clouded by emotion and loyalty, the Packers seemed headed back to greatness.

Groups from all over Wisconsin gather at the Packers' historic Lambeau Field for meetings: pharmacy conferences, corporate lunches, job fairs, annual employee gatherings, receptions, banquets, even weddings. Parents bring their children dressed in tiny Packers uniforms or cheerleader outfits, stroll upstairs, and before heading to their meetings, wander over to gaze at the field. The popular Lambeau Suite, closest to the 50-yard line, offers window views and rooftop access to breathe in the vaunted air.

It's practically a civic duty to buy a giant foam cheese hat, a Packers mug, a garden gnome, or perhaps a Lambeau Field serving bowl. With no rich owner or huge TV market to fund the team, they rely on steady revenue from selling Packers merchandise to help pay NFL salaries. They also make money from stock sales—six have been held. Stockholders earn no dividends, can't sell their shares, and have no real power. They don't get bumped up on the season-ticket list, but they can buy shareholder-only merchandise and proudly display a souvenir certificate. (The certificate can be sold as a collectible, but not the shareholder privileges.) This arrangement boosts the Packers' coffers—and feeds the mystique of modest Green Bay "owning" an NFL team.

Larry Francois chose his phone number based on his favorite Packers players' jersey numbers. He once wore a tuxedo to a game, then went straight to a wedding. He collected 8mm and Super 8 films of the Packers from the mid-60s through the early 70s; when the Packers Pro Shop later produced a *Legends of Lambeau* DVD, they used his clips.

When Ivery played, "there were so many 8-8, 7-9 seasons that we just came to expect it," Francois said. "It became a joke: Oh great, another 8-8 season. But we don't take being at Lambeau Field for granted. I never saw people wearing paper bags over their heads, no booing. That would be like doing something not right in your own house."

Francois might not have noticed—or perhaps chose not to recall it—but fans of the 1970s and 80s Packers? Oh, they booed.

Still, many players recognized the Packers' specialness even during mediocre years. Placekicker Jan Stenerud, who played for the Chiefs, Packers, and Vikings, said, "If you played a long time in the NFL and didn't play in Green Bay, you missed out on an exceptional experience." (He would know—he scored the first nine points of Super Bowl IV for the victorious Chiefs.) Offensive lineman Greg Koch said he went farther in the playoffs with his team after the Packers, but "playing for Green Bay, one of the NFL's most storied franchises, is a badge of honor." He added, "It's amazing how many Packers fans there are all across the country."

There was a time when an ordinary fan—someone working at a brewery, say—could call the Packers, ask for Bob Harlan, then corporate general manager and assistant to the president, and Harlan would pick up the phone. During the '70s and '80s, Harlan said he got three kinds of calls:

1. "Just who is making football decisions over there? We're not getting any better!"

2. "You don't care if we're 4-12 or 12-4! You're sold out every game, and you're making money no matter what!"

3. "The last great era was the Lombardi era—we had our day—but it will never happen again."

Of the five head coaches in the 24 years after Lombardi, Harlan said, "Each had a lower winning percentage than his predecessor. We were like a stairway going down." Only three other franchises had worse records—each of them expansion teams starting from scratch. In those 24 years, the Packers had 12 top-10 draft picks and still couldn't build a winning tradition.

"They hung onto the name 'Titletown,' but it got to be a joke," Green Bay sports reporter Don Langenkamp said. "There was more fan apathy than ever. The media were more objective and critical. We were pretty harsh. There once was a day no one booed at Lambeau, but they were getting more disgruntled under Devine. Then they were sure Bart would lead them back, but fans even started not liking Bart, which was sacrilegious."

That long slump finally ended with the hiring of Ron Wolf as general manager in 1991 and Mike Holmgren as head coach in 1992. Wolf replaced the quaint system of well-meaning local guys on the board of directors with a taut, no-sentimentality, coach-hiring machine, and the Packers won a Super Bowl in 1997.

When Ivery played for the Packers, though, that resurrection was still a long way off.

Harlan said, "Bart had a tough relationship with the media. Fans became apathetic at times, even though we were sold out since 1960." "Sold out," alas, did not necessarily mean a full stadium. There were periodic reports of empty seats at games, sometimes even setting new no-show records.

Tom Pigeon is a jeans-and-sneakers-wearing retiree. He keeps neatly filed newspaper clippings of every Packers game since the 1950s. Every game. He can recall by memory specific plays, yearly season records, and season summaries. Proudly old-fashioned, he thinks the NFL should revert to a 14-game season, that they shouldn't call the final game the "Super Bowl" but the "NFL Championship." He was surprised that he spent $1200 on an original Packer share certificate—a modest amount for serious collectors. Much of his collection he made himself, such as clippings and pictures that he framed and hung on the wall. He doesn't wear cheese on his head. He bought an early (used) VCR in 1978 for $700, taped every game, ran out of room in his house for the cassettes, then taped over losses with new games, keeping games untaped-over if the Pack won. A Lambeau tour guide, he always asks who in the group has season tickets. He said, "I met a guy who said his parents put him on the waiting list when he was born, and he had just gotten his tickets. He was 38."

Pigeon said of Starr's hiring, "I was caught up in it, too. I didn't think, *He has no experience.* I thought, *He'll save us.*" Like scores of Packers fans, Pigeon can recount the notorious, mid-season 1974 Devine-orchestrated trade for John Hadl with gloomy precision. Hadl, four-time AFL All-Star, had just led the Rams to the NFC championship game, but that turned out to be his last good season. Devine traded first and second round picks from 1975 and first, second, and third round picks in 1976 to get Hadl, so Starr had no high picks his first two years. (This came to be known as the Lawrence Welk trade: A one and a two, and a one-two-three.) They finished 6-8, third place in their division for the third consecutive year. Hadl was there one more season (he threw eight touchdowns and 14 interceptions). Green Bay sacrificed all those draft picks for an ineffective, past-his-prime quarterback for a season and a half. Devine resigned the day after the last game. Eight days later, Starr was hired.

Starr was named coach on Christmas Eve in 1974. He led the Packers for nine years, the first five also as general manager. He asked fans for patience and acknowledged his inexperience. In a press photo of that announcement, on the wall behind him and his wife, both smiling broadly, were banners featuring the Packers' many titles. The banners announced over his shoulder: Put more of us up here.

Fans did their best to buy in. Something positive would happen, such as a three-game win streak or an outstanding draft pick, and hopes would rise. "The Pack is Back" bumper stickers would reappear—for a while.

Harlan said of the fans' thrill at Starr's return, "It was almost like Jesus was reborn."

Again, Ivery played for a head coach returning to his place of player glory, with huge fan expectations. Like Pepper Rodgers, Starr would not live up to them. If Rodgers tried to revive Tech with personality, charm, fun, and celebrity, Starr tried to revive the Packers with determination, loyalty, smarts, and motivation based on character. Ivery would grow to love Starr, who treated Ivery like a son, even when Ivery let him down—which he did several times.

One of Starr's first decisions as head coach/GM flopped. The Packers lost Ted "the Mad Stork" Hendricks, one of their top defenders, to the Raiders because Starr refused to agree to a no-cut contract. Hendricks then played on four Super Bowl–winning teams, was an eight-time Pro-Bowler, and was elected to both the College and Pro Football Halls of Fame. The award for college football's top defensive end is named after him.

The Packers went 4-10 in Starr's first season. *He's still learning; give him time.* In 1976 they went 5-9; in 1977, 4-10. They traded for quarterback Lynn Dickey and his magnificent arm; he was promptly injured and missed nearly two seasons. In 1978, they drafted sublime receiver James Lofton but lacked the quality quarterback they needed with Dickey out. They started 6-1 but finished 8-7-1 and barely missed the playoffs.

"We thought Starr had it turned around, but we ended up 8-7-1," Pigeon said of the 6-1 start. "Then in 1979 we went backwards, again."

Starr's legacy of five NFL championships haunted the team, especially when former Packers visited: Jerry Kramer (five titles), Fuzzy

Thurston (five), and Dave Robinson (three).

Disastrous draft picks haunted Starr. Some were his fault; some were bad luck. Some were bad choices; some they passed over flourished elsewhere.

"It was one thing after another," Pigeon said.

The most painful omission, the one *what-if?* in their grasp that they let go was the quarterback who defeated Ivery twice in college and joined him in Tokyo for the Japan Bowl: Joe Montana. Along with every other NFL team but one, they said no thanks to Montana for three rounds and instead, after Ivery, chose two players who contributed almost nothing. No team thought Montana was worthy of round one or two, and he was picked at the end of round three, so perhaps the Packers should be given a pass. Who knew he would become one of the NFL's greatest quarterbacks: a Hall of Famer, two-time NFL MVP, leader of four Super Bowl–winning teams, the first player to be named the Super Bowl MVP three times? No one envisioned that.

But there's this: Midwest scout Red Cochran kept mentioning Montana coolly leading Notre Dame to a dramatic Cotton Bowl comeback victory, his precise passing, his leadership. He said he had watched Montana for years and insisted, "Bart, all he does is *win*."

Assistant coach Zeke Bratkowski wasn't impressed with Montana's workout (weak arm, he said), and Starr called Notre Dame head coach Devine, who did not recommend Montana even though he had helped make Devine a winner. In the second and third rounds, Cochran insisted they pick Montana. Starr ignored him. Perhaps Montana in Packers green and gold would not have matched his San Francisco scarlet and gold spectacular success. If Dickey—like Montana smart and savvy but with a stronger arm—had been healthier, maybe that pass-over would arouse hardly a shrug. But Cochran's unheeded refrain ("All he does is *win!*") echoed through the modest berg of Green Bay for a long time. And did the Packers ever need a winner.

In a pre-draft story in the *Constitution*, Ivery recalled having little clothing as a child, being teased at school because what he did have was shabby, and crying one Christmas Day when he received no gifts. He sometimes inserted cardboard in his shoes to hold them together. His family still poor, he was eager to buy them a nice house in appreciation for rearing him with no father.

Several sports agents approached Ivery, and he chose Michael Trope because he, though in his 20s, had negotiated several lucrative contracts. (Ivery primarily met with Trope's assistant Gene Burrough, who reported to Trope.) Media labeled Trope "Whiz Kid" and "Super Agent." In one stretch, Trope handled four of five Heisman Trophy winners. From 1973 to 1985, he represented more NFL first-round draft picks—including six Heisman Trophy winners—than any other agent. Ivery flew to Los Angeles for draft day, where he and Burrough took a limo to Trope's house. A Rolls-Royce sat in front.

In 1977 and 1978, the Packers had two consecutive drafts with two first-round picks each and landed four talented players. With another good draft in 1979, they hoped to become contenders. Reporter Christl speculated that Ivery might be the Packers' first pick. They may prefer a fullback, and among the top running backs, only Ivery had the toughness for that position. Christl spoke with Rodgers, who said Ivery was comparable to Chuck Foreman, a five-time Pro Bowl running back known for his elusiveness and versatility. Ivery, however, was stronger and "will do whatever you ask." Packers staff consulted Curry, the Tech offensive line coach from 1976, who remarked that Ivery was indescribably great and a "model citizen." Exactly what Starr wanted to hear.

When Ivery was selected 15th overall by the Packers, Bessillieu knew before he did. The Packers had only Ivery's number at his Atlanta apartment, so when they called, Bessillieu answered and gave them Trope's number. After Bessillieu hung up, he celebrated with Drew Hill.

"Green Bay! Eddie Lee!" he said. "Ha! A *cold* state. Man, ain't that something." When the Packers called Trope's house, the party erupted in cheers and champagne flowed, according to Ivery. Starr said they had watched film of Ivery and had talked to his coaches and were glad to have him. Ivery said he was eager to get to work. Starr said Ivery would help them be the team of the 80s. He told him to lift weights and stay in shape.

Ivery hung up and said, "Where's Wisconsin?"

Lee Corrick, the Packers' director of player personnel from December 1977 to 1987 and, for most of that time, Starr's closest adviser on personnel, was thrilled that Ivery was still available. He had studied him on film and seen him play in person, vividly recalling the Miami game—"When you think you have him down, he can explode out of there"—in which Ivery made an acrobatic over-the-head catch and gained more than 100 yards, mostly by breaking tackles rather than outrunning defenders. Later, Corrick said, "I thought he was a heck of a steal. I didn't think he would fall that far. I was so happy. He had great balance, elusiveness, strength. He was a heck of a receiver. He could block. Eddie Lee fit all the criteria for what you'd want, and they don't come along that often. He was a great kid, a class kid from a class university."

Harlan said, "We felt like we were getting the best running back in the country. Our coaches compared him to Gale Sayers."

That was a bold comparison. Without two devastating knee injuries that limited his career to only 68 games and four full seasons, Sayers would likely still hold some of the top rushing statistics in NFL history. He had one of the best rookie seasons ever, leading the league in all-purpose yards (rushing, receiving, kick returns), and his six-touchdown game—by run, pass reception, and punt return—remains one of the greatest offensive displays by a player. Possibly the game's most elusive back, Sayers was finished by age 29 and inducted into the Pro Football Hall of Fame at 34.

Years later, Starr described why he so strongly favored Ivery:

> We did our due diligence, with the position coaches and other staff. As we looked at our need for a quality running back, we always started with a quality person. That was critical. Physical talent was a must, of course, but also character and moral strength. That is a big, big factor. That's what he

> brought. Eddie Lee was a special young man. Talented physically, but he also fit the mold that we wanted, and he fit in personally, too.

Starr added,

> Eddie Lee was very nice to meet the first time. He presented himself as a class individual. He had a big smile and was very positive. He had a firm handshake. He was a hard worker in practice, prideful, diligent, smart, and he adapted quickly to our system. I felt he was warmly received by our veterans because of those characteristics. They saw a hardworking, well-conditioned young man.

Tech alumni who remembered the Packers' championship years were thrilled.

"We felt pride that Eddie Lee went to Green Bay," Hunsinger said. "We knew about Bart Starr. It was like the Green Bay Packers had recognized Georgia Tech."

"We felt big-time pride," Benatar said. "I watched Green Bay every chance I could. There Eddie Lee was, wearing the same number he wore at Tech."

"The Packers represented the best of pro football, so it lifted our egos for him to go to a revered program," Bell said.

Ivery signed a six-year contract worth $780,000, with the salary increasing yearly, plus a $250,000 signing bonus. He promptly went to Thomson, accompanied by Burrough, to buy a house for his mother and grandmother.

"We went all over Thomson," said the one who had grown up in the town's poorest neighborhood but now could buy in any part of town. He and Anna both got a Mercedes-Benz. "All of a sudden, I could buy anything I wanted," he said. That $250,000 seemed bottomless.

They bought the first Benz in Augusta.

"Anna picked out the car," he said, "and they gave me the keys, and we drove off. They said we could work out the financing later. I signed no papers. That was the first time I knew how different White people treated a pro football player. If I was a Black policeman or worker at the Uniroyal plant, they would not have treated me that way."

He and Anna bought a house in Atlanta from a relative for the off-season. He threw a party for his friends at a local club and covered nearly all the costs. Each person paid a small cover charge and drank alcohol for free.

"It was the most people that had ever been in that club," he remembered. "You had to squeeze through the crowd." His friends asked him about playing in the cold. He laughed and said, "It's a psychological thing," and recalled his record day in Colorado Springs. He often hung out at the gym, playing basketball. Youngsters asked for autographs. Everyone was impressed: He was the same ol' Eddie Lee. Money and fame hadn't changed him, they said.

Ivery had anticipated that the Falcons would choose him in the draft, so he felt misled. He thought the Falcons had told him and Burrough that they were going to make a trade that would move them higher in the draft so they could make him their first pick. He was excited to play near Tech and that close to Thomson. Instead of being the Falcons' top choice, however, he learned he was *one of* their top choices. The Falcons made no trade and remained at their original draft position. The Packers nabbed him. At some point after the draft, still feeling the sting from the Falcons, he had a snort of cocaine. That experience planted a thought: *This helps.*

Chapter 11

The Rare, Mystical "It"

Finally, Ivery's superb athleticism would be displayed alongside professionals, with a legendary player as his coach. The Packers recognized his talent and felt fortunate to have him; he would shine and get rich. He basked in the celebrity status that came with being a Packer in Green Bay.

"You knew you were special," he said. "There weren't many Black families in Green Bay, so they knew you were a football player, or you wouldn't be living your ass in that cold weather. Kids wanted my autograph on their arms, shirts, casts on a broken leg."

It was a tradition for children to offer their bicycles for players to ride from the locker room to the practice field, and Ivery loved it. "The players *wanted* a kid to ask them to ride their bike, and sometimes if a player didn't have a kid asking, they'd try to get someone else's kid's bike.

"They [the people of Green Bay] were so nice to me. It wasn't like they only liked us because we could play football. They were genuinely nice folks," Ivery said. Anna, a sociology major, got a job at a Montgomery Ward in Green Bay and wanted to live there after his NFL career. "I wanted to come back to Atlanta, but she loved it there," he said. "I couldn't believe a woman from Tampa would like it so much. She liked the cold weather, the snow. Green Bay had some good football weather, but those winters—whew! I hadn't seen snow of that magnitude."

In media interviews, Ivery—humble but determined—said he didn't worry about starting, that if you did what you were supposed to, it would come. Still, he admitted he was disappointed he might have to play fullback. He hoped for open-field opportunities, where he excelled—although that's not frequently the case for fullbacks. He said he had lifted weights to gain 10 pounds but hadn't yet "developed that power up the middle" that a fullback needs.

Coaches were impressed with his wishbone-honed blocking skills. "I had done it for three years," he said, "so I adjusted right away." They admired not just his ability but his willingness to block. "It was an attitude thing," he said. "You just got to want to do it."

He quickly realized he was no longer among college players. "I was excited to be in the big league," he said, "but while in college, you knew you were the fastest runner. At that level, you find out the defenders are as fast as you are, just as strong or stronger. There was a significant increase in size, speed, and ability. Even some linemen can chase you down."

Packers training camp, he said, was more demanding than Rodgers's:

> Training camp tested my desire. It was the toughest thing I ever endured, the closest thing to death I've ever been associated with. Some mornings I had to roll out of bed onto my knees and push myself up to get to morning practice. Bart Starr was in the Vince Lombardi tradition. He believed "Hard work will win over talent when talent doesn't work hard."

"A great running back," David Sims said, "is always a threat, especially if he can catch the ball well, like Eddie Lee. He can make a game-breaking run without a big hole in the line. He can make something out of nothing. A great running back is like a tank in the army: strong, lots of firepower. He can make the passing game better just because he's always that running threat. The defense doesn't know what to expect."

"The value," Curry said, "is incalculable. Jim Brown, Walter Payton: Eddie Lee could have been one of those guys. They dominate and attract attention, and then you have a guy like James Lofton running a skinny post, and no one can keep up with him. That would have made a big difference."

Ivery's performance turned the heads of Packers veterans who had seen players with more hype than performance. They knew the real thing when they saw it.

Larry McCarren, veteran Packers center and two-time Pro Bowler, rarely thought he was blocking for someone special. It had happened once before—in an all-star game, blocking for Purdue's Otis Armstrong, who became an NFL rushing leader. "I'm noticing a difference, man," McCarren said of Armstrong.

> I don't have to hold the block quite so long. You think you didn't hold it long enough, but he's 10 yards downfield, and it's like, wow, this is what a big-time back is like. The next time I felt that way was early in Eddie Lee's career. The speed with which he hit the hole, his instincts to find a hole… It made your job as a blocker easier. I thought, this guy has the rare mystical "it," the rare mystical it, who could be a difference maker. And there's not a lot of them.

Packers offensive lineman Greg Koch called Ivery

> one of the most electrifying players I've ever seen. We all had big expectations for him, especially the offensive line, after we saw what he could do. He was sneaky fast and had more power than you'd think for his size. His field vision was unbelievable, like the great ones. And he would bounce back to the huddle with a big smile and say let's do it again. You need some hard-asses, but you need guys like him, too.

Quarterback Lynn Dickey said at first, Ivery was just another rookie to him—until he saw him practice. "That kid is unbelievable," Dickey said. "He's quick and fast, has great hands, picks up the offense really fast. This guy is going to be something. He's everything you want. You just don't see guys like that come along." Dickey thought Ivery might set records they couldn't even imagine. "When I had a running back run for 100 yards, I never lost a game," he said. "He could be with the best of all time."

"Eddie Lee's versatility, wow," said tight end Paul Coffman. "Veterans said, 'He's the real deal, wow.'" Coffman recalled Ivery's field awareness, noting that he would stay in to block rather than run his route if he sensed pressure. "The coach would look at film and ask what he was doing, and Eddie Lee would say he saw Lynn looking the other way and a defender free he had to block. He somehow knew when to do that. He was football smart."

Packers fans noticed, too. "We thought with Dickey and our great receivers, Eddie Lee was the missing piece," Dennis Raabe said. "Finally, all the offensive pieces are there, and we're going to be a juggernaut." Tom Pigeon added, "I didn't know much about him at first, but then I saw him play. I can't think of any running back we had with his ability."

Bart Starr, Jr., who spent a great deal of time with the team, said, "He was so sharp in his ability to remember the context in which every play was taking place. Skills matter, but you also need to be a gifted thinker and understand what the team is trying to do. He had a feel for the game. He was very sharp and perceptive. He was a Gale Sayers–type, able to do everything well."

"I saw greatness," said defensive end Ezra Johnson. "We played Walter Payton twice a year, so I know. Watching Payton and Eddie Lee, he was on that level. He had moves like Barry Sanders. No telling where he would have wound up in the annals of the NFL."

Quarterback David Whitehurst marveled, "He just glided. He made cuts, would give the old lift-leg fake so smooth. He made catching the ball look like he had a baseball glove on, and the ball became a part of his hand. He'd see it coming, take his eye off it, and catch the ball cleanly every time. One-on-one, he'd win every time."

Packers historian Lee Remmel described Ivery as "the finest running back we had ever drafted."

"Everyone loved him," Corrick recalled. "He was fun and worked hard. He finished runs. He had a great pre-season. We were very excited. It looked like we finally had a difference maker."

From then on, Corrick said, "the nightmare began."

During training camp, Ivery endured traditional rookie hazing. "Everybody had to sing," Dickey said. "I hated that so bad. It's a long time, and every day I had to sing the Kansas State fight song." Nightly, Ivery had to stand in his chair at dinner and sing to players and coaches, sometimes coaches' wives.

"I couldn't sing," he said, "so I was embarrassed, and I was too scared to say, 'Kiss my ass.' They'd boo, throw bread. I didn't know many songs, so I sang gospel." One night, he sang "Will the Circle Be Unbroken?" and held out a bowl as if it were a church collection plate. The fun of it lasted four days, then he dreaded it.

He impressed in practice. What about against opposing teams? In their first preseason game, against the Chiefs, the Packers won 14-10, and Ivery was, according to the *Atlanta Constitution*, "clearly the dominant player." He scored on a 22-yard screen pass, rushed for 49 yards (over 5 per), and had three receptions for 32 yards. On the screen play, he faked out defenders and then outran everyone. Former Dallas Cowboys star running back Duane Thomas watched the game and said, "He reminds me of Leroy Kelley." Kelley is in the Pro Football Hall of Fame.

In the last pre-season game, Ivery rushed eight times for 23 yards and caught a 42-yard touchdown pass. In preseason, he led the Packers in rushing and running-back receiving. He impressed, powering through the middle and running around the end. Backfield coach Zeke Bratkowski said Ivery reminded him of Sayers and Willie Galimore, two of the Bears' greatest open field runners, and that he could be the best breakaway runner in Packers history. Starr wrote in his autobiography that he was excited to finally have a running back who could have the kind of impact Payton had for the Bears.

In his first predictions for the 1979 season, CBS sports commentator Jimmy "The Greek" Snyder picked Green Bay to win their opener and said their running game had greatly improved with the addition of Ivery. Several sportscasters predicted Ivery would compete for NFL Rookie of the Year. Starr told reporters that Ivery would start soon and added that the team had drafted him as much for his character as for his skills.

Ivery said he hoped to help return the Packers to prominence so they would be glad they chose him, and he often mentioned that after the season he planned to get his degree. Though he was disappointed that he mostly played fullback—blocking for the tailback rather than carrying the ball—he said, "I was just glad to be out there."

Reporters often commented Ivery was "all smiles." One reporter said he gave questions much thought and spoke in a "down-home slang." He said he wanted to start but just wanted to win and was still working on his blocking, that he noticed the difference between college and NFL football when he caught a pass across the middle and received the hardest hit he had ever had. He expressed amazement at the fan dedication in Green Bay, and said, shaking his head, that some people planned their vacations around *picture day.* Starr was asked if Ivery would play soon after the opener began, and he replied, "Very soon." Everything was in place for Ivery to become a new Packers legend.

The knee, the body's largest joint, performs a remarkable feat. Knees connect four rigid bones (the femur above, the tibia and fibula below, and the kneecap in the middle) so that the legs can bend smoothly while remaining firmly held together. Knees absorb stress and twist slightly to allow for a change of direction. However, due to their limited range of motion and the upper-body load they carry, they can be prone to injuries. The knee can rotate slightly inward (towards the other leg) by 10 degrees and outward by 30 degrees. Exceeding these limits can cause pain and potential injury. That classic Ivery move—nearly tackled, hand down, spring forward—depends on healthy knees. Their mechanism makes them dynamic—and vulnerable.

Flexible connective tissue—cartilage, tendons, ligaments—holds it together and allows flexibility. Tough and fibrous, ligaments connect bones to one another and keep them in position, preventing excessive twisting. Knees can't be too flexible, or we would fall down like marionettes; too tight and we're stiff-legged beings who would never have invented football. Two collateral ligaments function like straps on each side and prevent the knee from moving side to side too far. Two cruciate, or cross-shaped, ligaments inside the knee connect the femur to the tibia. They cross each other to create an X. The anterior cruciate ligament (ACL) is in front, and the posterior cruciate ligament (PCL) is behind it. Ivery's ligaments performed superbly, as designed, at Thomson High, Georgia Tech, and the Packers. Until the ACL didn't.

On September 2, 1979, Ivery entered Soldier Field on a cool, sunny Sunday to compete against the Chicago Bears. Packers and Bears veterans sensed their long rivalry in their guts, each eager to savor victory.

"We'd do anything to maul those guys," Curry said. Thousands of rabid Bears fans shouted for an opening day win.

"You couldn't ask for a better day," Ivery said.

The field was topped with an early type of artificial turf that most players didn't like—although place kickers did. Jan Stenerud, who played most of his career for the Chiefs, then for the Packers, loved the surface. Never muddy, it provided sure footing for his non-kicking foot, which kept him stable while the other swung to the ball. Many natural grass fields, he said, got muddy and slippery, but "artificial turf looked like a beautiful golf course fairway."

When he planted his left foot, the turf gripped football shoe cleats tighter than natural grass. In the lingo of the science of synthetic surfaces, as described in a National Institutes of Health report, synthetic turf lacks the ability to divot, the "complete shearing or removal of the turf/root system from the remainder of the root zone." The "cleat-release mechanism" of natural turf is better for a football player's leg joints because the foot is "released" from the grass in tandem with the movement of the player's leg and is thus less likely to cause a "potentially injurious overload situation," as when a player streaking downfield plants a foot and quickly changes direction—the move that enabled Ivery to buy two Mercedes Benzes. There is belief (though not conclusive evidence for any particular injury) that football players are more likely to be injured on that fake stuff—even if there is no contact with another player. The report concluded, "Studies that focus on lower extremity injuries caused by a twisting or shearing mechanism typically show greater rates of injury on synthetic versus natural turf."

"Those early turf fields were brutal. The traction was too good, and Soldier Field was never known for having the best turf," McCarren recalled.

Koch blamed his first serious injury on synthetic turf. "I planted," he said, "and everything turned from my knee up, but everything below didn't."

The Bears offense was led by future Hall of Fame running back Walter Payton. Throughout Ivery's career, when his team's defense was on the field, he usually rested or conferred with players and coaches. But when the opposition had a great running back, Ivery became almost an excited fan watching an idol, toes to the sideline, observing intently.

"I wanted to learn from them," he said. "Tony Dorsett, Earl Campbell, Walter Payton. I didn't sit. I was amazed." When the Bears had the ball, Ivery, for the first time in his life, watched up close Payton's moves, speed, and strength.

Anticipating Ivery's debut, television announcers Dick Stockton and Johnny Morris said Green Bay's first-round draft pick was "the one to watch." They said it was a "courtesy" that the returning fullback started the game, and they would see a lot of Ivery. Clearly, they had been briefed on the Packers' effusive enthusiasm for their hotshot rookie. When Ivery entered the game in Green Bay's third offensive possession, Stockton said, "We knew it was a matter of time" before Ivery became a regular running back and added that he broke all Georgia Tech's rushing records and is a "quick, hard runner who can go to the outside."

On his first carry, he gained 7 yards, but the play was nullified by a penalty. The next play, he was hit after gaining 4 and spun from the tackler's grasp to gain 2 more. An NFL audience saw his iconic spin move that exhibited his guile and ability to frustrate, to evade what seemed a sure tackle. Stockton noted, "It takes a whole bunch of blue shirts to bring him down."

Ivery said later, "I used my determination and balance. I expected you to hit me, then I'd use my instinct. He's thinking he's bringing me down, and I absorb the hit and either spin away from him or dip my shoulder, put my hand down and take off—something he doesn't expect." He usually decided what move he would make three steps from the defender. "Sometimes I tried to be the attacker, not the attackee," he said. "There are so many split-second decisions. You can't decide too early, or he'll react to what you did."

On the next Packers possession, Ivery's block helped tailback Terdell Middleton gain 7. On second and 4, Ivery powered through tacklers for 6 yards. First down. "So far, I like what I see of that fella," Stockton commented. "He seems to be tough to bring down."

Morris added, "Anyone who can gain 356 yards can run the football. He has good hands, is a good blocker. He's not real big for a power back, but he plays like he's bigger."

On third and 27, the Packers at their own 15, when a pass play is usually called, the quarterback handed the ball to Ivery as if to say *Let's see what the rookie can do.* Hit at the line of scrimmage, Ivery spun to his left and broke free (how many times had Tech fans seen that?). At the 25 (gain of 10 already), he faced a defensive back—and saw a blocker behind that defender and no other defender close by. In his first NFL game, if he gets past him, he scores an 85-yard touchdown on Payton's home field and gains over 100 yards before halftime. This would be a spectacular NFL introduction of one Eddie Lee Ivery. There was no guarantee he would do that, but all he had to do was get past one small defensive back—which he did routinely—follow his blocker, and he's gone. Just as he stunned a high school opponent when they kicked to him to avoid someone they thought was better, just as he stunned Bestwick, who suddenly changed his mind about recruiting a sophomore, just as he stunned spectators at the high school all-star game ("How did this team lose a game with that guy on the team?"), he was about to stun a packed Soldier Field.

Thomson and Tech fans watching knew what was coming. They had seen it before: Ivery speeding around the end, cutting inside, making a tackler miss—or letting the tackler think, *I've got this guy*—only to give him nothing solid to grab, leaving him behind with a spin or a bull rush. They had watched him blaze downfield, weaving through helpless defenders with precise timing.

He would give fans in Soldier Field, those watching on TV, players and coaches on the sidelines, and teammates on the field yet another thrill. His offensive linemen would fall even more in love with him: *We helped him do that.*

Ivery faked left and ran right—the move the Packers envisioned would propel him to stardom, starting with his very first game.

But as he cut back to his right, firmly planting his left foot, he stumbled and fell, hitting a defender on his way down. On Soldier Field's artificial turf, there was no tearing away of grass to release his cleated shoe. Because his left knee buckled, he had no power or speed to push past the defender. The pain in his knee was so great—the worst pain he had ever felt—he screamed and let the ball go as he fell, grasping his knee.

"Damn the ball," he thought. In the frenzy around him, the Bears recovered the fumble, and Ivery lay face down, barely moving except for tapping his right foot nervously on the cursed turf. Ivery writhed and sobbed. The tears, he said, were from the pain, not the sadness of possible injury.

Press-Gazette reporter Don Langenkamp had a direct view: "I, very clearly, could see that knee coming apart. It was horrible. It's so tragic because he had greatness. From then on, watching him, you winced, worried it would come apart again. If you saw it, it never leaves your mind."

In the stands were Jerry Ivery and their uncle Austin Ivery, an Army recruiter who lived in Chicago. Jerry's heart sank. He was so familiar with his cousin's movements that he knew something was wrong. "He went down and grabbed his knee," he said. "He didn't fumble much, and when I saw how he fell and how far the ball went, I said, 'That's it.'"

Curry said it was one of the saddest moments in his life. "I remember where I was standing on the sidelines," he said. "I watched him make the cut. He threw the ball away, grabbed his knee, and fell to the ground. It was awful. I couldn't believe my eyes. I played football for 20 years and didn't have my first serious injury until the 19th season. It happened to him his very first game."

Years later, when asked who some of the hardest hitters he faced were, Ivery said, "The Bears defense. That was the only time I was leery of getting the ball." But when his knee buckled, no one on that intimidating defense had touched him.

About the size of a finger, the ACL can withstand up to 500 pounds of pressure before tearing. Many athletes—basketball players, ice skaters, dancers, and skiers—who land and pivot suddenly at high speeds often experience tears. The remarkable and intricate knee can handle only so much. Some knee injuries occur with repeated use, such as tendonitis and arthritis. An ACL tear is sudden and violent.

TV analyst Morris misjudged the severity of the injury: "I think he may have pulled a hamstring or may have a muscle cramp." If only it were so.

Ivery had gained 24 yards on three carries. After a commercial break, the broadcast showed him lying on his back, still on the field, both knees bent. Two trainers helped him to his feet, and he limped to the sideline. A teammate slapped his butt. Stockton said he hoped it's not serious because the Packers "have a good young ballplayer who was going to help them this year."

Later in the second quarter, the broadcast showed Starr on the sidelines, while behind him, Ivery reclined on the bench, grimacing. An ice pack eased the pain somewhat. The announcers said without Ivery, the Packers have no long-gain threat in the backfield. During a play in which Payton ran with the ball, Stockton announced that Ivery had a "twisted left knee" and wouldn't return to the game. Ivery repeatedly picked up the ice pack and looked at it. Once, he thought it looked fine and tried to walk; the pain forced him back down. He began to think, *This might be bad.* The team doctor told him it might be a sprained ligament. He wondered, *What the hell is that?* and thought he might miss a couple of games.

Payton was terrific: agile, strong, fast, a powerful blocker. His fakes were quicker than Ivery's, and his style was more about coming to a stop to make a very fast cut, rather than changing direction in one power-fluid motion like Ivery. After one Payton block, Morris said, "Look at that block by a scatback runner." He finished with 125 rushing yards and 49 receiving yards. The Bears won 6-3. An Ivery 85-yard TD would have won the game.

While Ivery had been lying on the turf in pain, Payton walked over from the Bears' sideline and said, "God bless you. You're a hell of a running back."

The great Walter Payton had been watching him, too.

An MRI revealed a torn ACL and cartilage damage. Ivery would need surgery and miss the rest of his rookie season—after playing less than two quarters.

At the film session of the game, when they showed the play, Starr said, "Damn, Eddie Lee, you have to hold onto the ball!"

There was some laughter, but Starr was serious.

"That's the first time I really understood that professional football is about winning and supply and demand," Ivery said later.

> The attitude wasn't "Poor Eddie Lee got hurt" but "We need to win." If you fall, hold onto the ball, and then we'll look at the knee. We were on a drive and could have scored. I was on my way to a 100-yard day. We ran a slant, and I was the fullback in the split formation. I ran off tackle to the left. Our tackle made his block, and the guard picked off the linebacker. All I had to stop me was a little defensive back. I saw him coming and knew what I would do: cut against the grain.

He shook his head. "Now, I wish I had just run over him."

Koch echoed what many players were thinking. "Just dejected," he said. "You wonder who will start. I knew he would be a star and make all of us look good, so to see him hobble off the first game of his professional career, that's a killer. He was going to be the tool to help us get over the top. So unfortunate. He could put a team on his shoulders. We really needed Eddie Lee, and he needed to succeed. There's no telling how good he could have been."

Before surgery to repair the ACL and remove cartilage, Ivery was told that if he woke up with a cast on his leg, his rehab would take longer than they hoped. Sure enough, there it was, ankle to thigh. It remained for eight weeks.

While the injury ruined his rookie season, it changed his relationship with his mother—who rarely left Thomson, was scared of elevators and escalators, and had never flown on a plane.

"My uncle Nether," he said, "who had never flown either, got on a plane with her and reassured her everything was going to be all right." (Jerry was surprised they went: "We didn't have money for that.") When the plane backed up, she shrieked in fear—and again when it rolled forward.

Nether said, "Thelma, we ain't off the ground yet."

"She came to see me, and that changed everything," Ivery said. "She wasn't interested in seeing me play football, but she was interested in her child's well-being. That's a mom who loves you. The hell with football. When I get hurt, here she comes. She loved and cared for me. She had hardly left Thomson, and she got on a plane. I realized how much she loved me."

"Thelma" was now "Mom."

"Boy, you all right?" she asked.

"Yeah, I'm all right," he replied. She asked how long he would be there, and he said a few days. She said she just wanted to see that he was all right.

Satisfied, she abruptly said to Nether, "We can go now." Laughing, Ivery said there was no hanging around to visit.

"After that," he said, "I felt something special about her. It totally changed my attitude. She loved me enough to get on a plane, facing her own fears, to come see about her child."

Bennie Mae said she also eventually changed her view of their mother:

> I felt the shame. At PTA meetings, other parents would come,

> and I didn't want my mom there. She was illiterate, couldn't talk well. Then God revealed to me, you have that feeling about your mom, but if not for her, you wouldn't be here to be ashamed of her. From then on, I loved my mom, but when you're little, you want your mom to participate in school and drive you around. We didn't have things like other kids, but I now appreciate that we were never hungry, and our clothes were always clean.

She recalled her mother carrying water to wash clothes. "I get angry with myself. I wish it had been revealed to me earlier how silly I was. Back then, kids were ashamed of their parents if they couldn't read or write. She'd go to church and shout a lot. Some people dismissed her, but by the end of her life she drew everybody's respect."

On Sundays her mother, who had a large collection of hats, dressed sharp. "They'd ask me, 'Did you pick out your mama clothes?' I'd say, '*No*, she picks her own.' At her funeral, a friend made a display of her hats. She wore them mainly to church. She loved to keep her yard and wear her hats."

"As we got older, people started applauding her," Jerry Ivery said.

> If she wasn't at church, they'd call to check on her. It was ugly when we were younger, but not later. Everyone respected her. She'd get up early to pick up cans and walk four to five miles. There were maybe one or two incidents when people harassed her, but not much. People looked out for her. She never stopped picking up those cans. She put them in a certain place in the house, and everyone knew to leave them be. Don't mess with her cans!

When Ivery learned he was out for the season, he felt angry and confused.

"I was pissed off at myself," he said. "Why the hell didn't I run over that little defensive back? Why did I plant my foot? And I didn't know what happened to players who got hurt. Would they still pay me? Would they cut me? I was disappointed and scared." He heard that Sayers never recovered after he tore both his ACL and MCL in the same knee at the same time. Was his career over?

Sports psychologist Valdez said,

> That's a typical reaction for a great athlete. Once an athlete becomes elite, it becomes their entire identity. They feel like they have no other role in life, like they can't do anything else. They put all their all eggs in one basket, though maybe not consciously. It's so important for them, but society also puts a lot of importance on athletic performance and success. When some athletes don't have that to fall back on, they don't have an identity and that's part of the irritability. They're frustrated because of what a big role the sport plays in their lives. They can't adjust. They often don't know they even *need* to adjust. No one says that to them. Coaches often say, "Yeah, you have an injury, but when can you return?" There is implicit and explicit pressure to return to the role, so the longer it takes, the more frustrated they get.

Ivery said that he started drinking heavily. Beer was available at their seats on flights, and he helped himself.

"I felt like I lost who I was, and I drank to feel normal, to fill that void," he explained.

Eventually, he set aside his doubts and committed himself to rehabilitation, nurturing faint hopes that he might be ready if the Packers made the playoffs.

"Football was my life, my everything," he said. "I decided to take all my determination on the field and transfer it to rehab." He couldn't bear to watch the rest of the games and particularly dreaded the game against the Falcons in Atlanta. Without the injury, he would have played in front of family and friends, proving to the Falcons they were mistaken to think he wasn't worthy of the first round.

The Packers had a miserable 5-11 season. It was particularly painful after the 1978 (8-7-1) season had kindled optimism, in part because of the anticipated play of Ivery. Other injuries added to Starr's troubles. Twelve starters missed a total of 84 games. The 1979 season deflated Packers fans yet again. Fans at Lambeau booed. That last Super Bowl victory memory was fading.

Ivery was interviewed from his apartment on the *Bart Starr Show*. Starr asked about Ivery's rehab and said that he could tell by the gleam in Ivery's eyes that he would be back. Later, Ivery chuckled and said, "That wasn't no damn gleam. It was Budweiser and cognac."

When the cast was removed, he saw a small, stiff leg. He struggled to suppress doubts and fears, to exude confidence. He motivated himself by comparing his injured, weakened leg with his other leg, eager for the day they looked the same. When he wondered if his career was over, he reminded himself of what he had overcome in life and decided he would prove skeptics wrong, as he had before. *I'll show you.*

Ivery received a bill from the Internal Revenue Service for $90,000 in taxes owed on his signing bonus. A shocked Ivery, who had bought his grandmother a house and car, and cars for himself and his wife, and a house near Atlanta, thought, "I don't have $90,000." As was common, his agent received his percentage of the full six-year contract, deducted from the signing bonus, but players received their salaries over the course of the contract.

"If I don't make the team a couple of years later," Ivery realized, "he's gotten a percentage of money I'm not getting." In later years, the NFL players had programs to train athletes how to manage money, but when Ivery played, he was on his own. Lofton said Ivery was not alone.

"Agents didn't help," he said. "They were more for themselves. They don't alert you about taxes. In college, there's *no* tax return. I felt the same way, coming out of Stanford. My dad was a bank manager, and even I had never heard of that type of tax bill. We had no one to turn to, like they do now."

Frantic, Ivery called Burrough, who had left Trope to join agent Jerry Argovitz. Argovitz met with Harlan and suggested the Packers pay Ivery some of the money deferred for later so he could pay the tax bill. They agreed, and Argovitz became Ivery's new agent.

In the off-season, Thomson friends and family were impressed by Ivery's humility about being in the NFL.

"I always admired that when he was at the height of his Green Bay career he was just plain Eddie Lee, no celebrity status," Joseph Greene said. "Any person could pat him on the back, and he'd respond. He never left his roots, and I always admired that."

Greene took Ivery to the Masters, the prestigious golf tournament in nearby Augusta. "In Thomson," Greene said, "that's like going to heaven. He was like a kid in a candy store."

"I could have slept on that green, it was so beautiful," Ivery said later. "I was in the NFL, but I couldn't believe this country boy was there."

Around the same time, the city of Thomson received federal funds to expand sewage service. Finally, every house in Cherokee had running water.

Chapter 12

A Committed, Unselfish, Dedicated Young Man

Each time Ivery's leg was tested, the strength percentage rose, starting at 60 percent. He set his sights on 100 percent and reached 75 percent in six months. Allowing limited leg weight-lifting and light jogging, trainers advised gradually increasing his speed and running straight only. The first time he ran, he felt no pain. He smiled to himself and said, "I'll be back." He often ran with Lofton, usually several steps behind him. As he crept closer, his confidence grew.

"I worked so hard," he said, "that I came to training camp in the best shape of my life." But would his knee hold up when he changed directions at full speed? Without that, he was just another running back.

Frustrated Packers fans were again unhappy about the team's draft. They had the coveted fourth pick in 1980—a chance to land a standout player—and seemed to have it in Bruce Clark, a strong, quick Penn State defensive tackle who was the first junior to win the Lombardi Award as the nation's best college lineman. As a senior, he was first-team All-American. An excited Starr said Clark would play nose tackle.

But less than a month later, embarrassingly, Starr learned from reporters that Clark had signed with Toronto of the Canadian Football League. He would rather play in Canada than at hallowed Lambeau Field? The fourth pick—and they got nothing? Some draft disappointments weren't the Packers' fault, but, fans grumbled, they bungled this one.

Starr repeated that success would come as they followed his rebuilding plan. He said he had never been so enthusiastic or sure of his coaching and was confident in his assistants. Losing Clark was devastating, but, he added, some previously injured players were returning, and Ivery's recovery was particularly crucial. Bratkowski reminded reporters of last year's excitement over Ivery, mentioning his ability to cut, exceptional acceleration, reliable hands, determination, and dominance both inside and outside.

Ivery's first big test came in conditioning drills: players had to run four 440-yard dashes, each within 72 seconds, with only a one-minute break between runs. Ivery breezed through the first two. Fatigue gnawed at him halfway through the third, but he made it. Dickey said a not-in-shape player could "bluff his way through" until the last one.

Ivery's pride—and the fear Starr would make him run extra laps—kicked in.

"At the 110-yard mark," Ivery said, "my leg muscles were tight as drums. I wanted to fall because of the pain, but I kept going."

Someone with a stopwatch called out the seconds. Teammates, knowing this was a crucial moment for their young star, shouted, "Let's go, Eddie Lee!"

Propelled by their encouragement, he skimmed across the finish line at 71 seconds and collapsed.

"Walk it off, Eddie Lee!" a coach yelled.

Ivery stood, walked, and knew he was back.

The next challenge was practicing in pads and taking hits. The night before the first scrimmage, he barely slept. On the first play, he gained 10 yards around right end. There was no pain—and reporters noted he still had his "stunning acceleration."

"I thanked God," Ivery said. He added that he had "worked his ass off" and didn't cheat on his rehab regimen. He admitted he was eager but cautious.

It was noted he remained one of the most enthusiastic and popular players on the team, gaining respect from teammates who observed his grueling recovery.

"It's a dream to be in this league," Ivery said. He explained that he played for himself, his wife, and the Packers.

In the next preseason game, he carried the ball four times for 18 yards (9 on his first carry) and said he didn't yet feel like he was "bursting in there like I should"—but that would come with time. He admitted he was still apprehensive when he ran—not quite his hard-charging, hit-the-hole self yet.

The following week, against the Colts in a steady rain, the team played poorly and lost 17-3. Ivery left in the first quarter with a shoulder injury while blocking. When asked if his heart skipped a beat, Starr replied, "Four or five."

The injury, to everyone's relief, turned out to be a "stinger"—a compression of nerves, very painful but temporary.

In the final preseason game—described by reporter Cliff Christl as "one final wretched performance"—the Broncos smacked the Packers 38-0. Lambeau fans began booing in the first quarter. They even cheered when a Denver interception was returned for a touchdown—and booed when a penalty nullified it. It was Green Bay's first winless preseason in 26 years.

During that game, defensive end Ezra Johnson, coming off a Pro Bowl season, was spotted eating a hot dog on the sidelines. Starr fined him and required him to apologize to the team. Johnson insisted he hadn't meant any disrespect—he was just hungry—but the incident became a symbol of the Packers' dysfunction and lack of discipline.

If the Packers had been winning, some said, would it have been laughed off as a harmless moment of levity?

Outscored 86-17 in preseason, the Packers failed to score in three of five games. Oddsmakers pegged Green Bay as 1,000-1 to win the Super Bowl—the longest odds of any team.

In the regular season opener against the Bears, Ivery played his first full NFL game, wearing a knee brace as a precaution. Lambeau fans cheered loudly when his name was announced. Back in his favored tailback position, he had an 18-yard gain that helped set up a field goal near the end of the first half to tie the game 6-6. In the third quarter, after a tough 5-yard gain, his left knee gave out.

The stadium grew quiet as a grim Ivery limped off.

The team doctor determined he was fine—the brace had probably been too tight. Ivery removed it and never wore it again.

He returned late in the fourth quarter and finished with 73 yards and an impressive 4.9-yard average. The Packers' potential game-winning field goal in overtime was blocked by Alan Page, but kicker Chester Marcol picked up the ball and ran 25 yards for a touchdown to win it 12-6. Years later, Marcol revealed he had used cocaine at halftime.

Whatever optimism the Packers felt after opening with a win over the hated Bears didn't last. They lost their next three games by a combined 108-35, including a 51-21 drubbing by the Rams. In that game, Ivery gained only 12 yards rushing but scored on a 46-yard pass play.

Reporters described shouting and finger-pointing in the postgame locker room. In Milwaukee Stadium—where the team split its home games with Green Bay—fans waved signs: "Bye-Bye Bart" and "Fire Bart Starr."

In one loss, Ivery, still not at full strength from knee and shoulder injuries, gained only 31 yards on 10 carries, though he did score a 5-yard touchdown around left end. He began a new, low-key touchdown celebration: casually tossing the ball back over his shoulder.

After he scored, the stadium scoreboard flashed, "Congratulations to Eddie Lee Ivery, who became the father of a seven-pound daughter this morning."

Two days before the next game, the team held a players-only meeting, which is usually convened by fed-up veterans who demand a no-nonsense discussion made more serious by excluding coaches: We don't *have* to call meetings like coaches do; we're calling one because we *need* it.

Dickey said veterans "know who's working really hard and who's not." He said sometimes it works to say, "If you don't know who you are, ask, and someone will tell you." A player might then say, "Really, me?" A veteran might say if they're not hearing from the coaches that they're doing a good job, "You're probably screwing up."

Johnson laughed and said, "Airing things out without the coaches means something because it's your brother saying, 'We know you can do better than this, and we're in this together.' It's about guys having accountability without pointing fingers to individuals but letting guys know you're letting down the guy next to you. There is too much at stake, and we're out here working hard."

The next week, the Packers lost decisively to the Cowboys 28-7. Ivery gained 59 yards, averaging 6.6 per carry. In the Packers' one touchdown drive, he had runs of 26 (the Packers' longest of the season) and 9. As the 1-3 team left the field, the crowd of 54,776 in Milwaukee booed.

"I wanted to put a towel over my head," Ivery said. "That was the most degrading feeling. I took booing to heart and felt embarrassed. Green Bay had the best fans, but they were even booing Bart Starr." Ivery recalled once a backup quarterback replaced the starter and led the offense to a touchdown, and fans booed when the starter re-entered the game.

Although Ivery started the next game, against Cincinnati, which had the fourth-best rushing defense in the NFL, the Packers rotated four running backs, and he finished with 43 rushing yards and 15 receiving yards. Green Bay finally won again, 14-9.

They didn't lose the next game, against Tampa Bay, but they didn't win. The Packers dominated in all statistics but made critical mistakes (including two missed field goal attempts) and tied the Bucs 14-14, in a deflating non-loss. Ivery excelled at receiving: 128 yards on 11 receptions (a team record for most receptions by a running back in a game, not broken until 1992). He "made several tough catches in crucial situations," per a reporter.

They played well enough to win the following week but lost to Cleveland on a 46-yard touchdown pass with 16 seconds left. Ivery rushed for only 11 yards on seven carries. Years later, he said his shoulder injury was still bothering him, and he partly blamed Starr for his extensive physical practices.

"It was hard for us to heal," he said, "because we were full-speed tackling and blocking all the way to Thursday. Sometimes he'd have us do 80-100 up/downs [players run in place, and a coach shouts,

'Down!' and they drop to the ground and jump back up] before practice. That's ridiculous."

A reporter, reflecting on the poor season, suggested that if Ivery hadn't been injured, he might have been to the Packers what rookie Billy Sims was to the Lions. By the end of that year, the Lions would improve from 2-14 in 1979 to 9-7 and second place in their division, largely because of Sims—the Heisman Trophy winner—who made the Pro Bowl.

The following week, the Packers clung to a faint playoff hope after defeating the Vikings 16-3, with Ivery rushing for 63 yards. Their division was so weak that at 3-4-1, they sat in second place. Packers fans hadn't expected such fragile optimism under the saintly Starr—and it didn't last.

In the next game, Green Bay led the powerful defending Super Bowl champion Steelers for much of the afternoon, but Pittsburgh narrowly pulled out a 22-20 victory, despite the Packers gaining more yards. The Steelers' bruising running game dominated the clock while the Packers often scored quickly on big plays. According to Ivery, the Packers' defense wore down in the fourth quarter.

Still, they bounced back with a 23-16 victory over San Francisco. Ivery had -2 yards at halftime but rallied to finish with a season-high 91.

Regardless of how the Packers were doing, Ivery's high school teammate John Barnett, now a high school coach, would rush home from Sunday coaches meetings, turn on NFL highlights, and see how Ivery performed that day. The next morning, he opened the newspaper and, first thing, checked Ivery's stats.

The Packers started the season 1-3 but improved to 4-5-1, one game out of first place in the division. A reporter mentioned a "rejuvenated running game" led by Ivery and newly acquired Gerry Ellis, both strong, fast, and good receivers. Public criticism of Starr waned. Dickey was passing well (over 2,000 yards for the first time in his 10-year career), especially to emerging star Lofton. Despite having 16 players on injured reserve, they were favored on the road against the Giants, but the pattern of slight hope followed by disappointment continued with a 27-21 loss. Ivery gained 49 yards rushing and 37 receiving. The Pack had a cheerless record of 4-6-1.

On a cold, snowy day, in a contest considered one they "had to win," the defense held a Vikings team that had averaged 37 points in three straight wins to 13, and the running game excelled. Both Ivery and Ellis gained over 100 yards. The Packers committed no turnovers and won a road game for the first time in six tries. Championship-starved Packers fans tried to celebrate a 5-6-1 record, which put them in third place in the division.

Ivery finished with an impressive 145 yards rushing, marking his first 100+-yard game as a Packer, and scored a game-clinching 38-yard touchdown in the last minute, powering through the line and then running untouched. *This* was the Ivery the Packers had drafted No. 1. He blocked to free Ellis for nice gains, including a touchdown run. Often dragging defenders with him, Ivery quickly found and zipped through holes. He made sharp cuts with speed, gaining 12 yards with one fake that made a defender miss. He caught a pass in the flat, made a sharp cut, and gained good yardage. He caught a screen pass, despite briefly losing sight of the ball due to defenders and ran for a first down. On a run when a pass play was expected, he rushed for a first down and nearly broke free for a touchdown but was hit from the side. Frustrated that he didn't score, he slammed the ball between his hands.

With a chance to move to just one-half game out of first place in the division, the Packers squandered a game they could have won, losing to Tampa Bay 20-17. Afterward, before abruptly ending the news conference prematurely, Starr insisted the Packers, tied with the Bucs at 5-7-1, were still in contention for a playoff berth. He said Tampa Bay "came out and played like hell....but we were lethargic. I can't explain it." Stenerud—signed as a free agent that week—missed a 45-yard field goal try with 17 seconds left that could have sent the game to overtime. If they had won their last three games, they might have squeaked into the playoffs. But they lost every game.

They were demolished by the 6-8 Bears 61-7, the second worst loss in Packers history, the most points the team ever conceded. The Bears later said they had decoded the Packers' sideline hand signals to Dickey. Starr mostly answered reporters' questions with clipped replies.

He had said before the season that he needed a winning record to keep his job, but, with that now impossible, he said he wanted to stay for 1981. They lost to the Oilers when they were within 6 points late in the fourth quarter. Mighty Earl Campbell rushed for 181 yards. Mercifully, only one game remained, a disheartening loss to the Lions, 24-3. After being only a game and a half out of first, they lost the last four games and finished 5-10-1 (that tie the one meager improvement over the previous season). Starr now had five of six losing seasons.

Pleased with Ivery's season after his knee injury, Starr said,

> We were seeing in practice and games the reasons we had drafted him. It was heartwarming and rewarding. We saw a committed, unselfish, dedicated young man. Players like that recognize the true meaning of team and how to sacrifice for the good of it. Sometimes a talented person is not willing to commit, is selfish, so it's refreshing to be around people like Eddie Lee Ivery.

Though Ivery thought Starr tried to mimic Lombardi too much ("the way we practiced—beat each other up, grind it out"), Starr had Ivery's loyalty.

"If you didn't want to win for anybody else," he said later, "you wanted to win for him. He genuinely cared for his players. I wanted to win because of who he was, not just the Green Bay Packers."

Although Ivery had only one game with over 100 yards rushing in 1980—perhaps because their offense relied so heavily on passing—it was a successful comeback from serious knee surgery. He led the team in rushing with 831 yards (12th in the league), averaging 4.1 per carry, and, though a running back, was second on the team in pass receptions (50, a franchise record for a running back) behind All-Pro Lofton.

"I felt I was as good as ever," he said. "I was stronger. I had won over the coaches and fans. My confidence was back. I was a little disappointed because I could have gotten 1,000 yards, but I was taken out of some games that we were winning. I thought I'd rush for 1,000 the next season."

According to Christl's book, *The Greatest Story in Sports,* a four-volume history of the Packers, after the 1980 season, the executive committee held "bitter meetings" about whether to retain Starr. They kept him but removed his GM role. Starr insisted on keeping control over personnel decisions, which they allowed.

The draft, yet again, brought unwanted drama. They had the sixth pick, another chance to garner a star. Corrick favored University of Southern California defensive back Ronnie Lott, but the Packers chose University of California quarterback Rich Campbell—who never started a game in the NFL.

"I was dumbfounded," Corrick later said. "Lott was as high as you could go in our draft room." Chosen eighth by the 49ers, Lott starred in four Super Bowl victories with the 49ers, was named All-Pro eight times, was elected to the Pro Football Hall of Fame the first year he was eligible, and is considered one of the best defensive backs of all time.

The Packers shocked the world by beating the Cowboys in their first preseason game, (12-4 the previous season) 21-17. Those 21 points were more than the previous year's *entire* preseason and more than their total points in the final three games of the last season. Next up: defending Super Bowl champs Oakland Raiders. The Packers, before a sellout crowd in Milwaukee, celebrated their second straight "upset," 34-14. Forget last year's 5-10-1 record, fans cautiously hoped.

The Packers lost the next preseason game, then defeated the Browns (defending AFC Central Division champs) impressively, 35-18. Dickey looked sharp (18 of 27 for 250 yards), and Ivery and wide receiver Audra Thompson scored two touchdowns each—Ivery on a 41-yard run and a 15-yard pass. On the run, he broke through a hole off right tackle, faked out a cornerback, and cut cross-field. He continued to be the star they had drafted. Lambeau fans had booed after last year's final preseason game; this year, they cheered loudly. The Packers' 3-1 preseason record was their best since 1975, with their three wins against quality teams.

Ivery's preseason performance, particularly the 41-yarder, boosted his confidence. He exhibited his explosiveness, speed, and sharp cuts. Teammates praised his attention to detail and willingness to block. He sometimes winced while watching 1980 film, wondering if the knee injury had diminished his skills: *I should have crashed through that hole, broken that tackle, outrun that defender. Was I sometimes fearing re-injury, indecisive?* Those thoughts hampered him, he said, because "I'm not a second-thoughts kind of runner."

Now feeling more confident, he thought, "I'm back. No one's going to catch me again." The first game of 1981 would be back at Soldier Field, where his knee came apart. When asked about being leery of returning, he shook his head and replied defiantly, "That's over with."

But it wasn't.

"I had one of my best off-seasons," he said. "I worked harder than I ever had, and I was the healthiest I'd been." His personal life thrived. "Things were real good with Anna. She was my best supporter. She didn't pressure or worry me. She had waited on me hand and foot when I was in the hospital. I grew to love her as my wife. She said, 'Whatever you do, I'll stand with you.'"

In the off-season, they had lived in Atlanta and visited family in Tampa and Thomson. He felt especially proud as he visited his mother and grandmother in the home he bought for them. He hung out with cousins, played cards or basketball, drank beer, had cookouts. He was asked for autographs.

"I couldn't ask for a better life," he said. "I had a new daughter. Things were grand."

Chicago was a slight favorite, despite Green Bay's impressive preseason. Payton was set to defend another NFC rushing title. Pregame, an announcer asked, "Are the Packers as good as everyone says?"

Ivery scored the Packers' first touchdown, a 2-yard power run through a crowd, following a 28-yard gain in which he faked out a defender. He was having an excellent game with 14 rushes for 72 yards, a little over 5 per carry, likely headed for a 100-plus-yard game (30 more yards? Piece of cake). He blocked effectively, even against bigger men.

In the third quarter, the Packers ran a sweep, and Ivery burst into the Chicago defensive backfield—where typically he would romp—but was brought down by diving safety Len Walterscheid, whose helmet struck Ivery's left knee. The hit looked like a normal tackle, but Ivery felt pain and was helped off the field.

"I saw a hole and hit it," he recalled. "This was a rare time my peripheral vision failed me. I never saw him."

Green Bay upset the Bears 16-9 in a game filled with mistakes, bemoaned by both head coaches. Ivery walked gingerly to the locker room, thinking it didn't hurt as much as the first injury, so maybe it wasn't so bad. But the knee didn't feel right. Showering, he tried to feel hopeful.

When he learned he had torn a different ligament in the same knee, he wept. The first injury, he cried from the pain. This time, "I cried," he said, "not from pain but disappointment. I was devastated. I just knew my career was over."

It was a complete tear of the medial collateral ligament (MCL). The MCL, about 9 centimeters long, connects the femur and tibia. Like the ACL, it is tough but has limits. Unlike Ivery's first injury, this tear wasn't due to twisting but a direct blow. He was told rehab, after six to seven weeks in a cast, would take longer than the first one and require even more patience.

When Coffman learned of Ivery's second injury, he thought, "Oh no, not again. There goes our workhorse." Recalling his own experience with injury, Coffman said, "I only missed two games, but I felt like an outsider. You stand around and watch but don't participate. You feel like you let the team down. Mine was only two weeks, so I couldn't imagine what he felt like."

Injured players watch, unable to contribute, their competitiveness still raging, their eagerness to prove themselves just as strong—somehow feeling like they are to blame.

Starr remained optimistic and methodical.

"I think there's a natural concern," he said later, "when it happens twice to a player, but we didn't immediately think it would end his career. That's totally wrong and a poor attitude. Be calm, work it through, get a diagnosis, design a rehab program, then face reality. To say something negative going in is just not the appropriate way to face an injury."

Starr always had a plan—for the Packers' resurgence, for a player's rehab—and he confidently implemented each one. Still, he also knew the team was diminished. "It's a tremendous blow to our offense," he said then. "Everyone recognizes his value and versatility as a runner, pass receiver, and blocker."

Several days later, Ivery reflected that at least it was a different ligament this time. At first, he had been speechless with despair and worry, unsure if a second round of grueling rehab was worth the effort when no one was certain he would ever play again. He felt helpless watching the Packers lose six of their next seven games, then empty as they won the next three without him.

Worries crept in. Am I finished at age 23? What will I do? He regretted not earning his college degree. What would it be like to merely play—and not be Eddie Lee Ivery? He wistfully recalled preseason expectations just weeks earlier.

"I wondered if I should retire," he said. "But football was all I knew. The Goodyear plant had closed in Thomson, and I didn't have enough money to retire."

Anna said she would support whatever he decided. "She said never look back and wish you had tried," he said. She offered to get a job in Atlanta if he had to quit.

With Anna's encouragement, he decided he would work twice as hard this time. He spent two months in Atlanta with Anna and their daughter, then returned to Green Bay for rehab, planning to stay through mini-camp.

Ivery heard media reports that Green Bay should draft a running back. "Drinking and smoking weed," he said, blocked that out. "It gave me comfort. I had always wanted to make others happy, and I couldn't. I was scared because I hadn't graduated."

Despite Anna's support, he took his frustrations out on his family.

"I became crazy," he said. "I didn't want to be around my wife, daughter, nobody. I'd come home late. My drinking escalated. I drank every day for a month. I used cocaine. But Anna stood by me. She took my verbal abuse."

Once the cast was removed, his leg workouts were limited to stretching and light lifting. The Ivery known for his work ethic reemerged—despite his anger, fear, and drinking.

"It was pure desire and determination," he said, "especially when I read that no running back had come back from two surgeries on the same knee and been productive in the NFL. That inspired me." *I'll show you.*

"Once I made up my mind, I had that burning desire to play football. It meant a lot to be in the NFL, but it's just that the game—that's all I knew," he said. "It was the only thing I was good at that I didn't have to study. It came natural."

Teammates noticed his effort and attitude. Coffman said,

> We'd see him in the training room, and they'd be working on his knee, and we would see the grueling pain on his face. Then he'd come out sweaty and laugh and say, "That was a tough one today." It would be easy to give up, and some did, because you take baby steps in that kind of rehab. You see no change for a long time, until you keep at it month-to-month, and only in the long term see results.

"Rehab is horrible," Dickey added;

> I did it many times. More than once, at the end of the day, you're looking in the mirror and going, "God, I don't know if I can do this." The next morning, you think you might die

> doing this, but you're going to get it done. It's hard; it takes you a good month or six weeks to improve ever so slightly. It's like if you're doing something in inches, and you've been working at it, and two days go by, and you improve only a half inch.

With one game left in the season, the Packers had a slight chance to make the playoffs, but, after winning six of seven, they lost badly to the Jets, 28-3. Dickey was sacked nine times. They missed the playoffs for the ninth straight year.

"Yet another 8-8," fans said, rolling their eyes.

Receiver John Jefferson said the team lacked emotion and confidence. Some players said Starr was too nice and wasn't feared by anyone. Reporters criticized Starr's in-game decisions. Fans booed in Milwaukee and Green Bay. Some even chanted, "Bye-Bye Bart"—unthinkable when he was hired.

Chapter 13

I Was Truly Back

Between seasons, Starr's strongest backer in the front office was removed as president and replaced by Judge Robert J. Parins, known to be less supportive of Starr. Starr's contract was renewed, but not for the three years he requested. The committee suggested one year; they settled on two. His record was the lowest winning percentage of a Green Bay coach since Lombardi and the worst of any seven-year coach in NFL history. But he was *Bart Starr*; he got another chance.

In March 1982, Ivery was reported to be running at half speed and making slow cuts—and to be "highly motivated." In May, he was cleared to attend mini-camp and participate in team drills but was not allowed to cut at full speed. A trainer said he was working hard, very determined, running uphill and downhill—and shooting a lot of basketball. They instructed him to run only straight; he secretly made cuts when he was alone. He felt relieved that he experienced no pain.

"They'd say, 'We've done enough for today,' but it wasn't enough for me," he recounted. "I had proved to my critics and myself that if I work hard at something, I can do it. I didn't feel much pressure, but I wanted to get through the whole season. I worked twice as hard to get my knee as strong as possible." *I'll show you.*

By July, he was cutting at full speed in view of coaches, almost ready to take his first hit. In an early August scrimmage, he gained only a yard on his first run but emerged from the pile smiling.

"I didn't feel any pain," he said. He told reporters it "was a big hurdle," that it was good to get hit and perform well. He said, "I knew I was going to get hit. I did get hit, and I feel fine."

Some fans changed the lyrics of the popular Paul McCartney/Stevie Wonder song, "Ebony and Ivory," to "Eddie LEE Iver-EE." Sports journalist Bud Geracie overheard a group of boaters singing the song that way on a Wisconsin lake.

Ivery had been their best breakaway runner, and it was assumed that, after the two injuries, he would not have his previous explosiveness but would still be a valuable running back. Christl reported that the Packers should have a potent backfield, with Ivery and Ellis both being excellent rushers and receivers (with Ivery out in 1981, Ellis broke Ivery's Packers running back receptions record). Against two capable Packers backfield receivers, defenses might not double-team Jefferson and Lofton. The defense appeared, finally, to be better.

In what was now an annual tradition, reporters speculated on how Starr could keep his job: Have a winning record? Make the playoffs? Despite the Packers missing the playoffs the previous season with a clunker season-ending loss to the Jets, Starr expressed optimism for his eighth season.

"We feel we are on the threshold of really doing some big things here," he told reporters. "I'm very anxious to have this football team back in a championship posture, and we're closing in on it."

Starr said some of their offensive plans depended on a healthy Ivery, who he said has "recovered well. At this time, we're very optimistic."

Dickey watched Ivery and thought, "He's still good, but that burst of quickness is not there like it used to be." In their preseason opener, the Packers defeated the Jets (the game was a sellout, but more than 2,500 ticket holders didn't show), and Ivery gained 17 yards on four carries and had one reception for 5 yards. On one run, he scored a 3-yard touchdown and spiked the ball triumphantly—rather than his typical low-key toss over his shoulder.

"I was excited," he said. "That let everybody know I'm back." He said he was close to 100 percent. In a preseason win over the Bengals, on a near-touchdown run, he broke right, cut left, and was tackled at the 1-yard line. He was disappointed he didn't score but was thrilled to be in the open field and cutting. He gained 30 yards on three carries.

That summer, Ivery's sister, Bennie Mae, called and told him his father died. Ivery had seen his father only a few times and barely remembered him. He recalled people saying they had seen his father hanging out with other drunks and that he should visit, but he never did.

"I was ashamed and embarrassed," he said, "and didn't want to have anything to do with him." He skipped a preseason game against the Patriots to attend the funeral, wanting to see if he resembled his father. His mother was there.

He walked to the casket, looked down at his father, and said, "Thank you, Dad," in appreciation for any athletic abilities he inherited. He learned he had half-siblings, some of whom he had known. "Mom knew them all," he said. One half-brother, like their father, was an alcoholic. He saw a young woman he had had a crush on in high school, spoke to her, and learned she was his half-sister.

The opening game of 1982, against the Los Angeles Rams in Milwaukee, started disastrously and ended in triumph. At halftime, Packers fans were ready for Starr to go; boos echoed through the stadium. Dickey had thrown two interceptions and lost two fumbles. The Rams led 23-0.

Starr later wrote that he was furious at halftime and ejected everyone from the locker room except for players and coaches. Normally calm, he shouted that the first half was disgraceful and that if they couldn't show more pride, they should shower and leave.

It worked. The offense committed no turnovers, and the defense sacked the Rams quarterback four times and allowed no first downs in the third quarter—only four in the fourth. A 4-yard touchdown pass to Coffman: 23-7. A 3-yard Ivery TD run: 23-14. In the fourth, Dickey threw two touchdown passes in 17 seconds. The Pack led 28-23.

At 3:06 to play, Ivery clinched the game with a 27-yard touchdown run. The line opened a big hole, and he broke two tackles.

"I went through the middle," he recalled, "and a safety went for me. I made my move on him and high-stepped to the end zone. I was truly back. The team came off the sidelines and lifted me up. That was a great feeling."

High-stepping wasn't Ivery's style, but this was the time to celebrate. He was given the game ball. Ivery rushed for 109 yards (over 6 per carry), had runs of 32 and 27 yards, scored two touchdowns, and caught two passes for 32 yards. All that by a running back with two surgeries on the same knee and who had alternated at tailback.

Starr called the performance "the greatest comeback I've ever witnessed. I'm at a loss for words to tell you how proud I am of this football team."

Ivery appeared on *The Bart Starr Show* before an audience of Packers fans, wearing a suit with the shirt unbuttoned at the top, the collar visible outside the jacket. Coach and player joked easily on camera, exuding camaraderie and warmth. It's not hard to imagine a father-son type relationship.

Ivery joked about the cold weather in Green Bay, said his daughter had just turned two, and he was going to her birthday party after the show. Starr said Ivery had been very dedicated to his second rehab, adding, "Eddie Lee has a great sense of pride that we associate with a man like him."

Speaking softly, looking at the audience, not nervous, Ivery explained his rehab routine and said, "I feel comfortable running now. I'll be a reckless runner like I was in 1980."

A play featuring a nifty run by Ivery aired, and he complimented the blocking, saying he needed to work on his speed because he should have scored but was caught from behind.

An adoring little boy in the studio audience asked about the possibility of a strike. Starr said he didn't want to think about that, preferring to focus on the next game. The NFL Players Association was demanding 55 percent revenue sharing (among other matters), and the owners weren't budging.

Someone asked Ivery's opinion of rookie running back Mike Lee, and he was complimentary—especially of a block that helped Ivery sprint for a 27-yard gain.

A boy asked if it was scary running with huge defensive players. Ivery said, "I'm always nervous at first, but there's no time to be scared out there. Once I get into the flow of the game, I'm OK."

The show ended with two Ivery highlights. In the first, he powered through a crowd for a touchdown. In the second, he shifted directions quickly without losing speed and broke two tackles. Ivery commented, "I feel I'm 100 percent back now."

The next game was against the New York Giants on *Monday Night Football.* Pre-game, players from the opposing teams met at midfield for solidarity handshakes supporting the players' union demands, and the crowd booed.

The broadcasters' introduction highlighted the Packers' passing game: Dickey's strong, accurate arm (if he had time, since he wasn't very mobile), Lofton's speed and elegance, Coffman's toughness and reliability.

Ivery started and rotated with other running backs, but by the end he was the primary ball carrier. Announcer Frank Gifford mentioned Ivery's successful recovery from two knee injuries and his impressive career average of 4.5 yards. He said Ivery was a threat inside and out.

Throughout the game, Ivery displayed his versatility: short runs through a crowded middle, dragging defenders for extra yards; bursts around the end, making wise cuts, spinning free when hit, deftly changing speed.

On a 6-yard gain, he cleverly maneuvered through a crowd. On another, he ran through a big hole and likely would have scored except for a diving grab at his ankles at the 10. He jerked his head down in frustration. (Pre-injuries, would he have escaped?)

On a key 6-yard run for a first down, he used a rare stutter-step fake—right, then quick to the left—effectively. On a well-executed screen pass for a crucial first down to the 15, he danced through several defenders.

He blocked well but not perfectly. On one play, powerful linebacker Lawrence Taylor simply shoved him aside and made a tackle for a loss.

On a clinching touchdown run in the fourth, he faked left, took the handoff going right, quickly accelerated at the 3, and danced past diving tacklers into the end zone. The Packers had their first lead.

In the Packers' last two drives, they called on Ivery for most of the rushing, counting on him to protect the ball and use up time. He delivered: tough first downs, powering through the middle, darting around the end.

Ivery finished as the Packers' leading rusher with 98 yards on 24 carries. With the Packers' explosive passing, he wasn't the star of the game, but he was what they needed: tough, dependable, productive.

The Pack won 27-19. Two games in, Ivery led the NFC in rushing (203 yards, 4.5 average) and was tied for most touchdowns.

With their beloved team at 2-0, could fans feel hopeful? They had to wait two months to find out. NFL owners rejected the union demands, so the players staged a walkout while the owners initiated a lockout. Packers players held player-run workouts at nearby St. Norbert College. They shared moments of fun, including Jefferson tossing a football to Ivery, who attempted to hit it with a stick as if it were a baseball.

Ivery spent his time hanging out with family, playing cards with teammates, or drinking beer at a bar. Lofton, the Packers' player representative, relayed information to Whitehurst, who communicated it to the players. Whitehurst recalled feeling disappointed that Ivery favored ending the strike immediately although publicly, Ivery supported the union. He was eager to prove he was back in form, and he needed the money: he had an apartment in Green Bay, his mother and grandmother's house, and a house in Atlanta. After the NFLPA and owners reached an agreement, they played an abbreviated season with nine more games and then had the "Super Bowl Tournament." The playoffs were decided by seeding based on record rather than division standings. If the Packers made it to the Super Bowl, Starr would be the first player to return to it as coach of the same team he had played for in it.

In the first post-strike game in Milwaukee, Packers fans were still somewhat resentful about the strike and not fully convinced by the 2-0 start. There were around 4,700 no-shows, and reports indicated that the fans were less enthusiastic than what was expected of rabid Packers followers.

Thanks in part to Ivery's two touchdowns and a short pass reception on a third-and-22 that he turned into a 62-yard gain, they defeated Minnesota 26-7, becoming one of five teams in the NFL to start 3-0. They led the NFC in both rushing and rushing defense. They hadn't started a season with three straight victories since 1966, when they won Super Bowl I.

A *New York Times* story referred to Ivery as "the symbol of the Packers' return to glory" and noted that his running and pass-receiving hindered defenses from focusing too heavily on the Packers' excellent receivers. To reporters, Ivery said they hoped to restore the Packers' former glory, but years later he said wearily, "They always made that comparison. It became burdensome."

Dickey told a reporter that Ivery "does things you can't coach. He picks holes, picks his feet up, squirms, scratches, and all of a sudden, it's a big play." Ivery was the NFC's second-leading rusher and led the NFC in touchdowns.

Next up, the Jets at Shea Stadium, who had knocked the Packers out of the playoffs the previous year with a 28-3 walloping and nine sacks of Dickey. How would the Packers' impressive offense fare against the fierce Jets defensive line? Alas, they narrowly lost 15-13. Ivery had 29 yards rushing and 30 receiving. Ivery was in a three-way tie for the NFL lead in scoring among non-kickers with 30 points.

They followed that disappointment with an impressive 33-21 victory over the also 3-1 Buffalo Bills and their top-in-the-NFL defense, in intermittent rain on a slippery, muddy field, and at 4-1 were tied for first place in the NFC. Ivery scored a 1-yard rushing TD. Dickey, the NFL's top-ranked quarterback, passed for 195 yards and a touchdown. Stenerud's four field goals moved him into third place on the NFL's career scoring list. Starr chided the media for saying the Packers rarely beat a quality opponent and said it was a confidence boost for the team.

"It was just a matter of time until we were able to do that," he said.

But the following week they lost decisively to the 2-3 Lions 30-10. The Packers, 4-2, entered the game leading the NFC in scoring but didn't score a touchdown until the fourth quarter. Ivery had 26 yards rushing, 26 receiving. Overall, Ivery led the team with 314 yards rushing.

The next game, against the winless Baltimore Colts, was a chance to start a new win streak but the game, played in snow and rain, ended in a 20-20 tie. Both teams missed field goals in overtime. Green Bay's try missed; Baltimore's was blocked. Green Bay had led 20-6 early in the fourth quarter after Ivery's 1-yard power dive for a touchdown (an announcer said Ivery "was determined to get in that time"), and seemed in control, but the Colts scored two touchdowns.

"It's better than a loss, but not by much," Starr commented. Inconsistencies that haunted Starr's tenure as coach persisted. The running game was now called a weakness.

Receiver Jefferson said, "We need a balanced attack." Reporters questioned, and fans grumbled about, coaching decisions. Why didn't they go for it on fourth down?! The offense is too conservative!

The next game was against the 5-2 Atlanta Falcons, winners of three straight—the last a 17-7 victory over defending Super Bowl champs 49ers. With a win, the Falcons would secure the playoff home-field advantage.

"I was excited to be back," Ivery said. "My family hadn't seen me much, and they were there from Thomson." Plus, he still resented the Falcons for not drafting him.

Every aspect of the Green Bay team played well, and they dominated the Falcons 38-7, their most points in four years. An efficient Dickey, after two sub-par games, was 10 for 17 and threw touchdown strikes to Lofton of 80 (a perfectly thrown bomb as Lofton faked out and dashed past an overmatched defender) and 57 yards.

Ivery ran for two scores in front of cheering family. In one of his best games of the season, he averaged 6.6 yards per carry (9/59), caught two passes for 19 yards, and scored two touchdowns. Following a long kickoff return on the opening kickoff, Ivery was handed the ball up the middle, saw an opening to the left, tripped over a teammate's legs, put his hand down, regained his balance, broke three tackles, and gained 15 yards to the Falcons' 6. It took three defenders to bring him down. His second touchdown run went for 12 yards; he cut back perfectly to angle into the end zone, dragging a defender for the final two yards.

Green Bay, at 5-2-1, finally made the playoffs—for the first time since 1972. Starr said it was the biggest win of his coaching career. They made the playoffs, defeated a quality opponent, and had the third-best record in the NFC. They limited the top rushing team in the NFC to just 58 yards. Were they finally the Packers Starr had promised he would coach them to be?

Surely, they could handle the 3-5 Detroit Lions the next week. But they lost 27-24. Ivery gained 35 yards rushing (including an 11-yard score) and made one reception for 14. The loss didn't eliminate them from the playoffs, but it was a disappointing end to the regular season.

The Packers convincingly won their first playoff game, 41-16 over the St. Louis Cardinals, the first postseason game in Green Bay since 1967. The defense stifled the Cardinals, harassing the quarterback and knocking out their best rusher early. Dickey tossed four touchdown passes and completed passes to six different receivers. Jefferson caught six passes for 148 yards and two touchdowns. Ivery had 67 yards rushing. Now an integral part of a dominant offense, he scored their third and fourth touchdowns on a 2-yard run and a 4-yard pass.

Starr smiled broadly and revised his remark on the Falcons game, saying this was the best they had played in his eight years as coach. Before the game, fans were apparently not convinced the team was for real; Lambeau had its first non-sellout (10,000 tickets unsold two days before the game) since 1959. But the playoff-starved fans who did attend roared from an early goal-line stand to the final horn and stormed the field for a celebratory razing of the goalposts. Titletown denizens hadn't seen a title in so long that one playoff win meant damaging their own field in a frenzy.

Players expressed confidence they could beat a good 7-3 Dallas team with playoff experience, strong on offense and defense, led by legendary coach—and Starr's good friend—Tom Landry. The Cowboys, symbols of NFL excellence for over a decade, had made the playoffs 16 of the past 17 years and had two straight appearances in the NFC championship. Tony Dorsett led the NFC in rushing, and their defensive pass rush (part of their "Doomsday Defense") was formidable.

But Dickey was having his best season and could go deep to Lofton or Jefferson almost any time. Plus, there was dependable, rugged Coffman. All three receivers were headed to the Pro Bowl.

The Packers lost to the Cowboys 37-26, but it was a thrilling game with back-and-forth scoring. The Packers led 7-6 in the second quarter on an impressive 79-yard drive that ended with a precisely timed touchdown pass to Lofton, who out-quicked his defender. There were crucial Packers mistakes (five turnovers and four sacks), but otherwise, the game was about even. Aside from the interceptions, Dickey had his best statistical game of the season and threw beautiful pinpoint passes.

Ivery's best play was as a decoy. Lofton, considered perhaps the NFL's best athlete, scored another dazzling touchdown on a Dickey-to-Ivery-to-Lofton reverse in the fourth quarter, reducing the Dallas lead to four. Ivery rushed seven times for 24 yards and caught one pass for 25.

If a 49-yard flea flicker by Dallas hadn't worked after the Packers had closed the gap late in the game, perhaps the Packers would have pulled off the upset. Green Bay led in total yards and twice came within four points in the fourth quarter.

These were hopeful signs for 1983.

"It's disappointing to lose certainly," Starr said, "but we hope there will be a carry-over of the good things we've done this year into the next. We feel there has been a lot learned from the experience of the playoffs." Despite the loss, ecstatic fans greeted them at the Green Bay airport.

For the season, Green Bay was second in scoring in the NFL and fifth in total yards, but the offense was inconsistent. Ivery led the team in rushing and was second in the NFC with 10 touchdowns. The Pack didn't have the 1979 Ivery, but the 1982 Ivery was very good. Not a star like Dorsett or Payton, but tough, reliable, versatile, and smart.

He was rewarded with a new contract: a raise from $70,000 annually to over $200,000—with yearly increases, culminating in $375,000 in 1987—plus a $40,000 signing bonus and a $110,000 appearance bonus. Although this was just before NFL player salaries skyrocketed, if he were financially prudent, he would be financially secure for many years.

But he was not financially prudent.

"I was on top of the world," Ivery said, "up with the big boys." He paid off his mother's and grandmother's house and gave gifts to friends and family: Bennie Mae a car, Uncle Nether a truck, a cousin a stereo system, an uncle $500.

"I was spending money and having fun," he said. "I didn't think about tomorrow—just that day. I spent money and partied."

He decided to return to Tech for his degree, heeding his grandmother's words: *Get your butt in school.*

Soon after starting classes, he saw a former teammate, who had powder cocaine, which they snorted in a student center bathroom stall.

"It put me in a mellow mood all day long," he said. "I could hear the sounds of the world, but I couldn't hear them. It's like everything was music to my ears. The feeling that cocaine gave me fit the way I felt about life. So, I never went to another class."

Chapter 14

It Was Like Firing Jesus

One reporter's summary of the Packers' 1983 potential: Deep and talented, with a powerful offense, they ranked second in the league in total yards in 1982, second in passing yards, and fifth in scoring. Along with Dickey's leadership and accurate passing, they had perhaps the best wide receiver duo in the league (Lofton and Jefferson), as well as excellent linebackers. They needed Ivery healthy to prevent defenses from focusing too much on the pass. However, the defensive line suffered several injuries and, devastatingly, the departure of standout six-year starting defensive end Mike Butler to the USFL. Starr was determined to re-sign free agent Butler, and Parins assured Starr that Butler would be signed, but he wasn't, and Starr had already drafted a defensive back, leaving no replacement for Butler. This led to more unwanted, avoidable draft-day drama.

Ivery played little in the 1983 preseason (a disappointing 1-3) due to a pulled thigh muscle. He did have one "electrifying" 34-yard gain on a draw. Starr said this season Ivery would play more than last year when he rotated with another running back to relay offensive plays. It didn't make sense to have your best halfback on the sidelines half the time.

Ivery was relieved because, shuttling in and out, "It was tough to get into my groove. If I make a mistake, I want to make up for it the next play, do something positive after the negative." Adrenaline pumping, he didn't want to stew over it on the sidelines, waiting.

Packers fans hoped the 1982 season would carry over to 1983. Fan Raabe said finally making the playoffs after 10 years "was like throwing red meat to the fan base. We had a lot of good pieces, and we were ready to be respected."

In the season opener, the Packers defeated the Houston Oilers and

Earl Campbell (123 yards) in an overtime thriller, 41-38, in the Astrodome, on Stenerud's 42-yard field goal. A reporter noted Ivery was "starting to make people miss again." He gained 71 yards (an excellent 5.9 average) and caught three passes for 31 yards. A 17-yard gain through the middle featured his trademark shifts in direction and was a key play in the Packers' first touchdown—a pass to Coffman—on which Ivery blocked a blitzing linebacker, giving Dickey time. Dickey was spectacular: 27 of 31 (20 of 22 in the first half) for 333 yards and five touchdowns (tying a team record). He set a Green Bay record with 18 consecutive completions to start the game.

Ivery made a crucial first down on third and 10 that led to a touchdown just before halftime. The Oilers were expecting a pass; instead, he slashed for 21 yards. Ivery slammed the ball to the turf in frustration, thinking that before his surgeries, he would have eluded the tackler. On the game-winning drive, he made gains of 9, 12, and 8 yards.

Was Starr's vision coming true? *Be patient; my plan will work.* Perhaps the momentum really had carried over from last season.

They won the game, but in a blow to their defense, their starting nose tackle tore his Achilles tendon and missed the rest of the season. (His backup suffered a season-ending knee injury five weeks later.)

The next game featured a clash of offensive styles. The Packers scored on dramatic, quick-strike plays, while the Steelers' powerful running game marched steadily, eating up the clock. Pittsburgh won 25-21, running the ball 59 times, gaining 4.8 yards per rush, and holding the ball two-thirds of the game. Their first scoring drive featured 11 consecutive running plays and consumed nearly all the first quarter—after which the Packers scored on their second play, a 71-yard strike to Lofton. But the defense, given little time to rest, wore down. By the fourth quarter, the Packers' defense was whipped.

The Packers defeated the Rams next, 27-24, on a field goal by Stenerud with five seconds left after Dickerson fumbled. Ivery scored in the first quarter on a 1-yard run to make it 10-0. In the fourth, on a drive to tie the score 24-24, he made a key first down on a 10-yard run. When they reached the 6, he gained two yards, then four for the tying score. He finished with 54 yards rushing and 19 yards on two receptions. The Packers routinely relied on him in crucial situations, even though the passing game remained the stronger weapon.

The next game, on *Monday Night Football,* they flopped. A disastrous third quarter of turnovers and penalties contributed to an embarrassing 27-3 loss to the Giants. The Packers had more passing yards but couldn't score a touchdown. They had scored 89 points in their first three games but managed only 53 rushing yards against the Giants while losing three fumbles and one interception. Ivery gained 22 yards rushing and was replaced in the third quarter after fumbling. He said afterward that he wasn't into the flow of the game—which was odd for him, now that he no longer alternated at halfback.

The 2-2 Packers' offense ranked third in the NFC in yards gained per game (mostly via the pass), but their defense ranked dead last in the NFL against the run. Ivery was the team's leading rusher.

Whitehurst recalled that after someone in the press questioned whether Starr knew how to win, Starr pulled a watch from his pocket in a team meeting and said, "Coach Lombardi gave us this watch for winning the 1961 championship." He held up championship rings for 1962, 1965, 1966, and 1967 and declared, "Don't let anybody tell you I don't know how to win."

Packers fan Tom Pigeon noticed Starr getting testy with both the press and fans. At an event featuring Starr, Pigeon asked for an autograph, and Starr snapped, "How do you autograph people get in here?"

After the Giants game, there were two team meetings—one for offense, one for defense—to get back on track. And suddenly, the pendulum swung the other way: the Packers smacked the winless Buccaneers 55-14, the most points scored by a Starr-coached team. They scored an NFL-record 49 points in the first half.

Asked about the running game being ranked 24th out of 28 teams, coaches replied that the passing attack was so strong (first in yards gained per pass attempt) that they simply didn't rely on the run as much. Their offensive coordinator said they would like to give the ball to Ivery more but "can't afford to."

"I never said anything because I wanted us to win at all costs," Ivery said, "but I was not pleased."

Then the pendulum swung back. They fell behind 24-0 at halftime and lost to the 1-4 Lions, 38-14. The running game, with just 87 yards, was faulted in the press for not being a threat. Starr said, "I can't put my finger on what's wrong."

Then came another dramatic swing. On a beautiful night, the 3-3 Packers defeated the defending Super Bowl champion Washington team—who were on a five-game winning streak—in one of the most exciting games in *Monday Night Football* history.

The teams combined for 1,025 total yards (771 via pass), and the game featured six lead changes and three ties. There were 56 first downs and a staggering average of 9.1 yards per offensive play for the Packers. Dickey, throwing with laser accuracy, completed 22 of 31 passes for 387 yards. Packers running backs were used sparingly, but Ivery passed twice, completing both attempts.

Washington quarterback Joe Theismann and Dickey both threw beautiful, accurate passes. Running back John Riggins—fast, powerful, and the NFL's fifth-leading rusher—was mostly controlled by a swarming Packers defense that celebrated every time they contained him.

Green Bay opened the scoring with a Washington fumble that was snagged by linebacker Mike Douglass, who dashed to the end zone. An avalanche of points ensued. Sold-out Lambeau roared throughout the game. Washington promptly scored a TD, then Stenerud, the NFL's leading scorer, kicked a 47-yard field goal. Mark Moseley, the last full-time straight-on place kicker, the only special-teams player to win the NFL MVP award (1982), kicked a 42-yard field goal. The score was 10-10 at the end of the first. Green Bay had -5 yards rushing, 66 passing, and, true to their quick-strike offense, had held the ball only four minutes and thirty-nine seconds.

Green Bay's next possession, Lofton, whose track-star speed had to be respected, appeared to sprint straight downfield, but cut quick to his left. Dickey's pass was thrown before Lofton cut and landed precisely in his hands. After a beautiful long touchdown pass to Coffman—who faked inside, turned out, his defender so fooled he fell—Green Bay led 17-10. Riggins scored Washington's next touchdown by powering in from the 1-yard line, and the score was 17-17, with no punts so far. On third and short, Dickey pitched right to Ivery, who passed cross-field to Coffman. Coffman had faked a block and a stumble, then ran downfield, lunged to catch the underthrown pass, jumped up, and was tackled. A good pass would have been an easy touchdown. Still, it was first and goal at the 9, and Dickey promptly tossed a precise touchdown pass to Coffman, widening the lead to 24-17. The Packers led 24-20 at the half.

Ivery was on the field often, but this was a passing showdown. A 24-yard touchdown run by Ellis, weaving through defenders, was almost a shock since it was not a pass—the first rushing touchdown against Washington's rush defense in five games. Green Bay led 31-20. A Moseley field goal, 31-23. Washington scored from the 20 on a pass to smallish, quick scatback Joe Washington, 31-30. A Moseley field goal gave Washington the lead, 33-31.

At the start of the fourth, on second and goal, Dickey faked a handoff to Ivery and handed to a cross-field streaking tight end, who pranced into the end zone. Packers led, 38-33. The home crowd went berserk.

After a Riggins 2-yard bulldoze into the end zone, Washington led 40-38. Dickey passed Green Bay downfield for a touchdown. With 3:34 to go, Theismann threw a touchdown pass for a 47-45 lead. Dickey threw a 57-yard gain to Ellis, a pinpoint pass through a crowd. Ivery ran to the 4, then the 3. Ivery's job was to protect the ball and run down the clock. Leave as little time on the clock as possible for a winning field goal.

Forty-year-old Stenerud trotted onto the field, and just before the snap, the Washington coach called a timeout to "ice" Stenerud, a strategy intended to add pressure. Stenerud explained that when an opponent tried this, he concentrated on his rhythm and timing. He said kickers miss sometimes, and if it happens after an icing, "That's not the reason. Sometimes you just miss." This tactic had no effect on the cool veteran Stenerud, who by now had experienced many pressure situations—including three field goals in Super Bowl IV.

It wasn't bad for a Hall of Famer who became a kicker by chance. He moved from Norway to Montana State University on a ski-jumping scholarship. Once, while running the football stadium steps to stay in shape, he saw a placekicker practicing. Having grown up playing soccer, he asked, just for fun, if he could try. He kicked a few from straight on, as the kicker had, then asked if it could be done using the side of his foot, like a soccer corner kick. The kicker said there was one AFL kicker, Hungarian-born Pete Gogolak, who kicked that way. Stenerud tried it, and the school's basketball coach happened to be walking by, watched him kick a few, and promptly found the football coach, insisting he had to see this guy kick. As a junior, he kicked a then-college-record 59-yard field goal, and in his senior year, he was an All-American in skiing and football. He calmly aced the 21-yard field goal for a 48-47 Packers lead.

Theismann had 54 seconds, no timeouts, to get in Moseley's field goal range. A master of clock control, he efficiently completed passes to Washington, who ran for first downs and ran out of bounds—to stop the clock—until Washington reached the Packers' 21 (well within Moseley's range) with 10 seconds left. After Theismann quickly threw a pass out of bounds to stop the clock with 3 seconds left, the reliable Moseley, 4 of 4 this game, 82 percent from inside the 40 in his 10-year career, missed a 39-yard attempt to the right.

Ecstatic Packers ran onto the field, taking bows, waving to the championship-starved, frenzied Lambeau crowd. They ran around the field slapping outstretched hands of delirious fans. Starr told them to stay on the field as long as the fans cheered.

It was the highest-scoring game in *Monday Night Football* history (the record held for 35 years) and highest-scoring game in NFL history. Green Bay crept within one game of Minnesota, their next opponent, in the division race. If they could continue the momentum, they would be positioned well for a playoff spot. Would this high-caliber passing offense finally take them back to the Super Bowl?

That week, a newspaper story featured Green Bay police officers distributing Packers trading cards to children. The cards displayed pictures of prominent players on the front and offered crime-prevention and football tips on the back—a public relations effort to show children that police are helpful and friendly. An accompanying photo included an officer holding up an Eddie Lee Ivery card.

Football players hate to fumble the ball away.

David Sims said there's no worse feeling. You have let the team down in front of a crowd. "It's a *terrible* feeling," he said. "All you want to do is get back in there and make up for it, but you have to trot off the field and stand and watch."

Coffman, who rarely fumbled, said when the ball is loose, and you can't get it back as you scramble for it along with pouncing defenders, "It's almost like you're drowning, and you can't do anything about it. It's like, 'Noooooo! Come back!' You're desperately reaching and see the ball *right there* and can't get it. It's like your life depends on it. It's such a bad feeling. I only lost a couple, and it's a sinking feeling."

Dickey chuckled and said, "It's a sense of, 'Wow, have I screwed up.' It's humiliating, but it's a part of it. Some did more than others, and it makes it even more painful if you're not a fumbler, and Eddie Lee was not a fumbler. When Eddie Lee fumbled inside the 5 against Minnesota, he would be the first to say, 'We would have won if I hadn't fumbled.'"

Ivery was taught the "eagle claw": "You can swing your arms freely when you're in the open field," he said, "but when you're running in traffic, you use your fingers, palm, thumb, forearm, and chest to protect the ball. You compress the ball to your body. In Green Bay, they called it 'high and tight,' which is a little higher on the chest." He said fumbling is "the most embarrassing thing a runner can do. You let down 50,000 people and your teammates. Especially inside the 20-

yard line."

The Vikings were in first place in the NFC Central and a victory would give the Packers a tie in the division, but the Vikings won in overtime, 20-17. The Packers missed a chance to score just before the half when Ivery fumbled at the 2. A disappointed Starr said, "We've played half a season, and we're sitting here dead even."

Dickey, a keen observer of the dynamics of the game and his teammates, sensed something was off about Ivery.

"We were inside their 5," he said, "and it wasn't a big hit or anything. He went to the right side, and the guy casually tackled him, and he fumbled. He had another error in the game, and I thought, 'Huh, that's weird.' He nearly scored a touchdown that likely would have won the game, but he fumbled the ball away at the 2."

Dickey's hunch was right.

The following Wednesday, Starr called Ivery, the team's leading rusher, to his office and asked if he used cocaine. Starr held up what he said was a letter from "someone" saying he had sold cocaine to Ivery. Ivery denied it.

Starr said OK, we'll give you a drug test—right now. Ivery turned to leave, paused, knew he was busted, turned around, and confessed.

The previous summer, he had started using cocaine regularly, in addition to his heavy drinking. One dealer in Atlanta mailed drugs to him. His biggest supplier was a cousin in Chicago. He recalled a party where he used cocaine and marijuana, but he preferred to use alone or in a small group.

"I was paranoid I'd be found out," he said. "I'd show my face at the party but use drugs somewhere else." He felt more secure at the home of a dealer or a single teammate, so it would be just the two of them.

"I was caught up in the limelight. I was one of these young, country boys wanting to fit in. I said, 'Let me try it.' I liked it because it took away the physical pain and emotional pain I was going through," he said. That emotional escape eased his self-pity and anxiety over the knee injuries. "Everyone was telling me my career was over. 'He's washed up.' The only way I could accept those things was through drugs and alcohol. I thought."

Sports psychologist Valdez said,

> When you think of the high you get as an athlete, well, cocaine is about the only thing that gives you an even higher high than athletics. Once you experience that, sometimes that takes over and it's like, "Wow, that's the feeling I had when I was first playing football, and this is even more powerful." It works to help you cope with the injury and feelings, takes away the irritability and frustration for the moment, but then it takes more and more to get the same high. You develop a tolerance. It's a really powerful drug. It goes straight to those pleasure centers. There's no detour. You don't even have to play a game or put effort into it, so who wouldn't succumb to that, given everything else going on? Particularly in that time, that era in football, elite athletes in the NFL have money to burn, and it's readily available—and it works.

Valdez said the pressure to perform isn't only external. "Someone like him is not hardwired to accept mediocrity. They're always in fifth gear so to downshift into third gear, well, a Ferrari is not built that way. You don't want to drive it on the street. You want to drive it on the autobahn or the racetrack. Great athletes are not built for mediocrity, and it's very uncomfortable for them."

After the triumphant *Monday Night Football* game, like his teammates, Ivery had been thrilled. It was the loudest crowd he had ever heard, an exciting win, so he thought, *What the hell, I'll party all week.* He drank and used cocaine three nights during the week before a crucial game.

"I was so caught up in the excitement, I didn't worry about consequences," he said. He had enough money for a good lawyer and was oblivious to stories of pro athletes caught using drugs. "I didn't read the news," he said. "I only cared if *I* got caught." He celebrated all week, which culminated in a game that, as in 1979 and 1981, would be his last game of the season.

This time, it was his own fault.

When Saturday came, Ivery thought *What the hell?* again. He stayed up all night drinking and using.

"I was about to score. I had the ball on the 2. We could have won," he said. Did being high contribute to his fumble? "Without a doubt, absolutely. I tried to camouflage it and thought I was fooling everybody, but I wasn't. Some teammates probably thought I had it under control, but I didn't." Cocaine, he said, simply made him feel good. "I had no worries," he recalled. "I was on top of the world, man." But, he added, "When you're an addict, you use poor judgment."

Poor judgment, indeed. Ivery said he had a brief fling with a woman he recalled only as, "She looked like Brooke Shields." He secretly rented an apartment for six months so they (and others) could meet undetected. It was also a private place to use drugs.

After the fling and lease ended, he began using at home in the basement. "I got paranoid about getting caught," he said, "so I did it down there. Anna finally figured out what I was doing, and I lied my way out of it. I pretended I was down there playing with our dog. She believed it. But now, I think she really knew but wouldn't say so." His alcohol consumption was out of control. "By then," he said, "I crossed the 'imaginary white line.' I drank to get drunk."

There were teammates who used drugs and knew that others did, and they kept that among themselves. Addicts are strategic about whom to tell. Stenerud: "I knew nothing at all, nothing at all." McCarren: "I was totally unaware." Dickey: "I was pretty observant about what's going on with my guys, and that was one instance I had no clue." Coffman: "You knew they'd drink beer and whiskey and smoke pot, but for me everything was performance. If you perform on Sunday, everything is OK. Eddie Lee had two knee surgeries, and he was still performing, still picking up blitzes. I wasn't aware of hard drugs. He performed well, and that's the bottom line." Koch: "I was aware he used it but not the extent. He was the same ol' Eddie Lee to us. It's hard to go to another guy and slap him around and say something. Now I wish I had." Ezra Johnson: "I knew but not that it was a big problem."

That was the impression Ivery wanted: "Don't worry, I have it under control."

Koch added,

> He had lots of pressure. He was a top draft pick, had two injuries in three years. I don't know how well many others could handle it. Playing in the league is stressful. They're always looking to replace you with somebody cheaper. You're still a kid, haven't matured into an adult. I can imagine someone from his background—and getting that money? He thought he was on top of the world and thought it would last forever.

Starr managed Ivery's addiction with compassion and methodical planning. To protect Ivery's privacy, the Packers announced that he was "emotionally strained" and had been placed on "four-week non-football illness reserve" to address personal problems. Starr said if Ivery returned after four weeks, he wouldn't start but could likely play. Reporters were puzzled. At a crucial time, they make a vague announcement about their leading rusher? Starr said it was a private matter and provided no further details. Thereafter, Ivery always spoke fondly of Starr: "He was concerned about me as a person, *then* a player. I got no ultimatum from him. He said, 'Don't worry about losing your contract. We'll pay you.'"

In an interview years later, on *Packers Alumni Spotlight* on the Packers website, Ivery, tears streaming, said Starr didn't save only his career: "He saved my life.... I was headed to be one of those homeless, sleepless addicts, if it hadn't been for Bart Starr."

Starr hated drugs. One Packers fan recalled seeing Starr at a golf fundraiser, where Starr snapped at a photographer who wore his cap backwards, claiming it was a sign of drug involvement. The man explained that he normally didn't wear his hat backwards, but made an exception so the bill wouldn't interfere with his camera.

Perhaps one reason Starr was so compassionate toward Ivery was that he understood addiction's vicious hold. Around this time, Bart and Cherry learned that their younger son, Bret, a smart, funny, and shy college student, was addicted to marijuana and cocaine. Starr noted that while Bart Jr. grew up in Green Bay during the championship seasons, Bret grew up in the shadow of his father's struggles to succeed. He heard classmates and the media disparage his father, which stung deeply. It was a challenging childhood and adolescence.

The Starrs discovered his addiction when he performed poorly in college; they visited his dorm room, and he looked awful. They placed him in the Hazelden Foundation Drug and Rehabilitation Center in Minnesota, but he only lasted a few days before moving back in with his parents, pledging to continue outpatient treatment. This marked the beginning of years filled with hopes and disappointments, lies, deceptions, missed family gatherings, and heartbreak. It was their greatest anguish. During one hopeful moment, the Starrs helped Bret finance an exotic animal import business in Tampa, despite his lack of training or experience in business. But the Starrs were desperate and willed themselves to remain hopeful.

Over the years, Bret would call them sobbing, commit to recovery, and declare renewed faith in God, only for them to hope again—until he disappointed them once more.

It wasn't clear whether Starr knew that one of Ivery's cocaine dealers—also supplying other players—was Bret himself. In the locker room, they would arrange a place to meet for the deal. Sometimes, Bret sold drugs right there—in the locker room where his father was in charge. Later, Ivery wondered if Bret was the "someone" who claimed to have sold drugs to him.

When reporters came to his apartment, Ivery—Anna and their daughter next to him—was cordial but noncommittal, saying he might address the situation later. Players who were asked about it said they didn't know what was going on. Most truly didn't; some who had used drugs with him, of course, said nothing. Assistant to the team president Bob Harlan denied that Ivery's issues involved alcohol or drugs. Ivery also falsely denied it.

"It wasn't drug or alcohol related," he told the *Milwaukee Journal*. "That's why I want to get this thing squared up. No, it had nothing to do with that. Not at all."

Ivery tried to dodge the truth by saying, "I couldn't handle it anymore. I was at my limit. I wasn't performing real well. And a lot of things were going on in my life, and I just couldn't handle it anymore. That's basically it." He claimed he took leave because he feared getting chemically dependent on sleeping pills the team had given him—a claim the team doctor quickly refuted. Ivery said the emotional stress had built up over years, especially with his knee injuries. He mentioned trouble sleeping and that he had been nearly broke a year after receiving his signing bonus. He said the Minnesota fumble was his "peak" and that afterward he went to Starr. He said he couldn't concentrate during games or meetings and needed time off.

The Packers tried weekly outpatient counseling so he could return to the team and, they hoped, conceal the addiction.

"That didn't work," Ivery said. "I talked to the counselor high. I kept lying to him and everyone else. They did drug tests, and I used someone else's pee twice." Eventually, he was caught in a surprise drug test. He initially told Starr he had things under control.

"But when I walked out the door," he said, "I started crying. I went back in and said, 'Yes, I have a problem.'" They secretly sent him to Hazelden—the same treatment center where Bret had been.

By mid-November, Ivery was lifting weights and running, supervised by a team trainer. Starr said Ivery was eager to return, but the Packers hadn't decided if he would. In late November, a reporter revealed that a reliable source said Ivery had recently returned from Hazelden for drug treatment. Neither Starr nor Ivery initially commented. Starr said they had agreed any statement should come from Ivery, and if confidentiality wasn't honored, "They won't trust us to come to us with their problems." Then—and forever after—Starr refused to say how the Packers first learned of Ivery's addiction.

It was futile to hide what reporters had sniffed out. With Anna at his side, Ivery read a prepared statement (written mostly by Starr):

> Dear ladies and gentlemen. I made a very serious mistake in my life. I got involved with the drug cocaine, not knowing

> the seriousness of cocaine. I thought I could clean up this problem on my own during my absence from the team...but it was difficult alone. Therefore, I decided to seek help through the Hazelden program. It was a very tough decision to make. My life had become unmanageable. I had become very irritable with family and friends. I would like to thank my family who was there with me spiritually and emotionally...and also I would like to thank Coach Starr and the organization for their 100% support for giving me this opportunity to straighten out my life. Now I pray that I am forgiven for my mistakes and can go on with my life as a professional athlete.

Starr said Ivery, who had returned to practice, might play if the team made the playoffs but wasn't yet in good enough shape. Ivery would continue outpatient treatment. Starr said Ivery was a "prideful individual" who had tried to handle his problem alone. The Packers had provided resources for treatment, but Ivery had to make his own decisions.

Ivery had attended Hazelden for four weeks, but, he later admitted, "Hazelden was a get-away, a resort for the rich and famous. It was 28 days of vacation. I didn't go to fix my problem. I went to save my job. I was in denial. I didn't think I had a problem."

He ticked off reasons:

"I'm still married. I haven't lost my cars, pawned belongings, or lost my house. One guy there was paralyzed. Not me. I thought, 'Why am I here?'"

He even found a Hazelden kitchen employee who supplied him with weed.

"I smoked a joint with her and her boyfriend. We went to the back of the center and smoked reefer. I went in dirty, and I left dirty."

Flying first class back to Green Bay, he ordered a gin and tonic.

Reflecting later, Ivery said,

> The fame and money got me off track of who I really was. Some say money doesn't change them, but it changed me.

> Here was the first time I really had to take responsibility for my own life. In college, I had a scholarship, my bills paid, food provided, no car note. But now, life slapped me in the face. Like, wow. I was trying to learn how to be a husband and father as well as professional football player all at once, and that's a challenge. The biggest thing is that I had been a very God-fearing man. I loved church, then when I got drafted, it was like I told God, "You got me here, but I can handle it from here. I'll put you on the back burner." God wasn't at the head of my life. I had money, property, prestige, so I thought, "I can do this."

Valdez said,

> When you see it so many times, you think, "How could that possibly happen?" Not just athletes but public figures, celebrities, fame and money and the excess of money, having more than you need. All they hear is the adulation—another addiction that goes to the pleasure centers in your brain. It happens when you're an athlete; it happens when you're on drugs; it happens when you're getting all that adulation. All those things, it's too much, and you don't get the other side of it, that they are just a regular person. Great athletes are told how great they are. Sometimes it starts early, and there's this constant feedback that never says anything other than "Look at how good I am," so why wouldn't it go to your head? It's also the addiction talking.... It's a disease, a compulsion, that needs to be treated.

This analysis was true of Ivery, but he was many years from realizing he needed treatment. For now, he preferred eluding accountability as effectively as he eluded defenders. He falsely convinced the Packers he was drug-free and was confident he could keep up that deception. And he did.

Ivery said, "I'd use drugs until a month before summer training camp. If they had done drug tests at spring minicamp, I would have failed them all, after 1983." Packers quarterback Randy Wright said later, "His level of play was awfully high, so you wouldn't think those two would go together."

In the brain, dopamine helps generate pleasurable feelings. It doesn't create pleasure itself but helps reinforce enjoyable experiences and feelings. It links pleasurable things with a desire to repeat them. It helps us survive. We don't starve because it increases when we anticipate something good to eat and spikes when we bite into a scrumptious pork chop. Sex increases it, so we procreate. Addictive drugs increase dopamine dramatically. Eating a chocolate eclair may be pleasant, and we may immediately want another, but cocaine goes far beyond that, and it acts quickly. If the eclair taste is a battery, cocaine is a lightning bolt. Opioids are valuable pain managers, but when used according to one's own desires, they send dopamine levels soaring. In summer 1982, *Sports Illustrated* published a poignant confessional by former NFL player Don Reese about his torment with cocaine. Once he felt the euphoria of cocaine, he said, "From then on, I was available whenever it was available."

Cocaine is cruel. As someone continues using it, the brain is overwhelmed with the gush of dopamine and adapts by releasing less of it or modulating dopamine receptors so that less is absorbed. Perversely, the brain is less affected by the drug and the addict needs more of it. Dependency grabs tighter. The addict reaches what experts call "tolerance," the point when the pleasure—that sweet jolt of joy—is diminished even when consuming the same amount. The desire for a high demands an increased amount. And worse: Eventually, for many, the drug doesn't give euphoria, but makes life tolerable. All those risks—just to feel tolerably alive.

Many who knew Ivery were stunned.

Corrick said, "Eddie Lee opened my eyes to the world. It was a shock. I thought, 'If it could happen to him, it could happen to anyone.'" He recalled Ivery arriving early for rehab, running stadium steps before Corrick arrived. That kind of diligent hard worker would turn to drugs? "He did everything we asked," he said, "and everybody was happy. Then Eddie Lee failed a drug screen. That changed my whole outlook on people. If you can't believe him, you can believe no one. I was devastated."

Fan Raabe said some fans turned surly. "Some villainized him and made fun of him," he said.

> There were Eddie Lee Ivery jokes. Their expectations were so high. Fans think you owe them. He was supposed to be a great difference maker, and Packer fans got behind him and idolized him, and suddenly they found he was human, and some were not sympathetic but became bitter and angry. We put our idols on pedestals, but they're just people and make mistakes.

Raabe declined to repeat the Ivery jokes. "They were highly inappropriate," he said. "Some were vulgar."

Once the media reported Ivery acknowledged a drug problem, the dreadful news spread back home.

A crestfallen Bennie Mae heard from her football-fan husband, who read it in the newspaper. "I was so disappointed," she said.

Thomson teammate Barnett said, "I was devastated." He sadly told his father. He was at a bar with UGA fans who took snide pleasure in Ivery's drug problems, saying they figured that would happen.

Tech booster Hunsinger said, "When I heard rumors of his drug use, I was shocked. I tried to get in touch with him so he could tell me it wasn't true, but I couldn't reach him."

Tech teammate Carter said he had seen Ivery indulge in alcohol but never suspected it would lead to drugs.

Tech trainer Smith said, "It shocked me. I couldn't equate that to Eddie Lee. It was true, but.... He was nothing like that."

Tech running back Allen, whom Ivery, as a mentor, had advised to stay away from drugs and alcohol, said, "I said that is no way Eddie Lee, the person I knew."

Trainer Herrington said, "It was just a feeling of sadness because we knew what a good person he was."

Tech fan Copeland said it reminded him of another sports hero who let him down. "It's kinda like Mickey Mantle," he said. "He was our hero....He let me down like Eddie Lee did. He gave us so many thrills, so deep down I was disappointed. He gave Tech fans so much to cheer about, more than any player since I started following them in 1968. He went from the basement to the penthouse. From small-town Thomson, he grew up hard. How could he do that?"

Tech football broadcaster Kim King said, "I can't believe this is the guy I knew. I was naive. I was shocked and saddened. I have since learned of other 'good' people who used drugs, but I was really sad about him."

Ivery's childhood Cherokee friend Grant had seen Ivery use cocaine at an offseason party but, like many, thought it wasn't serious. "It was a shock," he said, "but at that time, cocaine was pretty popular in the NFL. Knowing some other friends in the NFL who did that, I thought, 'That's what they do.'"

That thought—*That's the world Ivery entered*—was in the air. Reese, who played for New Orleans and Miami, wrote that some Saints players sniffed cocaine in the locker room before games and at halftime, and that half of the Dolphins used it in training camp.

Ivery convinced the Packers he was free from addiction. He wasn't. Instead, he began 16 years of deception, dishonesty, and manipulation: the life of an addict, a well-loved, popular addict who was still a very good—though not as good as his pre-injuries self—pro football player. He was what Atlanta therapist Janet Fluker calls a "charming addict." He would put a teammate's urine in a small bottle and put it inside his jock strap, which kept it warm. He read that Drano would disguise the drugs, so before the next drug test, he pressed Drano crystals under his fingernails, then sprinkled them in the cup he had peed into. He passed that test.

"I guess it worked," he said. (It can work but raises the urine sample to a suspiciously high pH level that alert testers will catch.) By luck, deception, and careful planning, he never failed another drug test at Green Bay.

Abraham J. Twerski wrote in *Addictive Thinking* that whatever manipulation an addict may have done before becoming an addict, with addiction, it escalates. "People are forced into lying, covering up, and manipulating," he wrote. "Addicted people develop expertise at manipulating, and, over time, this becomes an ingrained character trait." It may begin to explain away using or to cover up problems. "But sooner or later it takes on a life of its own," he explained. "The addict manipulates just to manipulate and lies just to lie, even though there may be nothing to gain."

The Packers had a typical uneven season, but after a mid-November win, they were 6-5 and tied for first place in the division. Some media outlets suggested that Starr's job was in jeopardy if the Packers didn't make the playoffs and advance. Starr told reporters he didn't think his job hinged on that, as had been speculated over the last few years. In their final regular season game, the 8-7 Packers needed to beat the 7-8 Bears and for two other games to go just right to make the playoffs. A reporter noted that the Packers' board of directors had a routine quarterly meeting scheduled for the day after the Bears game and that Starr's future might be discussed then.

"I don't think too many people realize what kind of things we've had to overcome this season," Starr said. He mentioned that the Packers were better than when he arrived and reminded everyone he had had "on the job training" and that he was "just getting started"—in his ninth year.

Late in the game, with the temperatures a frigid -3 degrees and a strong wind blowing off Lake Michigan, the Packers learned the two games they relied on to allow a victory to put them in the playoffs went as the Packers needed. Win today, they're in. A Packers touchdown with under four minutes to play gave them a 21-20 lead, and the defense, the worst in the league, needed to hold. Payton had a superb game but was sidelined with a late-game rib injury. Though the defense had played well and Payton was sidelined, the Bears won 23-21 on a 22-yard field goal with 10 seconds to play—the fourth straight year the Packers lost the season finale, and the third time under Starr they failed to sneak into the playoffs in the finale.

Starr was criticized for not calling timeouts during the Bears' last drive, which would have given the Packers close to a minute to try to kick their own game-winner by the reliable Stenerud. Instead, they had only 10 seconds. Asked about that, Starr gave a clipped, "That's our business."

According to Whitehurst, after the game, Starr told the team, "I don't know what will happen. I don't know if I will be here or not."

"We were emotional because we loved him, and we knew he was a good coach," Whitehurst said.

The 1983 season had potential, mainly due to the Packers' offense. Dickey led the NFL in passing yards, touchdown passes, yards per attempt, and yards per completion. Lofton set a personal record with most yards gained in a season. The Packers ranked fifth in the league in scoring with 429 points (but allowed 439) and second in yardage. But Dickey's passer rating was low because he threw an NFL-high 29 interceptions, possibly due to their defense being the second-worst in points allowed and worst in yards allowed. When the Packers trailed, Starr allowed him to take risks a quarterback wouldn't normally take.

"Bart would tell me, 'Don't worry about throwing interceptions,'" Dickey said.

Koch said the Packers had "one of the greatest offenses in club history. Dickey, when on his game, had accuracy, velocity, and touch as good as anybody. He was mentally tough, a leader, savvy." But with the offense inconsistent and the loss of Mike Butler and several key injuries, the defense was weak. In one five-game stretch, they scored 27 points, then 3, 55, 14, and 48. They were 2-3 in overtime games. "We were really close to having a great team," Koch said. "No one wanted to play our offense, and *everybody* wanted to play our defense."

The morning after the loss, just before 8 a.m., Harlan saw Packers president Parins walk by his office toward Starr's. Parins was the last of the Packers leaders who was a local citizen—a circuit court judge in Green Bay—who worked his way up the 45-member board of directors: Board member in 1966, vice-president of the Board's Executive Committee in 1979, and president in 1982. He tersely told Starr he was relieving him—and all other coaches—of his position. Parins said he was going to announce this at 11 a.m. Starr could resign by 10 o'clock.

Starr declined, and Parins fired him.

He didn't thank Starr for his 26 years with the Packers, didn't say it was a difficult decision or anything supportive or compassionate. Starr wrote later that it felt like a "cold, unemotional sentence" the judge might deliver in court. Parins left. A shocked and furious Starr closed his office door and wept.

At 8:10, Parins peered in Harlan's office and said, "I just fired Bart Starr."

The gathered reporters assumed Parins would announce Starr was being retained, but he announced Starr's termination. He said the decision was his alone, and he made it that morning. Nine years after Green Bay was festooned with signs proclaiming, "A Fresh Start with Bart," Parins said the head coach position needs a "fresh look."

In his own news conference, an emotional Starr quoted Theodore Roosevelt's 1910 speech on citizenship given in Paris: It's "not the critic who counts" but "the man who is actually in the arena, whose face is marred by dust and sweat and blood; who strives valiantly, who errs, who comes up short again and again." Fault me, but I was *in the arena*.

Gentleman Starr expressed no bitterness but thanked the Packers for his nine years as head coach. He thanked his assistant coaches and other staff, from trainers to film people to secretaries. He thanked his players for their support. He declared, as he had before, that the team was better off than when he arrived and that he would continue to be the Packers' "number one fan" because "no one has more of his heart and soul in this organization as a fan than I do."

He mentioned his sons and how difficult it was to be Bart Starr's child in Green Bay. He thanked fans in Green Bay and around the world. He said the preseason goal was a 10-6 record, that they would have reached that if they had won two games that they should have.

He concluded by saying there were some good things he had done that he hoped atoned for others, and he gave as an example his relationship with Ivery—whose fumble against the Vikings, as well as his absence for the rest of the season as their top rusher, was likely one reason the Packers missed the playoffs. With a productive Ivery in the backfield, the Packers might have made the playoffs and saved Starr's job. Starr said he had talked with Ivery about "a particular situation and challenged him to continue to become the type of player that he has the capacity to be." Starr said Ivery told him he wasn't sure he could do that without Starr but promised he would.

Starr added that just a few moments ago they had "exchanged a few tears in the office and embraced." Ivery told Starr he had never had a father, and Starr told him, "You have one now." Starr concluded, "Maybe some of those things make it worthwhile. Thank you."

For Starr, his humane dealing with people made up for the lack of wins, and the relationship that came to mind—out of all the players he had coached, the coaches he had as colleagues, the fans that he had treated with kindness—was his with Ivery. In his painful farewell as head coach, the man whose son struggled with drug addiction concluded with a touching moment aching for hope. He didn't know Ivery was not free from addiction's grip, and would not be for many years, but Starr knew addiction's potential to destroy a life, and he placed faith in human connection rooted in compassion.

Much of Starr's compassion toward Ivery was Starr's character, but it was also because people loved Ivery, particularly father figures. Uncle Nether was the stern, demanding authority who expected obedience and responsibility. Willie Williams and Luther Wilson provided guidance and fatherly advice. Bestwick was the supportive, giving dad who supplied hand-me-down clothes. Rodgers was the wacky, fun dad who wanted his kids to have a good time. Starr was the firm, loving disciplinarian who forgave.

A reporter called Ivery for his reaction. His voice cracking, Ivery spoke touchingly of the coach who had cared about him when his addiction was revealed.

"I can't even talk about it," he said. "He was like a father, a teacher to me. I hate to see him go. I have never met such an outstanding human being." Ivery added later, "He treated me like family, even with my problems." Considering Bret Starr's addiction, Bart Starr had literally treated Ivery like family.

Starr had a worse record than his two predecessors, whom he had pledged to improve on. Against winning teams, he was 13-47-1. Opinions vary regarding why Starr didn't succeed: The offense was powerful but inconsistent. Starr couldn't coach defense. He didn't have enough veteran player leadership. He was not enough like Lombardi (not tough enough). Or too much like Lombardi (rough practices wore players out). He was tough on teammates as a player but not as a coach. He could be emotionally distant. He was too loyal to players. Too loyal to coaches. There was too much staff turnover. He preferred character over ability. He traded for players who didn't pan out. He sided with assistants over scouts when drafting.

Some players said he was fired right when he learned to be a good head coach and should have been given more time. Some doubted he would ever succeed (although they loved him). Maybe he was just unlucky (that disastrous Hadl trade—not his fault) and had many top players with serious injuries that ended or, like Ivery, diminished their ability.

Whitehurst said, "We just, frankly, didn't have the players to win championships."

Sportswriter Len Wagner said, "In Bart's case, talent was a problem, and he was in charge of drafting, so it still came back to him."

Over the last few years fans thought *We loved it when they hired him, but what do we have to show for it?* Fans, reluctantly, sadly, began to think: It's time.

Raabe said,

> Starr had plenty of time to prove himself. I felt sad. This guy who had the Packers on his shoulders all those years was such a fine, fine human being who had not succeeded. Some fans were angry and said he was a bum, but most still highly regarded him. To the day he died, he was the Green Bay Packers. Some couldn't fathom he would be fired because of who he was and what he had done for the team, but it was the right thing to fire him, although I still felt sad.

Francois said there was a morose feeling around Green Bay as it became clear the executive committee's patience was wearing out.

"When he was fired," he said, "we could feel it in the air. We knew it would happen. Will it be today? Next week? When it happened, it was a horrible day. He should have resigned and not have on his resume that he was fired. But he always thought he could do it." He added, "There is a statue installed in his honor almost forty years after his career. He was revered as a quarterback but not as a coach. He was successful as a businessman but not as a coach."

Starr was so beloved, Francois said, "It was like firing Jesus."

McCarren said,

> Fans were dying for the star quarterback to come back and save the franchise. He lived and learned. I thought he was coaching his best when they let him go. This is not a business that shows patience, and he got more patience than most. All I can say is, Bart Starr: Hall of Fame player, Hall of Fame human being. We missed the playoff by a hair, and I thought he was coaching his best, and I felt bad. We bear responsibility as players, but it is a performance-based industry, and if the team isn't good enough, the head coach picks up the tab.

Remmel recalled that Starr "got years of grace. No one worked harder than he did. He had a great relationship with the media, but it became adversarial, and that was the last thing he wanted. He had been adulated, fawned on, and lionized for his success as a player, so failing was hard for him to accept." Regarding that last game, he said, "What if we had won and made the playoffs? Would he have remained head coach? Who knows? Bart had become a very good coach. There was such a feeling of sadness. He lost sleep. Winning still didn't happen. I thought he would be very successful, and I'm still mystified why he wasn't." He shook his head.

Stenerud expressed strong support for Starr: "I had been around a long time, and I knew things like that happen in the NFL. It's a pretty cutthroat business." But, he said flatly,

> You don't fire a Bart Starr, an absolute legend. We all had so much respect for Bart, so maybe we don't always look at it realistically. We cared so much for the man. He was a perfect human being. We had so many injuries on defense, and the offense scored so many points.... If they had kept him one more year, get the injuries healed, and get a player or two, we could have been a hell of a team. How do you fire a man like Bart Starr?

Christl wrote a column titled, "Bart Starr: Why Did He Fail?" He mentioned staff turnover and all the trade and draft debacles—some the Packers' fault and some bad luck. (He quoted Corrick: "People will never know how great Eddie Lee Ivery was.") Christl mentioned Starr's work ethic (often arriving at 5:30 a.m. Monday to view film after returning home late Sunday) and said some of Starr's supposed bad qualities were true of other winning coaches. "Should he have been tougher, more emotional, less aloof?" Christl questioned. Starr arrived with little experience and "left as a coach who was loved and respected, who remained true to his character, but he didn't win enough games."

Harlan said later that when Starr appeared at Lambeau, he received the biggest ovation of all returning players. "Fans forget the coaching years," he said. At the 2004 unveiling of the Starr statue near Lambeau Field, he joked (21 years later) about his coaching career. He thanked everyone for their loyalty, smiled, and said with a laugh, "even during the coaching years." The crowd chuckled nervously.

Some players felt the way Starr was fired was an insult. Dickey said, "Parins walked into Bart's office and said, 'You're relieved of your duties.' That was it. He didn't have a conversation about appreciation, as in, 'You've been here years and years as a player and coach, but I think we need a change. If you'd like another position, we want to keep you.' He fired him like he was a towel boy. That was horrible."

The Packers replaced Starr with former Packers star offensive lineman Forrest Gregg. He played on seven NFL championship teams and three Super Bowl winners. Gregg, who was idolized as a tough (played in a then-NFL record 88 straight games), smart player, had coached the Cincinnati Bengals to a Super Bowl in 1982—two years after taking over a 4-12 team—and was named Coach of the Year. He had not only head coach experience but winning experience.

Remmel said, "I thought without question Forrest Gregg would succeed, but he didn't either." Gregg's tenure was a failure both on and off the field. According to Christl's book, Gregg's term was known for frequent bad headlines: player arrests, missed curfews, suspensions for steroid use, disturbances in bars, drug rehab, coaches misbehaving.

Raabe said fans were initially excited about Gregg. "He was another Packer player from the championship years," he said, "and now, instead of kind, considerate, thoughtful Bart Starr, we have someone who will bust heads. We need to be tougher. Gregg will come in and make things happen." But, Raabe said, "now I don't think a lot of fans have good things to say about Gregg. It was entertaining, but it didn't reflect well on the team."

While many players, even those who criticized Gregg, appreciated his directness and evenhandedness (he criticized stars as well as scrubs), he was widely despised. Ivery said, "Nobody liked Forrest Gregg." Dickey said that at one of Gregg's first meetings, he insulted them, saying they didn't work hard to earn their big money. He ripped into the well-respected stalwart McCarren (nicknamed the "Rock" after starting 162 consecutive games), saying he was overpaid.

"The whole damn team didn't like our damn coach," Corrick said. "Team leaders couldn't get along with him. Gregg was vindictive."

Coffman said when Gregg told him he was cut, he told Coffman he'd end up in Buffalo or Kansas City. Coffman said he preferred Kansas City, where he had family. According to Coffman, now in the Packers Hall of Fame, Gregg said, "It's not up to you. We'll let you know. Wherever you go, you will be *their* problem."

Gregg's winning percentage was lower than Starr's. Harlan said, "It was just another disaster." Starr's compassion didn't work. Neither did Gregg's ferocity.

Chapter 15

Half a Season

Between the 1983 and 1984 seasons, Ivery didn't stay in Green Bay to work out, mainly so he could use cocaine without being caught, and—to illustrate how drugs screw up a brain—he abandoned his lauded work ethic.

"When I look back," he said, "I wonder how good I would have been if I had worked out like, say, Walter Payton." How good he could have been is a mystery—without the injuries, the addiction, and if he had played on offenses that ran the ball more. There is a long list of sports what-ifs. How good would Gale Sayers have been without his knee injuries? Bill Walton without his foot and ankle injuries? Bo Jackson without his hip injury? Monica Seles without the cruel knife attack? Greg Oden: leg injuries. Grant Hill: ankle. Not all budding superstars bloom, but everything had been in place for Ivery in 1979.

In 1984, Ivery was on a fulcrum: No one had given up on him; his potential was still there. But given how his 1983 season ended—his knee injuries, a new coach who didn't have Starr's reputation for compassion, and his drug and alcohol abuse (though he hid it well)—he had to prove himself. (Raabe recalled he and his friends agreeing that "He's good, but he's not as fast and powerful.")

When he needed to show he was an NFL-quality player more than at any other time, he made a baffling, career-risking arrival at spring mini-camp. He was noticeably overweight. His standing with the team is precarious due to drug use, and he shows up pudgy? Here is how good an athlete he was: despite that inauspicious start to 1984 practices, he achieved one of the more remarkable NFL comebacks that almost no one knows about.

Lugging the extra weight, he lagged behind his usual pace in sprints. Whitehurst, who lived in Atlanta in the offseason, was not surprised. He regularly met other NFL players at the Georgia Tech baseball field, including Ivery, Kent Hill, and Drew Hill, for workouts.

"Eddie Lee did not work very hard to get in shape before the season started like the rest of us," Whitehurst said. "Eddie Lee was always late, and he would take a lap around the baseball field and go sit in the dugout and didn't do anything more. Drew and Kent were working their asses off, and he was not." The player who practiced like he was trying to earn a scholarship became a slacker.

"That's when I was using," Ivery said. "I did what I did without taking the weight room seriously. If I had taken my good work ethic and passion for playing and applied it to the weight room…." He didn't finish. "But I got introduced to 'my good friend,' drugs, and wasn't totally dedicated. As an addict, you want to think you are functioning and you can smoke and drink and go in the weight room and do only a little bit. You don't realize you're not in shape when you first get to camp." Ivery heard that the coaches said he looked like a fat pig. Embarrassed, he willed himself to lose nine pounds by the next minicamp in May, which was primarily for rookies and free agents. He attended voluntarily to show he had lost weight, to work out with the coaches, and to lose more weight. When he ran 440s, this time he finished in front, with other running backs and receivers. Gregg was pleased, but Ivery still had to make the team, then try to get his starting job back.

In Ivery's first media interview since acknowledging his addiction, he was convincing. He claimed he had moved past self-pity and indulgence to confidence and discipline. He said he had started using cocaine to cope with pressure and, on his own initiative (not true), had gone to Starr for help instead of risking arrest. He insisted he was as strong as ever, able to handle anything, and aware that he had hurt many people—including himself.

"I have a handle on it and I'm defeating it so far," he said, though it was a lie. He didn't want to dwell on his drug use, which he asserted was no longer part of his life. He spoke of attending addiction recovery meetings, said his wife had gone to Hazelden to learn how to support him, and that their marriage had grown stronger (also untrue). The birth of his second child, Eddie Lee Jr., he said, had helped him see what truly matters.

He planned to work toward becoming a starter and looked forward to a successful NFL career. He said he had overcome the physical challenge of returning from two surgeries on one knee, but this latest battle, he admitted, was harder. "It was a personal problem," he said.

According to Twerski, addicts often exhibit "distorted thinking." They think something that would seem contradictory to anyone else but makes sense to them ("I'm certain I can stop on my own") while simultaneously showing no self-control. An addict might not see the connection between their using and their life falling apart: I'm a "responsible user." Often, addicts do not purposefully mislead others but are "taken in by their own thinking." Especially in the early stages of addiction, the addict's family can be persuaded by this reasoning. An addict may sound convincing, statements appear to hold up, and accounts of events may seem valid. Family and admirers, after all, don't want to believe anything negative about someone they care for. They take them at their word.

In August, with seven running backs competing for five spots, it was not clear Ivery would make the team. He fumbled twice in a scrimmage, then again in the first preseason game. His play was described as "erratic." Against the Colts, the Packers led 31-10 at halftime. Ivery had played little in the first half, but coaches gave him extended time in the second half so they could evaluate him. The Colts defense keyed on him, knowing he'd be the ball carrier. He fumbled on his first carry—without being hit—but then played well, including a 7-yard gain on a screen and 15 on a draw. Gregg said he performed well despite being "in a pressure cooker." Ivery quickly exited after the game to avoid reporters.

Overall, his preseason performance was mediocre, but he'd shown promise in camp and that last game. Would it be enough?

Two days later, cuts were announced. Fearful, Ivery experienced one of his most anxious moments as a player. What would people think if he were cut? He was a superstar in Thomson and at Georgia Tech. Now, at 27, he might be out. He already carried the shame of addiction. What if his false claims of recovery were exposed? Addiction had robbed him of a rigorous offseason—an obvious truth to observers.

"I became determined to make the team," he later said. "I did what they asked. I worked my ass off. But now we had Forrest Gregg. Bart had been on my side, and he was gone."

Ivery explained there were two ways players were cut. At breakfast, a coach might sit in the cafeteria and call your name to talk, so players entering wouldn't even glance in his direction. The other method: an empty locker. "If you knew you were on the bubble," Ivery said, "your eyes zoomed in on your locker."

Monday arrived. His locker was still intact, and no coach summoned him. "I made the team on the last preseason game," he said. "I made that final cut."

When Gregg was hired, he guaranteed he'd coach a winning team. With a healthy Dickey, the 1984 Packers' offense could build on last season's club records. The running game, led by versatile Ellis and rugged Jessie Clark, was expected to be strong. Ivery, one of the backups, remained in the mix. Yet the Packers' top two draft picks again disappointed. Just before the season opener, Ivery injured his left knee and was placed on injured reserve for four weeks. Still, he was on the roster.

To the media, Ivery said he could return to 1980 form, when he rushed for 831 yards and caught 50 passes for 481 more. Regarding his drug use, he mostly lied: "It's a part of my life I feel is way behind me. I have a bright future ahead of me. I'm just a human being. I just made a very serious mistake. We all make mistakes. The people that survive in this world are people who know how to deal with those mistakes and know how to overcome them, like I have."

"I was in big-time denial," he said later. "I gave the media what they wanted, and I believed it when I said I didn't have a problem." Overcoming denial requires ceasing destructive behavior and beginning the hard path to recovery—steps Ivery had not yet taken. Twerski wrote that addicts often exhibit an "inability to reason with oneself," even if they seem logical to others. They may come across as intelligent and persuasive, but internally their thinking is distorted—something not always visible. Especially for someone well-loved and hard-working like Ivery.

He was reactivated in early October when another back was placed on injured reserve. Having lost 17 pounds since arriving overweight, he felt he had regained his quickness and was eager for game reps. Until now, he had only impersonated opposing players on the scout team. "I've been Dorsett. This week I get to be Eddie Lee Ivery," he said. "I've got a feeling of belonging now."

A few days later, while driving his four-year-old daughter to Hardee's, he was stopped for driving with a revoked license (too many traffic violations)—his second offense. The officers gave him a warning and told him he couldn't drive again without a valid license. Thinking his status as a Packer would shield him, he drove home anyway. It might have worked once, when the Packers were revered, but not anymore. Corrick said such incidents were once handled discreetly, with the police calling the team, but this incident, he said, "took place when things started to change."

The police were waiting. Five minutes from home, they arrested him. Wisconsin law required a minimum five-day sentence for second-time offenders. The judge gave him 10 days, a fine, and another six-month license suspension. He was allowed to leave jail for work and could delay the sentence until the season's end. He chose to serve jail time during the season because, after the season, he had no reason to leave during the day. To be there as little as possible, he said he needed to leave at 6 a.m. After practice, he pretended to work out and arrived at the jail at 11p.m. He served three days and was released due to good behavior.

"I had never been to jail before," he said.

> When I heard that door shut, I felt real fear. We all slept in the same room in bunk beds. I slept with one eye open, scared. I didn't sleep much. Gregg gave me a whistle to blow

> if there was trouble, and I kept it around my neck. He may have been kidding, but I kept it there. After that, I never really enjoyed drugs again, and I became paranoid about the police. I'd look out the window and wonder if the police were watching. I never enjoyed drugs again.

But he didn't stop using.

Publicly, Gregg shrugged it off: "If he was an ordinary guy, you'd probably never know about it. But he's Eddie Lee Ivery, and that's news. A ballplayer has to understand they're expected to be above all that. But they're not. They're human." Privately, though, he was furious it happened during the season.

After starting 1-0, the Packers lost seven straight. Ivery hadn't played.

In 1984, Ivery's NCAA single-game rushing record was broken by one yard. Rueben Mayes of Washington State ran for 357 yards. Later in life, Ivery wished Rodgers had left him in longer; had he reached 400, he would have held the record until 1999, when LaDainian Tomlinson of Texas Christian rushed for 406 yards.

Three weeks after returning from injured reserve, Ivery finally played—as a backup. The Packers' season turned around. Inserted in the second quarter, he was electric: 116 yards on just nine carries, nearly 13 per attempt in less than three-quarters of a game. Dickey passed for four touchdowns, the defense had three interceptions, and they routed the Lions 41-9. It was the team's first 100-yard rushing performance of the season.

Flashes of the old Ivery returned. His first carry went 27 yards to the Detroit 3. The next: 9 yards. In the second half, he ran for 50 and was caught from behind. He wasn't quite as fast, but still elusive. On another play, he made a short gain but dragged defenders. Still powerful. On a second-and-3, he picked up the first. On a long gain, he broke tackles with power, then speed and a quick cut. On one play, he turned a sure loss into 3 yards. *Pro Football Weekly* named him offensive player of the week.

"Eddie Lee is back," Ivery declared after the game. "There's no self-doubt. My quickness is definitely coming back to what it was two years ago. I don't think I've reached my peak. I think I'll be a damned good football player before it's all over."

The Saints were next. Their defensive backs said they needed to rush Dickey hard, but Ivery would make that difficult. "He gives them a new dimension," one said. Green Bay won 23-13. On one 14-yard run, Ivery weaved through the line and cut right, leaving two lunging defenders on the ground. He was tripped by a diving ankle tackle—so close to breaking free. If he had made it past him, he had Jefferson blocking the cornerback, and Ivery could have cut back to his left. He and Jefferson slapped hands in frustration. Later, on a swing pass, Ivery picked up a first down, before being tackled by three defenders. He picked up a critical third-and-1 first down to burn clock, then ran for 12 more. On third-and-7, he didn't make the first down but gained enough to set up a manageable field goal from the 24. Coffman scored a touchdown Coffman-style—hit at the 1, dragging a linebacker into the end zone.

With the Saints focused on the Packers' stellar receivers, the running game—finally—was key. Ivery had 78 rushing yards, Ellis 86. In two games, Ivery had 194 yards on 25 carries—almost eight per carry.

Next up: the Vikings, tied with the Packers for last in the division. After a lackluster first half, Gregg spewed a scathing, screaming halftime denouncement with language the *Press-Gazette* wouldn't print. The Packers dominated. A productive ground game (Ellis 110, Ivery 55) complemented four passing touchdowns. With the win, they pulled within three games out of first place.

With 249 yards on 36 carries—6.9 per—since returning, Ivery had powered the team's three-game win streak.

After playing as backup and alternating with other backs to relay offensive plays, Ivery was named starter. Clark was out with a season-ending injury. Ellis moved to fullback; Ivery returned to tailback—his favorite position.

"I'm sorry for what happened to Jessie," Ivery said. "But I look at this as a real opportunity to prove I should be a starter."

After defeating two teams with losing records, they faced the 7-4 Rams, who had the great Eric Dickerson and a formidable defense. Starting for the first time in a year, Ivery scored three of the Packers' four touchdowns and gained 77 yards rushing, 22 receiving. The Packers crushed the Rams 31-6. A four-game win streak had seemed impossible mid-season, and it was their first in six years.

Suddenly, Gregg's gruff, no-nonsense style looked like what the team had needed. Gregg said Ivery is "playing the type of football that we felt he could play. He can help us control the ball." Ivery, averaging 6.4 per carry, told reporters, "The real Eddie Lee Ivery is back." His injuries, he said, were behind him. His drug addiction, he insisted, was history.

Asked whether it was psychologically difficult to rebound from his struggles when others had doubted him as an athlete and a person, Ivery paused. It was a tough question, he said; it had been difficult. "But it wasn't as hard as I thought it would be," he said. "I had a lot of support from my teammates and coaches."

He smiled. "I feel good now. Very aggressive. Hard running. This is one of the best moments in my life. I'm just enjoying myself now. You can't sit around and worry about doing it. You've got to go out and do it."

The Packers were resurgent—but it was late in the season, and a playoff run was unlikely. Still, they just needed to beat the 3-8-1 Lions—whom they'd walloped a month earlier—on national television on Thanksgiving.

They led 21-7 at halftime. Ellis ran for a 36-yard touchdown. Dickey hit Coffman for a 46-yard score, and Ivery caught a 7-yard touchdown. Then, the Lions roared back to win 31-28.

An embarrassed, furious Gregg called it "the worst 60 minutes of defensive football I've seen. It was horrible." The Packers' slim playoff hopes were gone.

Ivery had 44 yards rushing and 46 receiving. He was strong, tough, elusive. On one tough 3-yard gain, he was hit by a big lineman but powered forward and was tackled by two defenders. On his touchdown, he broke an arm tackle and dove into the end zone. On a pitch to the right, he quickly cut back toward the middle, avoided a defender, and almost broke it big, but was stopped by an ankle tackle that, pre-knee-injuries, he probably would have foiled.

Even as Ivery thrived on the field, off it, a scandal erupted. He and Lofton were accused of sexual assault by 18-year-old dancer Katherine Magestro in a private room at a Milwaukee strip club, The Marque. Following his lawyer's advice, Ivery made no public comment. Prosecutors ultimately didn't press charges, saying they couldn't prove guilt beyond a reasonable doubt—though they called the behavior "reprehensible, shameful, and depraved."

Both men admitted being in the room but denied assault. They were convicted only of trespassing in Magestro's dressing room and fined $500 each. While this seemed a harmless resolution, the incident was publicly embarrassing because the slow-moving case remained in the headlines for many months.

Parins denied rumors that the Packers offered $25,000 to Magestro to avoid a lawsuit. She stated she wanted criminal charges, not money. It was said she had drinks with them and got their autographs after the alleged assault, which led some people to interpret her accusation as false. In January 1985, the club's owners sued Lofton and Ivery for $5.5 million, claiming that the publicity had harmed their business. Çoverage of these stories heightened the embarrassment. After many months, a settlement was reached, which included a non-disclosure agreement. Ivery said Anna was angry, "but she always stayed in my corner. I told her the sexual assault didn't happen, but I told her what *did* happen, and she didn't leave me. She stayed with me until my addiction ran her off. And now I can't talk about it."

He later admitted that the temptations that come with being an NFL player—a Packer in the smallest market with avid, adoring fans—got the best of him. He enjoyed it and indulged. "I was the worst husband and father," he said.

> There was something missing in our marriage, and that something was me. I grew up around an all-female household, and I tend to relate better to women, but as a boyfriend or husband, I didn't have a role model in my house. Anna was married to me, but I wasn't to her. I was *Eddie Lee Ivery*, so I only provided for her financially and then did what I wanted. There was no real communication. If there were problems, I'd buy her a Mercedes or a fur coat, and that seemed to make her happy.

He frequented the Carlton West bar with other players and slept with the "Green Bay Groupies" who made themselves available every Tuesday night. "We called it boys' night out in town." He added, "If someone treated me as I treated her, I'd probably kill them."

With no chance to make the playoffs, how would the Packers perform in their final three games? The following week, in snowy, muddy conditions at Lambeau, the Packers scored four touchdowns in the second half to defeat Tampa Bay 27-14. There were 55,973 tickets sold, but 9,173 fans chose to stay away. Reporter Christl wrote, "Two teams that are going nowhere played a meaningless football game here Sunday on a field fit for pigs and mud wrestlers." They trailed in the first half 0-7; the Lambeau crowd booed. The sportscasters said the Packers' offense wasn't "crisp." Ivery generated the bulk of their first half offense, primarily on tough runs for 2-8 yards, using quick, strong moves. Even with two knee injuries, it was rare for a single defender to tackle him, such as when the great Lee Roy Selmon grabbed his upper body and flung him.

At halftime, according to Ivery, a furious Gregg entered the locker room, flipped over a table topped with pre-autographed footballs, and told the "bleeping players in skill positions" to remove their underclothes and "put these on." He threw down a box of pantyhose. Ivery said he cheated by removing only one pair of his two thermals and putting the pantyhose over the other pair. The Packers scored 27 straight points to win.

Ivery continued in the second half with tough runs, usually gaining 10 or fewer but making crucial yards. Ivery's two touchdowns were 4 and 2 yards, the first by powering through a scrum and the second a dive. The Packers took the lead by faking a handoff to Ivery and passing to another running back. Ivery had been used so often that the defense went for the fake. On a 10-yard gain, two defenders missed him, and a sportscaster said, "You can't do that with an Eddie Lee Ivery. He'll hurt you." Coffman and two teammates did celebratory belly slides through the mud after the game. The Packers were 6-8.

The next Sunday, they played at Chicago—led by Payton and the NFL's top-ranked defense—the NFC Central Division leaders who needed a win to possibly secure home field advantage in the playoffs. The Packers played for pride. In their first meeting, Chicago edged the Packers 9-7. In this game, with Dickey unavailable due to severe headaches, the Packers won 20-17 in a match filled with injuries and mistakes on both sides. Ivery rushed for 50 yards and caught two passes for 27. Rich Campbell, a former first-round pick now a third-stringer, threw a last-minute, game-winning 43-yard desperation touchdown pass.

In the season finale, they faced the Vikings, who had lost 10 of their last 11 games and fielded the NFL's lowest-ranked defense. Could the Pack reverse their 1-7 start and end the season 8-8? Or would they repeat the Thanksgiving Day disappointment against the lowly Lions? Ivery gained 59 yards rushing and scored on a 5-yard run as the Packers dominated 38-14. Dickey threw two touchdown passes and *ran* for another. Lofton caught five passes for 91 yards, setting a single-season Packer receiving yardage record.

After a miserable start, Green Bay finished as one of the hottest teams in the league in their final eight games (second only to the Super Bowl champion 49ers) and had good reasons to be hopeful for 1985, with their high-powered, prolific passing game returning and a resurgent Ivery in the backfield. Rookie defensive back Tom Flynn led the NFC with nine interceptions. Players, buoyed by the gritty pride they exhibited in the second half of the season, said perhaps Gregg's harsh demeanor and ferocious tirades were what they needed. Coffman declared, "Under Forrest, the Green Bay Packers will be a championship team again."

They never would.

In a retrospective of 1984 Green Bay news stories in the *Press-Gazette*, the Ivery/Lofton sexual assault allegation made the top 10. When the prosecutor declined to press charges, Magestro invoked an obscure law that allowed a judge to intervene and demand charges be pressed if the judge believes there should be a prosecution. She made that request to a judge. This extended the story further because the players' lawyers requested that the hearing on that decision be held in private while Magestro's lawyers wanted it to be public. Those deliberations were covered avidly.

The top Packers story was the second half of the season's resurgence, and Ivery was praised for overcoming "several personal problems" to ignite the running game. Considering that Ivery hadn't played in a year, arrived at camp overweight, had a middling preseason, barely missed being cut, missed half the season with an injury to the *same knee* that sidelined him for two seasons, and was a backup when he finally played (plus being a cocaine addict)—it was an amazing comeback.

He was a major contributor to the team's unexpected turnaround; in his first game, he gained 116 yards on only nine carries and was one of the league's most consistent running backs in the season's second half when he rushed for 552 yards (5.6 per). Only he and Dickerson rushed for over 500 yards and averaged more than 5.5 yards in the season's second half. (And, Wright noted, their offense "wasn't a Dickerson-type offense where they ran the ball a lot. That was a lot of yards for that offense.") He led the team with six rushing touchdowns and was the Packers' third-leading scorer while playing *half a season*. He caught 19 passes for 141 yards and a touchdown. He had almost as many rushing yards as Ellis but with 24 fewer rushes. There is no guarantee half a season would match the other, but if he had played the entire season, he likely would have rushed for over 1,000 yards—in a mainly passing offense.

The Packers were optimistic about their running game in 1985. The previous season, the running backs rushed for 4.4 yards per carry, ranking fourth in the league, and Ivery finished magnificently. They planned to keep Ivery at starting halfback and Ellis at fullback. In their first preseason game, Ivery gained 27 yards on his first carry. The running backs coach said Ivery ran "quicker, harder, more decisively than in recent seasons. He's stronger than you think." Coaches said no player was in better shape than Ivery, and they were amazed at how much better he was compared to the previous preseason. Imagine having him for a full season. Yet again, however, an injury would hamper what seemed to be a path to NFL success. The first two major injuries involved the body's largest joint, while this time the culprit was a much smaller one.

In August, Ivery sustained a minor hip injury, then injured his right thumb in practice while blocking on a pass play. That injury also seemed minor, but it was later discovered that his thumb was both dislocated and broken. A surgeon inserted two pins and placed it in a cast, which sidelined him for six weeks. Later that month, still wearing the cast, he participated only in noncontact practice and made one-handed catches.

"As soon as Eddie Lee gets healthy, we're as good as anybody," commented offensive coordinator Bob Schnelker. Gregg was confident that Ivery would make the opener.

The limited practice frustrated Ivery.

"It throws your timing off to not practice full speed," he said. "Going through the motions won't cut it in the NFL." He worried that, with a hand injury, he might play less aggressively to avoid fumbling. No one had ever seen an unaggressive Eddie Lee Ivery play. Plus, he was eager to continue the success of the end of 1984. He missed the first game, a loss to the Patriots. In the second game, as a backup, he scored the game-winning touchdown against the Giants, a 1-yarder, with four minutes left. He rushed for 28 yards and caught one pass for 7 yards.

By this time, legal and illegal drugs were taking their toll. Running backs in the NFL are repeatedly banged up as linemen and linebackers smack into them, and injuries add onto injuries. Bones and tendons and muscles and ligaments are resilient but not invulnerable. Many injuries don't keep a player off the field but need attention.

"They shot me up," he said later. "Every time I complained about my knee, they injected a pain reliever. I got that for my knee and my back. The shots didn't take away *all* the pain but helped me continue to play. There was pressure to perform. I wasn't a young buck anymore, but I loved playing for Green Bay, and to keep my job, I had to play hurt." What about long-term effects? "I'm sitting here right now as a result of back and knee problems. I experience it daily. Pretty much from my neck down, I have problems."

His addiction was wearing on Anna, who threatened to leave if he didn't get help. He fooled the Packers but not her. "She wanted to raise children there," he said. "She thought it was a great place to live. If you're the wife of a Green Bay Packer, you get treated special, and she enjoyed that. I'm an NFL player, and she actually wanted to work, so she worked and built relationships in the community." She wanted to stay in Green Bay—but not if he continued using.

Next, the Packers lost to the Jets 24-3. Ivery, coming off the bench, rushed for 25 yards and had 32 receiving. He still didn't feel in sync after so much missed practice. Then came a 43-28 loss to the Cardinals, where he rushed for just 23 yards and caught one pass for 8. After the game, the locker room was somber; players gave terse replies to the media.

Then, in what felt like a we-finally-got-it-all-together performance, they routed the 3-1 Lions. The Packers blitzed relentlessly, sacked the quarterback four times, and forced six turnovers. Dickey-to-Lofton dazzled for the first time all season. Though not the featured back, Ivery scored the team's first touchdown on a 2-yard pass reception and rushed for 33 yards. He showed glimpses of the 1984 Ivery.

When asked about being a backup, Ivery placed team above self: "It's a little disappointing, but you know me, I just go out there, do what they tell me and do the best I can." He said he would be patient and give 100 percent on every play. After all, that's what had happened the previous season—he missed games, came in as a backup, then became the featured back credited with helping turn the season around.

A broken thumb may not sound severe, but it hampered him in ways he hadn't expected. Limited practice disrupted his rhythm, and he questioned whether the injury made it harder to hold the ball securely. Should he avoid contact to protect it? Indecision was his enemy.

The Packers then played a complete game—highlighted by a goal-line stand and a crisp two-minute drill—to beat the 3-2 Vikings, 20-17. Ivery, suddenly, was the leading rusher with 83 yards (6.9 per carry). But the next week, they lost 23-7 to the powerful Bears, who would finish the season 15-1 and demolish the Patriots in the Super Bowl. Losing to the league's best team wasn't shameful. But the following week's loss to the 2-5 Colts stung. Reporters overheard shouting from behind the closed locker room door. Then came a rematch with the Bears—more competitive but still a 16-10 loss, marred by fights, cheap shots, one ejection, and five personal foul penalties.

Against the Vikings, Ivery was listed as "probable" but played. He took a hard hit early and felt pain in his back the rest of the game. Still, it was his best outing of the year: 111 yards on 15 carries (7.4 average). It was also the team's first road win, 27-17. Was he finding his late-season groove again?

He ran powerfully on a 19-yard gain, finishing with a collision that added three more yards. On a pass near the goal line, he caught the ball in the right flat, bounced off two defenders, and was taken down by a third. On another play, he sliced through a crowd for 12. Later, he took a sweep for 3 yards, then, after a fake handoff, caught a 2-yard touchdown pass to give the Packers a 20-17 lead. To close out the game, he broke off a 38-yard run, weaving through defenders. The Packers were 4-6.

They handily beat a weak Saints team, then lost to the Rams.

Then came one of Lambeau Field's most famous games: the "Snow Bowl."

The 2-10 Buccaneers, on a 17-game road losing streak, traveled from 80-degree Tampa to 28-degree Green Bay. Twelve inches of snow fell before the game; five more during. Packers fans pride themselves on braving brutal weather, but this game was exceptional. Two-thirds of ticket holders stayed home—a franchise record for no-shows. Only 19,856 fans (some arriving by snowmobile) showed up, the smallest Lambeau crowd since 1957.

Bucs quarterback Steve Young, making his second NFL appearance after the USFL, had grown up a Packers fan and looked forward to a classic cold-weather game—until he got one.

Receiver Preston Dennard made it only because neighbors shoveled a path from his house. Johnson drove, but his wife had to walk after their driveway was snowplowed shut. Harlan's car got stuck; he walked the rest of the way and called home to tell his wife to stay put. Corrick didn't even try to drive—he walked.

Fan Tom Pigeon went but left at halftime with his two young sons. "They wouldn't say they wanted to go," he said, "but I could tell. Our feet were wet. We got stuck driving home in our Chevette." His sons pushed the car, and when it finally got moving, he kept going, afraid to stop. "I left the kids to walk home," he said. "They still tease me about that. Then I got stuck in my driveway."

The field's tarp was frozen to the turf. Push-broom crews scrambled between plays to clear the yard markers, which were quickly covered again by snow. When Ivery emerged from the tunnel, the wind made his eyes water. "It was uncontrollable, like I was crying," he said. A teammate told him to smear Vaseline on his face, which helped. By game's end, 10.7 inches of snow had fallen in under 24 hours. With wind swirling between 20 and 30 miles per hour, wind chills dipped to -7. Snow puffed into the air when a player hit the ground. When Tech had traveled to Colorado Springs in 1978, Air Force coaches thought the frigid weather would hamper and intimidate the visitors from the South. It didn't then. This time, it did.

Tampa's coach said their game plan wouldn't change—they'd just wear more layers. But Dickey noticed the Bucs took their time leaving their locker room for warmups and retreated inside after only 20 minutes. Tampa wore white jerseys, normally an inconsequential decision, but, with the swirling snow, they had a hard time finding each other. Punters could barely see the snapped ball. Defensive backs strained to see opposing quarterbacks. Receivers hoped to see the ball in time to catch it as it emerged from the mist. A Tampa safety said 80 percent of the time he couldn't see the ball.

Expecting a run-heavy game, Dickey was told to pass. The receivers knew their routes; defenders didn't. They'll slip around, and we'll eat 'em up. The coach was right.

The Packers shut out the Bucs 21-0—their first shutout in eight years. They gained 512 yards and 31 first downs. Tampa managed just 65 yards and five first downs. Lofton topped 100 yards receiving by halftime. Young, future Hall of Famer, was frozen and flustered. He mainly threw short passes—with a frozen ball he couldn't grip—and was sacked five times, face down in the snow. "I never suffocated in the snow before," he said. He passed for only 53 yards and threw an interception. After the game, Wright spoke to Young, who told him: "We wanted absolutely no part of being up here."

The veteran Dickey coolly, steadily ran his offense: 299 yards, even scoring on a 3-yard run. "Mind over matter," he said. Receivers ran their routes, knowing Dickey would pass the ball where it was supposed to be, even though they couldn't see it until it was halfway there. Ivery and Ellis both rushed for over 100 yards. Ivery averaged 4.5 per carry, often grinding out tough 7- to 9-yard gains with power and speed. He caught two passes for 18 yards. A picture of Ivery being tackled by four Buccaneers, just before they all land in a pile of snow, hangs on the wall of the Packers Hall of Fame Museum.

Sportswriter Christl praised the game as a boost to Green Bay's mystique. Fans dressed in their fortress-against-the-winter hunting gear. It was messy, raw—memorable. A meaningless game between two losing teams became iconic.

Next came the 9-4 Dolphins. They jumped out to a 20-3 lead in chilly but snow-free 18-degree Lambeau. The Packers rallied and took the lead 24-20 in the fourth on a 1-yard touchdown by Ivery. But Dan Marino threw two more touchdowns. Miami won 34-24.

Against the 7-7 Lions, both teams out of the playoff race, the Packers won on a last-second field goal. Ivery played little but contributed on the final drive.

They closed the season with a win—but not much celebration. They trailed the 2-13 Buccaneers in the fourth quarter, squandered red zone chances, and finished 8-8 for the fourth time in five years. On a third-and-12, Ivery made a crucial 18-yard catch on the game-winning drive. His 20 rushing yards made him the team's leading rusher—for the season—by just 3 yards. He totaled 636 yards (4.8 per carry) on a pass-heavy team.

Ivery's season did not end spectacularly like the previous season, but he remained reliable in crucial moments—rugged, dependable, experienced, if a step slower and physically and mentally hampered by the thumb injury. After the season, Gregg announced an impending roster overhaul. He also said he wouldn't require end-of-season physicals to include drug testing—he'd leave that to each player's conscience.

Music to Ivery's ears.

Chapter 16

I Bet There's Not That Many

In April 1986, there was a media report that Cowboys coach Tom Landry wanted to trade for Ivery. When told this years later, Ivery, contemplating life in a warmer climate on a winning team, said, "Damn, I wish I had known that. To get out of Green Bay…." He paused and continued, "I don't think I would want to go. The Packers, they saved my life. If my addiction had been handled differently, I could have possibly died. They could have found out I was using drugs and violating team rules and cut me, but Bart Starr cared for me as a person and wanted to help me. And the Green Bay organization allowed him to do that."

In the 1986 draft, the Packers selected first-team All-American halfback Kenneth Davis from Texas Christian University in the second round. He didn't have the high expectations Ivery faced in 1979, but the Packers hoped he would be a breakaway "difference-maker," helping the team surpass the dreaded 8-8. As a junior, he ranked third nationally in rushing yards and gained 152 yards in his first game as a senior. However, it was discovered that he was receiving money from boosters, resulting in his dismissal from the team. That didn't bother Gregg, who stated that if *his* college had offered *him* money, he would have accepted it, given his financial situation.

Despite the addition of Davis, coaches believed Ivery was too talented not to be utilized. (Since his 1983 hiatus, Ivery had averaged 5.1 yards per carry.) A reporter noted, "Knee surgery robbed Ivery of his chances for greatness, but he has become a surprisingly strong, dependable runner with a knack for making tacklers miss. He plays virtually mistake-free football and is excellent in the passing game."

In June 1986, University of Maryland basketball star Len Bias, one of the college's most dynamic players and recently drafted second overall by the Boston Celtics, died of cardiac arrhythmia due to cocaine use. As a junior and senior, he was an All-American and the Atlantic Coast Conference Player of the Year—and seemingly destined for NBA superstardom. Would that startle Ivery into quitting cocaine?

"I remember reading about that, but when you're using and see events like that, you try to minimize your usage compared to his," he said. "Len died using a purer cocaine, like 100 percent, not diluted. That was my excuse: *That's* not what I'm using."

In July, Gregg said Ivery was still the starting tailback, and he expected the offense to run the ball more. The Packers were shifting to a ball-control offense with less emphasis on long bombs to Lofton. Good news for Ivery, it seemed. However, he began to sense his role might change. He recalled that earlier, the running backs had all lined up as receivers in certain formations, and Ivery had run routes the best and made the fewest mistakes. The receivers coach noted, "He has great hands, and his hand-eye coordination is excellent." Possibly, it could throw the defense off if they didn't know which position he would play.

At an August practice, Ivery was preparing to do calisthenics when a coach directed him to join the receivers, and he remained there all day. He was puzzled but said later, "They tell me to line up at center, I'll line up at center."

Gregg said, "Eddie Lee's done well, as we expected he would." Gregg said they already knew he could play tailback and were trying to find other ways to utilize his talents. He said Ivery might be a backup wide receiver.

Ivery practiced at receiver partly because he maneuvered himself there. He said later, "I saw my value as a running back going down, so when practicing against the defense, running other teams' plays, I would volunteer to go to wide receiver." Cards indicated which receiver would get the ball, and when they held up a certain card, he would quickly say, "I'll take that position," knowing that receiver would be thrown the ball. "They saw how well I could run routes and catch." He also practiced on special teams and led the preseason in special-team tackles.

Gregg had spoken of rebuilding the Packers, and he did so by releasing 21 players, including Dickey (who ranked behind only Starr in the team's all-time passing statistics) and Coffman. Gregg said, "What I'm trying to do with this football team is get a fresh start." He noted that some were "just playing out their time" and not "good enough to win with." Ivery chuckled to reporters, "There are still a few of us left."

New fullback Paul Ott Carruth, like others, recalled a "jovial, happy-go-lucky" Ivery lightening the mood at practice. Carruth was also somewhat in awe. A football fan since childhood, he read about Ivery's record-breaking Air Force game in high school and remembered it. At Green Bay, he thought, "There he is in person. I'm in the pros, and he's standing beside me. Wow." He was not familiar with Ivery's knee injuries—or his cocaine addiction—and was impressed with his versatility and skill. (He said of Ivery's addiction, "I never knew until you just told me.")

Being new, he evaluated Ivery as a veteran NFL player. He didn't say, "He's good—considering everything." Instead: "He probably could have been in any position on the field, especially on offense: halfback, fullback, and block; he did split-outs as a receiver. He could catch the ball. He could do it all. He was *good*." He said casual fans aren't aware that being that good is more than physical ability. "A lot goes into that," he said, "knowing what to do, how to do it.... I remember him being a *leader* of special teams, being the guy who shows you: This is how you do it. This is how you play football—on special teams or whatever they ask you to do."

In a preseason loss to the Bengals, Ivery led the team in receiving after only one week of practicing as a receiver. Gregg said Ivery was their third-best receiver and said he was "pretty smooth out there. He made some big catches, and he worked hard to get open." He said Ivery may play in the shotgun formation (quarterback stands several yards behind the center instead of crouching directly behind) as a slot receiver (between the tackle and the wide receiver, a few feet behind the line of scrimmage) and, with his running skills, would match up well against linebackers. With Wright as quarterback, the Packers emphasized quick-release passing and focused less on long passes to wide receivers—which could mean more passes to Ivery.

Meanwhile, the Wisconsin Supreme Court heard arguments regarding the constitutionality of the law permitting a circuit judge to compel the filing of charges against an individual when local prosecutors refrained from doing so. Lofton and Ivery's attorneys used the separation of powers argument, asserting that the current law violates due process. The Court did not issue a ruling immediately, and the story continued to unfold, keeping the embarrassment in the news.

Ivery was now practicing with the number one shotgun unit in practice, and coaches expected him to make an immediate impact, but he suffered yet another injury—a neck strain—and missed the first four games (all losses). He finally played in the fifth game against the Bengals and caught two passes for 18 yards. The Packers lost 34-28. Pack 0-5. Lofton became the Packers' all-time leading pass-reception leader. The previous season, Lofton had become only the fifth receiver in NFL history to gain 1,000 yards in five or more seasons.

They fell to 0-6 in a loss to the Lions. Gregg's guarantee of fielding a winning team faded further. At least Starr was personally popular with players and fans—and pretty much anyone who met him—but Gregg was disliked *and* had a losing team. Ivery had one rush for 15 yards and caught seven passes for 71 yards, second only to Lofton. On one play, Ivery was open in the middle of the field, but the ball was thrown elsewhere; he slapped his helmet hard with both hands and shook his head in frustration. The Packers finally won a game, 17-14, over the 4-2 Cleveland Browns. Ivery caught two passes for 30 yards and made one tackle on special teams. According to reporters, the postgame celebration was low-key. How does a Packers team celebrate 1-6?

When coaches were asked about the running game, Ivery's name was not mentioned. In an injury report, he was referred to as a wide receiver and would undergo X-rays on his ribs after an injury from the previous game was exacerbated by an acrobatic diving catch in practice. When asked about not playing running back, Ivery said he was happy to find a way to stay on the team. He said later, "I did whatever I had to do. I was not ready for my career to end."

In the next game, a 31-17 loss to the 49ers, Ivery caught three passes for 24 yards. The Packers were driving for a potential tying touchdown when a pass intended for him was intercepted and returned 88 yards for a touchdown with 33 seconds left. The Packers were 1-7, halfway through the season. Two years earlier, boosted in part by Ivery's return to the lineup, they went from 1-7 to 8-8. Not this season.

Green Bay reporter Bob McGinn, commenting on why they were 1-7 (not enough great players), praised Ivery as "an unsung contributor" but who "isn't the full-time answer," although he was a player quarterback Wright trusted on third and 5. Wright said later,

> When they moved him to receiver, he was fabulous, a lot better than anybody would have imagined. He was always in the right spot, always made the play. In a year when we had Lofton, the best athlete I ever played with, and [Phil] Epps, an outstanding wide receiver and one of the fastest in the league, Eddie Lee was the guy I felt the most comfortable throwing to. He wasn't a deep guy. We had Lofton and Epps for that, but he probably had more first downs on receptions. I had tremendous respect for his ability to go from being what he was pre-injury, switching positions to something he'd never done before, to be as good as he was. That speaks for his character.

He added, "I can't imagine having *two* of those injuries and *still* play running back. It would be scary how good he could have been based on what I saw. Playing arguably the toughest position, running back, to be able to come back from *two* injuries in three years and play six years after that. I don't know offhand if there is another running back who did that. I bet there's not that many."

After a 27-3 loss to the Steelers, the Packers and two other teams were 1-8 (including the Oilers, who had beaten the Packers 31-3 in the season opener). As they prepared for a visit by Tampa Bay, Gregg said sarcastically, "Tampa Bay's a better team than us. They've got two wins."

The Packers equaled that by winning 31-7. Ivery had one carry for 9 yards and caught three passes for 56, including a 42-yarder. The game, played in Milwaukee, was blacked out locally since it was not a sellout—the first time that had happened since after the 1982 strike. The first two games at Milwaukee that season would have been blacked out as well, but the local television station scheduled to telecast the games had bought the unsold tickets so they could air the game.

Such was the tepid interest in a 1-9 team by fans known for their fervor. For the 1986 season, the Packers averaged 5,500 no-shows at home.

The Packers lost a close game to defending Super Bowl champion Chicago, 12-10. Their record: 2-10. The game was marred by a vicious late hit—a body slam from behind—on Bears quarterback Jim McMahon by defensive end Charles Martin, who was ejected. McMahon's shoulder injury sidelined him for the rest of the season, likely extinguishing the Bears' hopes for a repeat Super Bowl championship and denying Mike Ditka the opportunity to become one of the rare head coaches to win consecutive Super Bowls. He called the Packers thugs: "They had high character when Bart was there. I don't see that anymore." Under Gregg, the Packers went from the third-least-penalized team in the NFL to the second-most penalized.

On dirty tactics, such as Martin's late hit, Ivery said, "In those days, you'd find guys who did that kind of thing. Refs don't see everything. One Steelers defender tried to spit tobacco in my eye while I was on the ground. [Ed] "Too Tall" Jones, he would grab my nuts."

A few weeks later, Martin was accused of grabbing a woman without her consent at a bar. Initially, Gregg cursed angrily at reporters who asked about the incident, which was settled when Martin apologized to the woman and gave her $500, an arrangement made after Gregg called her brother.

The Packers dedicated their Thanksgiving Day game against the 5-7 Detroit Lions to Martin, who was suspended. The Packers won 44-40 on a dramatic 83-yard punt return for a touchdown in the final minute. Ivery caught a pass across the middle for 11 yards, clinging to the ball even after being hit by two defenders, and made three special-teams tackles. On the punt return, Walter Stanley started left, saw a wall of unblocked blue jerseys, reversed field, put his hand to the ground, and then sped around to the right. Ivery was there to block, and although he didn't physically block anyone, he strategically obstructed a defender's direct path to Stanley, who dashed untouched to the end zone. Parins awarded each player a $50 dinner bonus. "I think this is a big chance for this football team," Gregg said. "It's good for their mental health. We have a lot of kids with a lot of pride and a lot of character, and we're quite proud of them."

In a new low even for this era of the Packers, they lost again—the first team to lose every game at Lambeau—clobbered by the Vikings 32-6. Ivery had one rush for no gain and caught three passes for 51 yards (second to Lofton in receiving yards). In the five Lambeau losses, the Packers, outscored 125-42, scored only three touchdowns and seven field goals.

In a profile of Ivery in the *Press-Gazette*, he said his goal was to play for at least 10 years. He was currently in his eighth. It was noted that he had arrived at camp in excellent shape and had played more than expected due to another receiver being in a contract dispute. He said he didn't want to fully switch to receiver but acknowledged that he adjusted to it and now considered it a good move since running backs tend to have short careers.

"If I stay there, without injury," he said, "who knows how long I can play this game?" He played halfback when the Packers were in the shotgun formation but mostly played in a four-receiver formation in passing situations. As a receiver, he had caught 23 passes, which was the fourth-best on the team, despite being a backup. Gregg said he can also play fullback: "That's the advantage of having someone like him, who is as knowledgeable about the game as he is. He can come in and bail you out at a lot of positions." Ivery expressed frustration at seeing younger running backs make mistakes that he didn't make. He noted that other than the 1982 playoff team, "We've been pretty much mediocre. You can't be satisfied with just being mediocre. I know, myself, I'm not mediocre."

In a win followed by little celebration, the Packers defeated a struggling Tampa Bay team 21-7 in their penultimate game. Ivery caught three passes for 40 yards, second on the team. Then, an incident occurred that further tarnished the Packers' already low public reputation, resurfaced the tawdry charges against Lofton and Ivery, and led to the suspension of one of the NFL's greatest players—yet also set the stage for one of Ivery's most remarkable achievements. It was also the last time he would touch a football in an NFL game.

Lofton was arrested and charged with second-degree sexual assault in the stairwell of a Green Bay building that had a penthouse bar. It was the third sexual assault allegation against Packers players since Gregg had become coach. Lofton claimed the sex was consensual. Starr—still loyal to his players—appeared in court to support Lofton. Gregg ordered practices and the locker room closed to media and canceled a news conference. Lofton was suspended for the final game against the Giants.

Reporters recounted other events that had damaged the team's image: Magestro's accusation, safety Mossy Cade also facing sexual assault charges, and the Martin bar incident. The judge approved a motion by Lofton's attorney preventing the prosecution from mentioning the Magestro incident, but that meant Ivery's name was once again publicly mentioned in a disparaging light.

Lofton was traded to the Raiders with the condition that if he was found guilty, the trade would be off. Corrick said later, "Judge Parins made me trade him. He was very embarrassed." The Packers received almost nothing in return for a future Hall of Famer.

The Lofton and Cade sexual assault trials were held in the spring, across the hall from one another. Reporter Langenkamp said he was interviewed by ESPN, ABC, and CBS in one day. They asked about having two felony trials for two players on the same team at the same time.

"Those were bad times," he said later.

Lofton was acquitted, but Cade was found guilty and sent to prison.

With Lofton suspended, Ivery started at wide receiver for the first time in his career against the 13-2 New York Giants. Coached by Parcells, the Giants would win that season's Super Bowl (Parcells's first of two). The Giants were securely in the postseason but needed a win to secure home-field advantage through the playoffs, so this was not a rest-the-starters-for-the-playoffs game.

The Giants were motivated and dominating. They had eight Pro Bowlers, with their stout defense led by the quick, powerful, and disruptive Lawrence Taylor (that season's NFL MVP, one of only two defensive players to be so honored), perhaps the greatest defensive player ever. "He had such power and speed that no one could stop him consistently," Ivery said of Taylor. Ivery used a great defense like that of the Giants as motivation: "I would think, 'We *want* this team. We want to be the team to score on them.'"

Ivery, when he was a running back, had faced a blitzing Taylor before, and he never forgot it. The first time, Taylor trampled over Ivery and sacked Dickey. "I was embarrassed," Ivery said, "because I was proud of my blocking. My pride was hurt."

For the next Taylor blitz, Ivery had a new strategy. "I knew not to cut him low. He'd jump over me. He tried to bull rush me like the first time, and I put my head under his chin and stopped him in his tracks. His head snapped back. He threw me to the side, but we got the pass off." Ivery said that when the team watched the game film, the coaches said *that* was how you stop a blitzing linebacker.

"I walked around all day with an 'S' on my chest," Ivery said, thinking of Superman. In this game, as a wide receiver, he might be *tackled* by Taylor, but he wouldn't have to block him in the backfield.

Also on the Giants team was wide receiver Stacy Robinson, a player Ivery had not heard of but who would play an important role in the Giants' Super Bowl victory—and years later a crucial role in Ivery's life when he was at his lowest point, desperate for help.

The Packers lost decisively 55-24, becoming the first Green Bay team to lose 12 games. They gave up the third-most points allowed by a Packers defense. Gregg said after the game that the arrest of Lofton was an "emotional drain" on the team but offered little else. Players refused to comment. There were good plays but failures aplenty: dropped passes and penalties. Still, it was an exceptional game for Ivery.

In the first quarter, Ivery almost caught a 50-yard bomb in a diving attempt. He beat his man, who hit him as the ball arrived inside the Giants' 10. It was catchable but would have been a spectacular grab. Ivery stood and snapped his head down in frustration.

On another pass, Ivery was open, but the ball was overthrown as Taylor hit Wright just as he threw. Ivery caught one 14-yard pass for a first down near midfield on a down-and-out, dragging a defender for the last three yards—still a strong runner. He dropped a pass right to his hands on a third-and-long that would have been a 21-yard first-down gain. Unusually, it was his fault. ("It was a great pass," he said, "but I didn't get my head turned around in time.")

He caught a 13-yard TD pass in the second quarter to cut the score to 24-7. He ran his route straight, then stopped. The defensive back kept going as another Packers receiver ran by, and Ivery drifted to open space in the middle. He caught the pass and ran freely into the end zone. Toward the end of the first half, with the Packers trailing by 10, Ivery caught a 21-yard pass and stiff-armed for a couple more yards. The drive led to a field goal.

The Packers trailed by only 7 at halftime, but the stampeding Giants scored on their first five possessions of the second half. Ivery caught a 14-yard pass across the middle—smacked by a linebacker in front and a safety from behind. He said Lofton had taught him to survey the field when running middle routes: to know where everybody is, to prepare his body for the hit, and to be aware of when and where it's coming. ("And don't close your eyes," Lofton said later.) Maybe you'll avoid the hardest hit and get hit by someone else. And catch the ball no matter what. Ivery absorbed and enacted those lessons exactly. He spun free and made it to the 15. In agony, he writhed on the ground but was back for the next possession. A pass was thrown behind an open Ivery when a catch would have made a first down.

The Giants kept scoring.

From deep in Packers territory, Ivery missed a pass and threw up his arms, wanting a flag—which he got. Another pass intended for Ivery was intercepted before it reached him. It wasn't a superstar performance, but it was solid—even though this was another position change, from the slot to wide receiver. He proved he could not only play receiver in the NFL—he could start. He scored the Packers' first touchdown and was the leading receiver in the game, with 67 yards, against the league's second-best defense, which would go on to dominate the Broncos in the Super Bowl.

For the season, after missing the first four games, Ivery rushed four times for 25 yards. He caught 31 passes for 385 yards, the longest being 42, and scored one touchdown. On special teams, he made 14 tackles and assisted on four others. A sportswriter said Ivery was a "football-smart jack-of-all-trades" who "made a smooth conversion to wide receiver."

In March, Lofton and Ivery won their Wisconsin Supreme Court case in a ruling that deemed the law invoked by Magestro unconstitutional and in violation of the separation of powers. No charges were filed, but the publicity was once again embarrassing. The Marque Club owners sued Ivery and Lofton, but unsuccessfully.

"It got aggravating and frustrating," Ivery said, "because you want to move on. I guarantee if we had been winning, we wouldn't have heard about it as much." In spring 1988, at an event honoring the Packers-Bears rivalry, Remmel noted that one speaker made a crack about the Packers' bad reputation. Remmel shook his head and said,

"We had to put up with that. We were tarred with that brush. It was a difficult time. Temporarily, we got a reputation we didn't deserve. I got a sick feeling in the pit of my stomach when we had two sex charges in the news at the same time."

When the Packers finally won another Super Bowl in 1997, a Madison columnist mentioned the strip club incident in an article titled "Packers No Longer an Embarrassment." Columnist Mitch Albom mentioned it, along with the sexual assault charge against Lofton, in a piece about Lofton during one of his three Super Bowl appearances with Buffalo. In 1999, when the Packers considered drafting a college player with questionable character, a columnist brought it up. In 2003, when Lofton was inducted into the Pro Football Hall of Fame, a Wisconsin newspaper columnist mentioned both incidents. The embarrassment seemed to never fade.

Ivery had legitimate hope for 1987 and perhaps a few additional years. No longer playing running back, a position notorious for punishing hits and short careers, he had proven himself as a receiver and special-teams player and thus could be a valuable contributor for the Packers. That is, if he could still hide his drug use and remain free of any new injuries. He managed one but not the other.

In 1987, the Packers expected to continue using Ivery, their only backup receiver with experience—a nine-year veteran—in their shotgun offense and as a reliable third-down receiver. He would also play on special teams as a blocker and tackler. No longer the potential game-changing running back that Dickey and Coffman thought might break Packers records, he remained skilled, smart, and reliable. Wright said Ivery "reacted well to changing coverages and seldom made assignment errors" and made clutch catches. Despite his injuries—large and small—he was valuable to the team.

In an August scrimmage, he was hit in the back while reaching for a slant pass. He grasped his lower back in pain. Two days later, the pain had become so severe that he couldn't practice. An exam revealed that a small fragment of a disc had protruded into his spinal canal.

With his 1986 neck strain, this was his second spinal injury. The team physician recommended surgery; Ivery sought a second opinion. At the end of August, he said he preferred physical therapy, hoping it would heal without surgery and allow him to play that season. He was placed on injured reserve.

Packers fans were not enthusiastic about the 1987 season. In the spring, shockingly, more than 200 people declined the opportunity to buy season tickets when their names rose to the top of the waiting list. In the final two exhibition games, there were more than 12,000 empty seats in the first and 18,000 in the second. Potential new players gave Green Bay the side-eye. According to Christl, young players preferred to play in warmer weather in a bigger city with a more diverse, vibrant social life, and with better endorsement possibilities. They didn't want to play for a head coach they heard was a jerk, nor for a franchise that, rumor had it, was stingy. *Sports Illustrated* ran a feature by Frank Deford giving the reasons Green Bay might no longer be suitable for an NFL team. (He mentioned, among other issues, the Lofton/Ivery/Magestro embarrassment.) He said only four players lived there year-round and suggested the Packers abandon their quaint hometown for Milwaukee.

As a strike loomed, the Packers opened their season against the visiting Los Angeles Raiders, Lofton's new team, and suffered a 20-0 loss. Weary and leery, fans booed Gregg as he exited the field but cheered Lofton before and after the game. They chanted, "Strike! Strike! Strike!" seemingly preferring to end the season rather than endure another disappointing performance. In late September, the NFLPA initiated a strike that lasted 24 days. Meanwhile, Ivery remained on injured reserve. Players picketed outside the Packers' practice field where replacement players were training, shouting insults such as "Scabs!" and "Whores!" at the intruders.

Ivery found himself in a difficult position; having opted for back surgery after a month of physical therapy, he supported the strike but was uncertain about his prognosis post-surgery. Joining the strike would mean losing several weeks of pay—what if his back injury jeopardized his football career? He had a family to support and a future after the NFL to plan for. If he chose to stay with the team for financial security, he would be betraying the union. Ultimately, Ivery remained on the team, aligning with about 15 percent of NFL players, while continuing his treatment. Fortunately, the Packers' union representative did not criticize him, understanding Ivery's circumstances, and noted that Ivery had attended meetings and supported the union.

By early November, Ivery underwent back surgery to remove a disc. The strike ended after three games primarily played by replacement players. When the Packers' replacements achieved a 2-1 record, the small Lambeau crowd cheered, finally seeing the win column surpass the loss column. Ivery could not return to play for the remainder of the season, which the Packers finished with a 5-9-1 record. Ironically, it was the replacement players, not the veterans, who managed to secure a winning record.

In early January, the Packers "relinquished the right of first refusal" for Ivery, which meant he was a free agent and could pursue another team or consider retirement. He hadn't played in 1987 and had undergone back surgery, leading the Packers to determine they no longer needed him, despite his performance in his final game in 1986.

Ivery realized his time in football was over when his surgeon warned him that playing could increase his chances of spinal cord damage with just one wrong hit to his back. He reflected, "All those injuries plus the back surgery.... Cocaine and injuries wore me down." His body had endured various injuries—knee, shoulder, thumb, neck, ribs, and especially his back. Other injuries he had managed through medication and determination, but the risk to his spinal cord was not one he was willing to take.

Like many who struggle with addiction, Ivery's drug use influenced how he perceived this transition in his career. He shared, "Shit, Jerry, for me, at the time, I was content with it. I was given an opportunity with the Packers, which I appreciated, but I was still taking random drug tests—they could call me in at any moment. So, I said to myself, 'I don't have to worry about pissing in the cup no more.'" Ultimately, he wrote a letter officially declaring his retirement from the NFL.

He believes that his illicit drug use (and alcoholism) combined with prescription drug use to create a powerful addiction that seized him physically, mentally, and emotionally. Regarding the pain medication administered by the team, he said, "That played a part, no doubt. Before, I didn't know what drugs made you feel like. I had never taken pain medication. My medicine was always ice. After my first knee injury, I started experiencing drugs that make you feel no pain, emotionally or physically. Pain-relieving drugs became more routine after that first injury."

Dickey, summing up Ivery's career, said,

> I've told people he had everything that could have led to a Hall of Fame career. Others who have made it were uninjured, unscathed. Take Barry Sanders. What if he injured the same knee twice in the first three years? Or Walter Payton? It doesn't matter who it is. Sometimes you got to be lucky. Especially when *no one touches you*? Like his first injury. He was just unlucky. Some are drafted by good teams where it's almost easy. Franco Harris was drafted in 1972, and the Steelers had a really good offensive line, and he's running through huge holes and playing fantastically, but if he had been drafted by an expansion team with a bad offensive line? You need all the pieces around you, and not everyone has that.

"To remember how terrific he could have been just makes you sick," Corrick said.

We lost him before he had a chance. He ran with power. He ran with speed. He ran with elusiveness. He could catch the ball. It was just a shame. He had a chance to be really special. He was one of those deceptive guys. He really carried his pads well. I thought he was everything you wanted in a back, just a complete guy."

Corrick said without the injuries, Ivery "might have turned out to be a Hall of Fame kind of guy. He was just tremendous, and he was a good person. He got into those drugs because of the pain. I liked his running skills: the God-given natural running ability. I liked his durability. He had been such a workhorse for Georgia Tech." In another interview, Corrick said, "When people ask me my greatest disappointment, I tell them the Eddie Lee Ivery story. The fans of Green Bay have never had a chance to see how great this young guy really was."

Langenkamp said, "Even after his second injury, he could still have one of those long runs, and it was like a flash of nostalgia. His career could have been so much more productive. I always felt for him. He had a trace of sadness in him."

McCarren said, "He averaged around 4.5 [4.4] for his career, and to have those two injuries—guys don't *do* that. *Healthy* guys don't do that. If you're averaging 4-plus, it's amazing especially after having serious injuries two of your first three years." (Walter Payton averaged 4.4 yards per carry; Tony Dorsett, 4.3; Eric Dickerson, 4.4. All are in the Hall of Fame.)

Koch said if an offense can gain 4 yards on first down, the defense has to prepare for a pass or run on second down, which makes it more possible to deceive the defense. He said Ivery "could make linemen look a little better than they were. We all saw the potential. What could we have been if we had had him full speed?" With a chuckle, he said, "But at three-fourths, he was still pretty damn good."

In answer to a newspaper reader's question in 2002 about all-time great Packers running backs, Christl wrote, "If Eddie Lee Ivery had stayed healthy, he might be the standard by which others were measured." In a 2017 story on the Packers website, about the many critical injuries in the 1970s and 1980s that "sucked the life out of the franchise," Christl, who by then was the Packers historian, listed five players, his top example Ivery, who had shown "flashes of greatness" in his first preseason.

Harlan serves on the committee to select players for the Packers Hall of Fame and said when the committee meets, Ivery's name is mentioned every year, not as a nominee but as a "What if?" Harlan said, "Someone will say, 'There's a guy who could have been as good as anybody in the NFL.' Think about what records he would probably still hold today because he had that kind of potential.' Not just to be a Packer all-time great but an *NFL* all-time great. But he was never able to stay healthy long enough. To this day, his name still comes up."

Ezra Johnson said that, in that era, injured players were rushed back into action too soon:

> They were so foolish. He's a running back and gets injured, and when training camp starts, he's back practicing. Unlike today, these guys have to get cleared, and they know how to take care of somebody they're going to count on. Nowadays, they don't wear them out in preseason and camp. He had to jump right back in, like he had never gotten hurt. They didn't ease him back into things. You have something special, and they treat a diamond like it was glass. Just throw him right back in there. In practice we hit him, tackled him. Physically, it takes a year, with those types of injuries, for a guy carrying the ball, to get right back in it.

Former NFL players say when they retire, they miss the camaraderie. Johnson said,

> The locker room, my teammates. I miss the money, of course, but in that locker room, you have lifetime friends, a bond with guys that is unparalleled. You can't understand it unless you lived it, to be a part of something where everyone is in it together. What I do has a direct effect on what we're trying to accomplish. To grow to love guys as brothers and friends, to have a bond that's awfully hard to be broken. I miss that. Nothing else is like it. You're talking about blood, sweat, and tears, giving your all, every bit of yourself. If I quit on a play, it affects everybody. What I do has a direct effect on somebody else's career. I've been retired thirty years and we're still buddies when we get together. It's like a family reunion.

McCarren said he misses "doing something at the highest level, playing against the best in the world. That's a special deal, and you don't get those opportunities often." Like others, he misses "the guys."

"You're all pulling on the same end of the rope. You meet people that you don't always have a lot in common with, but you fight together. You don't find that often in other areas of life. You might not see each other for years, then you pick up where you left off."

Koch agreed. "Everybody will ask if you miss the money or the fans applauding," he said. "It's not the money, the people clapping; it's the people you work with. You sweat bullets with them. You see them injured and feel for them. It's a special place to be, on an NFL team, pulling for that one goal. I became a lawyer after football, and it's not the same."

Ivery joined that community of ex-NFLers navigating life without football's toil and purpose. Former Tech teammate Stover, who was a resident at the same addiction recovery program as Ivery in the late 1990s, said, "There was no one to mentor Black athletes back then. Many of us needed guidance and weren't prepared for fame and money. Then, after football, you ask yourself, 'Who am I now?'"

Ivery said retiring from the NFL "left a void in my life, so to fill that void, I went back to using cocaine heavily. I had stopped using for a while but not drinking." Only later did he understand the scope of his addiction and the web of connections that underlay it. "Now that I know about addiction, I think my street drugs were replaced by my prescription drugs, like the drugs for my back and other injuries: Percocet, Tylenol 800, all that. I didn't realize I was—I might as well say even if I stopped using illegal drugs, I didn't stop using drugs."

As Ivery's addiction worsened, it affected Anna and their children. At first, they remained in Green Bay, and the combination of cocaine, weed, alcohol, and free time provided Ivery with ample opportunities to make poor decisions.

"When I retired, I didn't care anymore," Ivery explained.

> I put drugs and alcohol before her and the kids. I was staying out all night. I'd close clubs down. I'd come home high and maybe drunk. My wife got tired of my abuse: sexual and physical. I put drugs and alcohol before her and the kids. I was devastated over not playing anymore. I didn't know what

> to do with my life. Once I went to Chicago—I said I had to go there for something—and didn't come back for two days. She finally got fed up.

One night, he went too far one time too many. "I was pretty tore up," he said, "I came home drunk and high and demanded sex. We got to arguing and I pushed her."

Anna picked up a cast-iron skillet and swung. His football instincts—peripheral vision, quickness—may have saved his life.

"As I turned, if I hadn't seen that pan, I wouldn't be here today." He ducked, and instead of his head, she clanged a hole in the wall. He fell asleep and woke up alone. She called from Kentucky and said she and the kids were headed to Tampa.

He was angry, then relieved. He said, "I thought, 'How could you leave me without telling me?' But that also meant I didn't have to hide my drug use from her or the kids. I didn't have to worry about her arguing with me. I could do what I wanted. There was less hassle, and I didn't have to use the basement." For an addict, coming home to an empty house wasn't so bad. He soon realized there was nothing for him to do in Green Bay, so he moved to Atlanta.

According to the ESPN documentary *Broke*, by the time NFL players have been retired for two years, 78 percent are bankrupt or under financial stress. They may have heard such stories but think it won't happen to them. Most don't realize how short their careers will be or think about retirement and decades of expenses. In what careers do people retire in their 30s? Ivery was no exception. When he moved to Atlanta, he had $75,000 in severance pay and some money left over from his salary but little else. He had plenty of money while playing but didn't think beyond that (he suspected Anna secretly put away money for her and their children).

Over the years, college football media reports featured his name less frequently as more running backs broke the single-game rushing record, and his yardage fell down the list. (As of summer 2024, his 356 yards against Air Force was tied for 15th.)

He reappeared in the news, though, when someone at an Atlanta hospital broke the law.

Chapter 17

Betrayal

The timeline in this chapter may be off here and there. An addict's memory is not always clear. Readers of an addict's story should expect some ambiguity.

According to Twerski, an addict who expresses denial about reality isn't technically lying because a person *knows* when they're lying, but addicts *believe* they're telling the truth.

"You can often tell if someone's lying, but if *they* think they're telling the truth, you don't get those signals," Fluker said. Denial and other mental defenses function to "protect the addict from some intolerable, unacceptable, and catastrophic awareness." That awareness is that the consequences of using are worse than those of sobriety, which is obvious to non-addicts, but reaching that stage for addicts is arduous. Ivery was nowhere near that point when he returned to Georgia. He needed to acknowledge his distorted self-perception and change his behavior, but "addictive thinking" would not allow that. Fluker said that since long-term abstinence and recovery are difficult, an addict thinks, "Who wants to do that?"

Twerski wrote that addicts are sometimes in denial due to the stigma of being an addict ("That's not the Eddie Lee I knew"). Most people viewed Ivery as a family man, a fun-loving, hard-working athlete they could rely on. Admit you're powerless over something? Show weakness or moral failure? Not someone of his stature. Accepting that they can't control their drug use is humbling because they struggle to accept being powerless over life—particularly for someone known for his power.

Denial allows for fantastical thinking, and until denial is overcome, addicts are not lying when they say they are not addicted. They believe it, so they give "good" reasons for their lifestyle. An addict might say to themselves, "I use because…" and whatever comes next is valid to them. These reasons may be convincing, particularly when spoken by someone as engaging as Ivery, making it easy for family to get taken in. Fluker, who has counseled addicts and families of addicts, noted that it's part of the self-deception that accompanies addiction. She said, "It's hard for families because they believe what they're told by the addict, so it doesn't feel like they're being lied to. And they *want* to believe them."

Addicts often project the blame for their addiction onto others or circumstances. It may have been legitimate if Ivery blamed his injuries, the pain meds, or pressure to perform, but to begin recovery, he needed to accept his part in his addiction. A mantra in the addiction/recovery world is, "You can't change anyone but yourself." It's one declaration an addict will do almost anything to avoid. And he did. For 15 years, Ivery's life was marked by betrayal, dishonesty, and manipulation. His wife and children, his Thomson family, and his alma mater all felt the fallout from his addiction. They would all be hurt and exasperated.

Carrying the football, Ivery was known for his power and deceptive speed. Driven by his addiction, he learned another kind of deception. He parlayed his big smile, his lovable nature, and his football fame into ruses. He learned to charm people into helping him get drugs. Thomson residents might recall his final heroic game at The Brickyard, and he would reminisce—and perhaps ask for a little money to tide him over. *Did you know Bart Starr was my first NFL coach? Did I tell you about the time I blocked Lawrence Taylor? When I was the leading receiver against the Super Bowl champ Giants? What about when we beat No. 10 Notre Dame without throwing a single pass?*

His family deeply loved him, repeatedly forgiving him and giving him extra chances, often looking the other way. He took advantage of their hopefulness and love. It is easy to criticize such families, but when an addict is in *your family*, you want to believe them and root for them. Recognizing yourself as an enabler doesn't mean you stop being one. You search for any small hint of hope and cling to it.

Ivery's family clung to hope, prayed, and believed. From the moment Bennie Mae learned of her brother's drug use, she joined her grandmother in praying for him and never wavered.

Fluker said,

> Everyone makes fun of enablers, but if family sees the addict is in danger, they'll do everything they can to try to prevent something bad from happening. They're scared to death that something bad will happen. They orient themselves around this. If somebody had cancer, you'd take them food, take them to treatment, etc., and it would be good. But with addiction, when they do that, they're supporting their use without realizing it.

Ivery's family was in that hazy zone: how to help a loved one but not perpetuate addiction. Fluker said that if family can maintain a relationship with the addict while they're using—though that's difficult—then being loving and supportive when the addict finally, genuinely realizes they need to change can work. However, the addict needs that realization to sink in. And the family needs to find a way to keep that relationship without enabling. That is tricky.

Once addiction takes hold and draws the family in, Fluker said it's typical for everyone to feel shame. Families may not be the ones addicted, but the addiction of one family member tends to warp the lives of the rest. Ivery's addiction brought shame to his family, but they continued to love him. The family in denial hears people tsk at them, and they tend to believe those judging them have a point. Like many families, some of Ivery's excavated their shared past like coaches watching game film, looking for why Ivery's addiction happened—and inevitably asked, *Did I have something to do with it?*

In Ivery's mother's and grandmother's home, above the living room sofa, was a large, framed picture of Ivery in a Packers uniform, mid-stride, airborne, leaping with a football. Sitting beneath the picture, Bennie Mae said,

> When I was five years old, I couldn't walk, and my grandmother stayed with me in the hospital. Eddie Lee's wife always wanted to know why he is hurting. Anna thought there was something he wouldn't talk about. I thought and prayed about it. Did he think I got more attention because I was sick? All the attention was on me, the only girl.

She added, "I think he used drugs also because he thought, with him coming out of poverty, he had disappointed everybody. Made them envious? Thought he had the big head? Somehow thought he was above his raising? Because he made it big, stood out?"

She shook her head. "But he had *always* stood out. Even before he made it big." She paused and said, "We let him know we loved him."

Anna and the children remained in Tampa, and Ivery convinced her to let him join them, saying he was no longer an addict. She loved him and believed a father should be with his children. He got a retail job at a Tampa sporting goods store—a job often held by teens or college students.

"It was humbling," said the former professional athlete who now sold shoes and rackets. He should have been naturally successful, with his personality and sports knowledge, but his addiction caught up to him. "I was disappointed, embarrassed, so I eventually turned back to drugs." He wasn't familiar with Tampa, but, he said, "An addict has the instinct to figure out where drugs are sold, so it wasn't hard to find them." He started using again, staying out late with drug buddies.

Bret Starr had also moved to Tampa to start the business financed by the Starrs, which involved importing exotic animals. It was a desperate act of hopefulness, placing trust in him with money and independence. But it was perfect for Ivery, who resumed buying drugs from Bret, sometimes at Bret's house.

"He had a python with a head like a football," Ivery said. "He had an anaconda that had to be 8 to 10 feet long. I went there only a little. I was scared of those snakes."

When Bart Starr was asked over the phone about Ivery's drug use for this book, he feigned ignorance: "What drug use? Talk to some other folks and see if they remember." Newspaper stories with Starr commenting on Ivery's drug use were faxed to Starr—evidence he knew of it from nearly the beginning.

He called back and said, "I don't want to get into this" because it hadn't been a good time for him or the team. He talked about a minute. He claimed the first interview took place during a busy week, and he wasn't thinking clearly but wanted to talk as soon as he could. So, he denied knowing what he knew.

It was a painful topic.

In summer 1988, the Starrs hadn't heard from Bret for three days. They had paid for addiction treatment in Tampa, and Bret had quit. Sometimes he wouldn't respond for a long time, but he had been calling regularly. His parents would agonize over his silences, and when they heard from him, they tried to feel hopeful. After years of seeming sobriety followed by relapse, Bret could at least be counted on to call every day or two. The lack of a call often meant bad news.

Starr flew to Tampa, knocked on Bret's door, and shouted his name. From inside, he heard Bret's two rottweilers and loud rock music. Something smelled bad. No one answered, so Starr drove to a police station and returned with a deputy. They looked in a back window and saw Bret's body on the dining room floor. Tests revealed he had a small amount of cocaine, enough to stop his heart—which is what happened to Len Bias two years before.

In an interview for this book, Ivery said he was told one of Bret's snakes suffocated him. When told it was cocaine, he became quiet and stared at the floor.

The reunion with Anna lasted about a year. "I hid it for a while, then Anna figured it out again. She told me to go. This time was even more embarrassing because her parents owned the house we lived in." In the past, when Anna had confronted him about drug use, he had lied or lashed out. "I didn't get angry this time," he said. "I was just ashamed and embarrassed. I knew I was wrong." He moved to Thomson.

Once, Ivery's Aunt Naomi catered a birthday party, the bartender got sick, and Ivery took his place. "That was perfect for me, as an alcoholic," Ivery said. He charmed the guests while helping himself. "Everybody wanted their picture taken with Eddie Lee," a Thomson friend said. It's easy to overlook drinking when awed by fame.

Another tactic: payback. Childhood friend Grant, still one of Ivery's best friends, said, "He might have done you a favor when he had money, so you felt like you should pay him back."

Jerry Ivery said Eddie Lee used his fame without appearing to do so and manipulated people who didn't know of his fame.

"If you didn't know him, you wouldn't know he was in the NFL," he said. He added, "All addicts lie."

Jerry's path out of poverty wasn't through sports; it was the Army and a work ethic ingrained in Cherokee, where he toiled as a child, drove his father's wood-delivery truck, and, at 10 years old, ran a gas station on Saturdays with Grant. "*Everybody* did something," he said. (Jerry's mother told one of her sons she would pay for four years of college and no more. He didn't graduate after four years, so she stopped paying. Years later, he finished, paying his own way.)

Jerry announced his intention to join the Army in the 11th grade. "Everybody said I was crazy," he recalled. "I said, 'It's gotta be better than here.'" He enlisted two months after graduating from high school and served 20 years and five months, enough for a nice pension. While enlisted, he earned a two-year college degree. For a time in the Army, he worked in personnel, and when he retired, he was an E-8 Master Sergeant (E-9 is the highest). By then, he said, "I bossed people."

While he was in the Army, his family started a day care in Cherokee, and he ran it after his discharge. He also opened a construction and remodeling business. He modestly stated that, during that time, he was "surviving," but he owned a 5,000 square-foot house on six acres.

Many of Eddie Lee's awards, dusty and broken, ended up in Jerry's storage building behind that house. One plaque was empty where a football was originally attached. Observing the disfigured award, Ivery said, "People tell me it's a shame I let this happen."

Jerry had had an inkling about the severity of Eddie Lee's addiction when he and his wife visited Eddie Lee and Anna in their Atlanta home during one off-season. "They had visited me in Germany," he said,

> and we reciprocated. It was an upsetting experience because at first all was good, but then they both left and left us there. And we had come to visit *them.* That's when I figured his drug problem was really bad. She came in at 2:00 and then Eddie Lee 30 minutes later. They went out together and came back separately. I said to my wife, "Let's go." I was upset, and we left in the morning.

Bennie Mae also worked her way out of poverty, first as a school secretary and then as a teacher's aide. Next, she worked at a shoe store, eventually becoming its manager. She stayed there for 30 years. She enjoyed living in small-town Thomson and was able to take care of her mother and grandmother. When she retired, she continued to care for them, along with an aunt. She said Eddie Lee told her a drug dealer he owed money showed him a picture of a dead person and warned him, "That will be you if you don't pay what you owe." She said, "They didn't care nothing about you but money, so I prayed even harder."

> Eddie Lee would ask me for $5, and I wondered what he could do with $5 and, him being my brother, I gave it to him—even though I knew. I didn't want him in jail for stealing. I'd pray as I gave it to him.... He stole from our aunt who came from Chicago. He stayed with her. He stole a check out of her checkbook and forged it. I paid the liquor store where he wrote the check, and they gave me the check.

She kept that canceled check in case there might be an occasion to use it. Years later, there would be.

Fluker said enablers worry they're punishing the addict they care about if they allow natural consequences to follow bad behavior. Not wanting to seem uncaring, they help the addict avoid consequences. *If we don't pay the rent, the addict may become homeless.* Family members might concoct excuses for the addict's behavior because they don't want others to worry or because they don't want to feel embarrassed. They will clean up a mess because they are tired of looking at it; it is easier just to act instead of arguing. Enabling prevents the addict from perceiving which is worse: using or quitting. Enablers, Fluker said, also have the "illusion of control": If I say the right thing and do the right thing, maybe they will stop. However, addicts *need* negative consequences from bad behavior to motivate change. Everyone looking in from the outside—not the addict, not their family—can see that's obvious. But addiction distorts normal thinking.

On the other hand—maddeningly—according to *Beyond Addiction* by Jeffrey Foote, Carrie Wilkens, and Nicole Kosanke, confronting an addict is often futile. Addicts tend to get defensive and resist change more fiercely. Well-intended and no-nonsense-we-mean-it-this-time interventions can increase denial and other defenses. They recommend instead, "Treat people with respect and present them with a range of options, and their resistance will decrease. Nobody likes to be bossed around." It seems paradoxical, but that approach can help addicts feel understood and accepted, rather than judged, which might lead to changed behavior. (It may not work right away. Starr tried it; Ivery wasn't ready.)

Families of addicts are trapped. They know and they don't know. They suspect things that are likely correct but want to remain hopeful. They're unsure if vigorous intervention will help or drive the addict to something worse. They eventually realize they're being hoodwinked but believe they can navigate through the maze of deceptions. How can you give up hope when it's family—someone you toiled with in Cherokee, who, like you, carried the piss pot, sweated in the garden, and learned to work hard for everything.

Driven by their cravings, addicts fall into survival mode (you can't live without it, the brain tells them) and take crazy, impulsive risks. Addicts don't weigh pros and cons. Possible consequences that make most people hesitate (jail, sickness, death, public humiliation) are brushed aside. *I haven't been caught yet.* They don't worry about reputation or morality. Or safety. According to *Beyond Addiction*, repeated drug use alters the prefrontal cortex, where we weigh consequences, and revs up the brain's limbic system, from which urgency comes, so, "the hell with possible consequences; go for it! Smell marijuana, anticipate a good feeling, and go for it."

Ivery took dangerous chances. "I went out once," he said. "I was not familiar with Tampa, but you don't care where you go." At 3 a.m., he drove his Jeep Cherokee to a public housing project and got out of his car to engage a drug seller. "I gave him the money, and he gave me the drugs, and he tried to take the keys to my car. As I was going back to my car, he hit me in my jaw. I wrestled my keys from him and got in my car."

Another time, he drove to a club. He said,

> you could drive by, almost like a convenience store drive-thru. I rolled down my window, handed him $20, and he grabbed it. I wouldn't let go, and he pointed a gun at me, and I held my head down and just drove. I couldn't see where I was going. There were cars on both sides of my car, and somehow my car stayed straight. I was guarding that $20 with my life. That's how sick that disease is. I risked my life to keep $20 to buy drugs.

Later, after leaving Tampa, he convinced Anna once again that he was clean and stable, so they reunited in Thomson. Maybe having Anna and the children with him and living near his family would be good for him—that desperate hope families cling to. While looking for work, he approached town leaders who remembered his football exploits at The Brickyard. He wanted to coach football but lacked a college degree. With former Brickyard ol' Dog Ralph Starling and others as advocates, the school hired him as a teacher's aide, allowing him to work with the football team, though not as an official coach, alongside former teammate John Barnett.

During this stint with Thomson schools, Ivery successfully hid his addiction. Barnett said, "I never saw any evidence of it, and we were at times around each other outside of work. He was never late, never missed work, none of the things you associate with a substance problem. When coaches went scouting, we'd usually go out to eat and have drinks with our meals, and he'd have a drink, but the rest did, too."

Several years later, when Ivery again returned to Thomson, Barnett wasn't fooled. "I could tell," he said, "even though I wasn't around him a lot. I saw him at a basketball game, and he was very red-eyed. I could tell he had been drinking—at least." Barnett asked someone who knew Ivery what happened to the fellow they all liked so much.

The reply: "He went from Eddie Lee Ivery to Eddie Lee Asshole."

While addiction drove Ivery to drugs day after day, eventually the *euphoria* of cocaine—which lures an addict with an irresistible explosion of pleasure—became a distant memory. The enjoyment that makes the risks worth it diminishes as the brain adapts, but the grip of addiction does not lessen. Drugs and alcohol turned into something his mind and body *demanded*—less a pleasure he once relished.

Former Tech teammate and NFL veteran Ben Utt said one can't be sure if pain meds lead to addiction. However, he noted that once those meds lose effectiveness, the athlete still needs relief, and the mindset can easily become, "I'm a first-round pick not performing like one. I'll try something else." Utt explained that coaches can subtly pressure a player: "You're a first-rounder, but we can get someone to replace you." Utt added, "Nobody teaches you how to be in those circumstances. Sometimes drugs take away the pain, but they don't necessarily make you happy."

Ivery: "He got that right on the head."

Ivery and Anna attempted to repair their marriage in Thomson, but it didn't last long. Anna moved back to Tampa, leaving their daughter, Tauvia, with Ivery in the hope that the daughter could "save" her father. They moved into his mother and grandmother's house, where Bennie Mae also lived. He had nearly lost the house when the IRS planned to place a lien on it to cover unpaid taxes. Ivery beseeched Thomson mayor Bob Knox, Jr., whose office walls showcased University of Georgia degrees (undergraduate and law), a drawing of "The

Arch," a famous entryway to the UGA campus, and a certificate announcing Knox's membership in the Sphinx Club, a UGA honor society. With Knox's help, a judge in Augusta transferred ownership to Bennie Mae.

They were able to keep the house, but what happened inside it became unbearable. "When he would come home," Bennie Mae said, "you could see fear in his eyes. He was looking foolish, paranoid, looking behind him to see who was there, saying the police were outside. My brother scared me so bad he was so paranoid. I thought he was going crazy."

She said she smoked a little weed and drank alcohol when she was young, but "I didn't know what I was doing. I'd feel miserable the next day if I got drunk. So, I didn't understand the appeal of it. I knew he was hooked when I saw that. To see my brother like that—my heart melted. I'd think why would somebody—? How is that a good feeling? They say you're trying to get the next high, but it looked like misery to me."

"They got tired of my addiction, too," Ivery said. He and Tauvia were asked to leave. His behavior was poor, and he put them at legal risk if drugs were found in their home, so they moved into an apartment. Bennie Mae said Tauvia faced teasing at school, where both she and Eddie Lee were called "junkie."

"They picked at her," Bennie Mae said. "We're a praying family. That could have broke her, but she laughed it off. She didn't let it hurt her." One evening, he left Tauvia home alone while he bought drugs. When he returned, he found a note from her next to his drug paraphernalia; it said she didn't want to stay there and watch him kill himself.

Not even leaving his daughter at risk shocked him out of his addiction. Jerry said Eddie Lee, high and in tears, once told him he took Tauvia with him to get drugs and left her alone with a stranger while he went down the street to buy. When he returned, they were gone. It took him 30 minutes to find her. She was fine, but, Jerry said, "He got scared. That was a breaking point. He said he wouldn't forgive himself if his daughter was hurt while he was trying to catch a high. I said, 'It's got you that bad?'"

But it was not a breaking point, even when Anna returned Tauvia to Tampa.

Fluker said, "When you're in seeking behavior, your brain says nothing else matters. They do harmful things to family, and it's not that they don't love them, but their primary loyalty is the drug. They think: 'If I don't get it, I'll die.' It's fight or flight. Judgment goes out the window. Their brain is not working correctly."

Anna realized that even during Ivery's periods of abstinence, he was just one drink or snort away from an ugly relapse. He did not yet understand what he would eventually come to learn: "I was *abstinent* but not in *recovery*." Tired of heartache and betrayal, Anna filed for divorce. "She did her best to save the marriage," Ivery said. "But something was missing, and what was missing was me." In an interview years later, Anna stated that God placed her in a marriage with Ivery to help him, but eventually it was time to let go. She ultimately learned the recovery mantra: No one can help him if he won't help himself.

The dissolution of his marriage was a (temporary) jolt for Ivery. He had, for a while, been able to manipulate Anna and take advantage of her love for him and her desire to have a complete family, but now he realized she was serious about staying away—and taking his children. So, he sobered up—for a while—and obeyed his grandmother.

Ivery getting his Tech degree came about by Dick Bestwick once again using a bit of manipulation—this time at Tech. By the late 1980s, he worked in athletic administration at Tech's rival UGA and periodically called Ivery's grandmother to ask about him.

"I had heard stories about *things*," he said. He eventually called Ivery to see if he was interested in completing his degree. Ivery expressed interest, and Bestwick contacted the Tech athletic department to suggest they assist him. Bestwick noted their lack of enthusiasm, so *he* proposed helping Ivery finish—at UGA. Shortly after, someone in the Tech athletic department called Ivery, arranged for him to enroll, and found him an apartment near campus. It would not do for one of

Tech's greatest athletes—addict or not—to hold a UGA degree.

Ivery's return to Tech was facilitated by the National Consortium for Academics and Sports (NCAS), which helped former college athletes complete their degrees. (It was renamed in 2018 the Institute for Sport & Social Justice.) Ivery received the Courageous Student-Athlete Award from the NCAS and the NCAA Foundation a few months before graduating in 1992 with a degree in industrial management.

Assistant athletics director Jack Thompson was still enamored with Ivery, who stopped using drugs (though not alcohol) while finishing at Tech, despite stories he had heard. "He had a fabulous personality," he said, "even during his bad days. He had that smile. He just sparkled." He said Ivery was watched closely and given regular drug tests. "I was on top of him constantly," he said. "I had to treat him like he was a new student. We put all our resources into him because he really wanted to get his degree. Therefore, I was so surprised when he relapsed."

After Ivery graduated, a Tech alum helped him get a job as a sales manager with Russell Athletic in Alabama, which manufactured athletic apparel and uniforms. This should have marked the beginning of The Great Eddie Lee Ivery Redemption Story: a superb athlete messes up, finds help from people who care for him, quits using cocaine, graduates from a prestigious university, leverages one of the touted Tech connections to get a job, and transforms his life. A touching, inspiring story. However, that story would have to wait. The job lasted about a month.

After completing job training, he drove toward Thomson with $1800 from a freshly cashed check. He planned to celebrate his sobriety and job and tell his family about a delightful woman he met with a bright smile. He intended his first stop in Thomson to be a basketball court; while football was in his past, he could still shine playing hoops. The thrill of basketball was not like besting an NFL linebacker, but it satisfied his desire to compete and win. As he passed through Atlanta, he stopped near the house where he and Anna once lived to fill up his Mercedes. Spotting a nearby liquor store, he bought a Heineken, took it to his car, popped it open with his teeth, and drank it in one swig. The alcohol surged from his bloodstream to his brain, prompting a snap decision that would ruin the life he had so strongly desired and had briefly achieved.

Fluker said, "That's relapse. That's not being vigilant. Maybe he should have had someone with him. That's the addiction thinking: 'I can have one beer and be OK.' That part of his brain gets that dopamine rush, and there you go."

There he went.

Twerski wrote that addicts often say they can quit any time because they have a different conception of time. Stopping for one day or several hours? That's "time." Outsiders think it's *obvious* an addict can't stop any time because they keep relapsing, but, he wrote, "the addict thinks in terms of minutes.... All of the substances addicts use produce their effects within seconds or minutes." That quick high is instant gold. If an addict were offered a drug that would give them the best high they ever had but took two to three days to take effect, they would decline because "part of addiction is the immediacy of the high." An addict who abstains for a few days or months will convince themselves they can quit any time. They think they've accomplished something. That is abstinence, not recovery.

As Ivery had changed directions to fool defenders, after downing that Heineken, he reversed himself. Looking back, he couldn't explain his rash, consequential decision. He said, with a snap of his fingers, that something popped into his mind. "I started east towards Thomson," he said, headed to a normal life, "but then turned around to my old stomping grounds. Just like that, I was back in my addiction."

He didn't resume slowly, as when he first started. He picked up where he left off and burned through all his money. Then he drove to Thomson without having slept all night, heading to the gym. He didn't reach it. He woke up in a hospital with a broken arm and a state trooper asking him what happened.

He didn't know.

Apparently, he had fallen asleep—or passed out—and hit a tree in front of a church near Thomson. His Mercedes was smashed. He thought he reached—or fell—to the right, so his chest and face didn't crash into the steering wheel. No charges were filed.

When his family took his mother to see the car, before they knew he was not seriously hurt, she cried out in despair, "Oh my child."

Ivery said, "They hadn't seen me yet, and she thought I was through. Nobody should have survived that crash." Jerry said in the hospital Eddie Lee "acted like a clown, goofing around"—and on the way home bought a bottle of Hennessy cognac.

Ivery returned to Russell Athletic, but they had heard about what happened and fired him immediately. "They told me it was best we separate," he said.

Ivery returned to Thomson and again moved in with his mother and grandmother. Bennie Mae said, "We got embarrassed about him, the drugs. I didn't want to be around him. He disappointed so many people who were so hurt and gave up on him. But my grandmother and me, we prayed and persevered."

Once, Ivery was speeding and braked as he approached a car in front, but a car hit him from behind. He had been up all night drinking and began yelling at the driver who hit him. When the police arrived, he was stunned that the officer placed him in the back seat of the police car. He asked why he was being detained since he had been hit from behind, and the officer said he could smell alcohol. His lawyer arranged for the charges to be dropped.

Ivery saw his children rarely from 1993 to 1995. Then, he found some degree of abstinence and was once again persuasive to Anna, who allowed the children, but not herself, to move in with him in Thomson. Perhaps having parental responsibility would set him straight. However, he soon resumed using, prompting Anna to summon them back to Tampa.

Joseph Greene arrived in Thomson in 1959 as an insurance salesman. Without a car, he walked from house to house selling policies. He sold a life insurance policy to Ivery's grandmother for 17 cents a week.

Every week, he walked to her house to collect the payments. He rose through the company to become vice-president, later became chairman of the Georgia Board of Regents, which oversees all public colleges, and taught at Augusta State University. Greene said when Black Thomson residents learned of Ivery's addiction, they

> felt very hurt and highly disappointed, but also helpless. He was a shining knight, and then there was a chink in the armor. Thomson Blacks felt more *pain* than anything else. Many of his former teachers felt pain and anguish. My wife was personally hurt. But some of us never gave up on him. It's like he was a child who makes a mistake. You're hurt and angry, but you don't toss him out.

Once, in Thomson, Ivery's former high school assistant coach Dale Ricks (who nabbed Ivery's jersey after his final high school game) saw Ivery fishing with some buddies. Ricks said, "He was so high I don't think he knew who I was."

No one in Thomson would hire him, so Jerry gave him a job at his daycare working with the children, where Ivery worked for about a year.

"He's family," said Jerry. "When he's of sound mind, he's a good motivator and he was a really good mentor to the kids." Still, Jerry was wary. How do you love an addict and be compassionate yet not feel like a sucker? Knowing Eddie Lee might still be using, Jerry underpaid him, hoping that less money would mean less ability to buy. But Jerry discovered Eddie Lee and a friend were entering the office at night to steal money. Eddie Lee would leave the back door unlocked so there would be no sign of a break-in. He didn't steal all the money, hoping the theft wouldn't be noticed, but businessman Jerry did. Jerry let it go, figuring—between the stolen money and his reduced salary—he was getting what he would get anyway.

"He thought he was sneaking it," Jerry said, "and I knew. I might have raised sand if I was paying him the full amount for that position." Then Eddie Lee stole too much; Jerry could ignore it no longer.

He confronted the friend, who said it was Eddie Lee's idea. When

Jerry asked Eddie Lee, a contrite Eddie Lee said, "The only person that can help me is myself. You can talk to me all you want, but until I decide to change, I won't change." Eddie Lee told Jerry he had made up his mind to get clean. But he didn't.

A newspaper reported that police had said there was a "domestic dispute" between Ivery and his girlfriend. "Yep," Ivery admitted. "That was another part of my addiction. We were staying together, and we argued one night. I left, and she wanted me to stay away, and I came back, so she called the police. More bad judgment due to addiction."

This could be about when the Nissan incident happened. Eddie Lee told Jerry he was serious about rehab, that a program in Atlanta had accepted him, but he needed to borrow a car to get there. How can family decline that? Eddie Lee zipped off in Jerry's prized Nissan 280ZX, a sporty two-door muscle car. Paul Newman raced in one.

"He took my car to go to rehab," Jerry said, "and I've never seen it since. He doesn't know where it is, either. It wasn't my main car, but still—he came to me all upset and said he's gonna get his life together but didn't have transportation. I gave him gas money, and he used that to buy drugs. I asked where my car was, and to this day I don't know."

Out of options in Thomson, Ivery moved to Atlanta and became one of the city's drug-addicted homeless, sometimes panhandling for money. He stayed nights with "random folk who smoked" and gave him space on shabby sofas in filthy apartments. He worked day labor at labor pools. Day laborers arrived very early in dark mornings (to allow time for transportation to the worksite) in dingy rooms to get hired for the day, doing menial work such as construction site cleanup, truck loading, garbage collection, hotel room cleaning, window washing, or landscaping. They usually got about half of what the labor pool company was paid for their work, due to deductions for fees, transportation, lunch, and equipment.

One labor pool company was called "Temporary People." At the end of work, soup kitchens were usually closed, so laborers often had to choose between work and dinner. Day labor suited an addict's haphazard life. Just do the one day's work and get meager pay. Often, the nearest place to cash their check was a liquor store, purchase required. Many received their pay and promptly found a dealer.

Precisely how long this Atlanta phase lasted, Ivery can't recall.

Ivery now mostly used cheaper crack cocaine. Crack, he said, gives a high that lasts only a few seconds, but it is a doozy. Crack can drive you crazy, one nearly insatiable desire at a time. He said, "That first hit of crack, you spend the rest of the time looking for that same high. You'll chase that first hit for a week. Then you'll stop for a day, get that first one again. You get that only if you get a break. Each new time, you start searching for that same feeling."

That's quite a dilemma. Dare they take a break for a day or so to feel that first high again, only to again be dragged unmercifully along by its irresistible pull? Ivery said,

> It's a sensational feeling, not really a high, a sensational feeling. Powder cocaine is more mellow, and crack cocaine is a 10-second sensational feeling. You suck it in, blow it out your mouth, feel it, then it's gone. If it's real good stuff, it will last longer than 10 to 15 seconds, but if it's a little piece that costs $20, it's gone in five seconds.
>
> My first hit of crack, I was addicted, like the pain shots I got in the hospital. I got so many of those shots, my butt was so sore that I had to take it in the shoulder. I'd get a euphoric feeling and fall asleep, but with crack, you get the good feeling, but you don't fall asleep. You keep hitting all day to keep it going. Now, I think, what the fuck, damn, what did it really do for me? It gave me a divorce; I lost my house; I wrecked cars.

He was amazed that he kept his will to live and wasn't convicted of a crime or killed. "It became like I didn't care with all I had lost. My wife and kids were gone. She took care of them with no help from me. I had nothing to live for."

Many of Ivery's former Tech teammates gathered regularly for camaraderie, to work out, and to recall that era at Tech when being a

Black athlete disrupted expectations. They loved seeing their fun-loving buddy Ivery, but during this part of his life, he didn't show. "I'm not sure if they tried to find me," Ivery said. "But I was unreachable. I don't remember having a stable contact method." Bessillieu said he once saw Ivery at a Tech football game, and "he looked bad. We'd invite him to stuff, and he wouldn't come."

Once, after using drugs at an apartment in East Lake Meadows—a notoriously dangerous public housing complex rife with drugs—he began to hallucinate. His heart raced, and he tore up the apartment.

His hosts thought he had overdosed. Did they call 911? No, they kicked him out. He continued to act wildly outside the door, prompting someone else to call the police.

When the police arrived, they knocked on the door where Ivery was standing. However, the residents had scrambled out the back via a balcony. As the police spoke to him, he calmed down and "called out to Jesus to help me." He attempted to open the locked apartment door and told the police he was okay, so they left.

"I felt that the Lord was watching over me," he said. "Somehow, I was never caught red-handed with drugs."

Lawrence Lowe spoke candidly about Ivery's addiction: "When I learned about that, I had been experimenting myself, so I wasn't one to point fingers or judge because he was my friend. Once I learned how severe Eddie Lee was, I said if he can't handle it, I can't handle it. We met several times, and before we knew it, it was too late. He lost his family, and soon after, I lost mine. That's how powerful that stuff is."

Lowe, who had been a Georgia state trooper for a time, recalled a visit to Ivery's home in Atlanta. Already high, Ivery spotted the patrol car and feared the police were after him. He was relieved that it was his friend Lowe. They got high together.

Ivery and Lowe made a pact to support one another. Lowe said, "We talked religiously because we had to beat this addiction. That was a promise we made to each other. We talked, and if not, we knew one of us had slipped. We made that promise in the late 80s." They attended AA meetings at an Atlanta hospital, but that attempt at rehab didn't work.

David Sims, who played in the NFL for four years before a career-ending injury, later reflected on Ivery's addiction and wished he had kept in contact. "Maybe he wouldn't have had his drug problems," he said with a resigned shrug.

> Maybe I could have showed him the ropes. We went to school together, so I feel that what he did later is partly a reflection on me. Maybe he thought he was ahead of what he could handle, but there were still lessons he needed to learn. When I first heard about his drug problems, I assumed he'd come right out of it. But then I came home, and some friends told me what he was doing. I didn't know it was that bad.

Donnie Sewell said he didn't hear of Ivery's drug use until Ivery hurt his back. "Then I started hearing rumors," he said.

> I don't believe rumors unless I see it. Plus, I was dumb and naive about drugs. Once I was with the Miami Dolphins, and I saw someone sniffing something out of a camera film canister. I didn't know what it was until later. I asked him, "Do you do this before a game?" He said it made him feel better. I didn't know for sure about Eddie Lee until his family left him. I saw him in Atlanta, and he didn't look good. Then, later in the 90s, Lucius Sanford told me he was living in East Lake Meadows. I thought, "How could he be at the top of his game, make all that money, live a good lifestyle, and do that?"

What does it take for an addict to become desperate enough to seek help? Losing a job, losing family, going to jail, getting shot at, getting shot?

The *Beyond Addiction* authors wrote that addicts change when it becomes worthwhile to them, when the benefits of change appear to outweigh what they gain from using. Even though this means breaking a habit hard-wired in their brains, a habit that drives their every moment toward the next high but doesn't truly satisfy, then sends them careening off again. Even though treatment seems unbearably arduous, and stopping addictive behavior seems impossible. When making *that* kind of difficult change finally appears better than using, they become open to rehab. The Hazelden Clinic? That was a paid vacation where Ivery scoffed at the losers who genuinely needed rehab. Ivery had to believe deep down that he was also someone who needed rehab and that without it he was lost. Something had to shift to make real change worthwhile.

Sports journalist Bisher wrote an occasional column titled "For What It's Worth," an assortment of unconnected, brief statements or questions. Not top-quality journalism, it gave Bisher a chance to use thoughts he had collected. On February 3, 1997, that column included the following: "The Braves' first interleague game is scheduled June 13 at home against Baltimore. Good, I get to miss it. That's the week of the U.S. Open in Washington.... Did anybody say this after Brett Favre beat New England in the Super Bowl—that it was a case of over-Kiln? ... And whatever became of Eddie Lee Ivery?"

Two weeks later, Bisher wrote, "Folks from Thomson call in to say that Eddie Lee Ivery is back in his hometown working with youth in a social services program. Got his life back in order, and when you get back to the people who really know you, you'd better have."

Except, it wasn't true.

Chapter 18

This Ain't Football in Here

In the late 1990s, Ivery, who had lost just about everything important to him, started telling people close to him that he had had enough of drugs. Bennie Mae said, "He said he bought some crack and said he started doing it and said he thought, 'I'm tired of living like this. I don't want to do this anymore.'" He sounded weary and worn down. How many times had his family heard that? Ivery had attempted recovery several times, including when Tech paid for rehab, but then Jack Thompson said, "The next thing I heard, he was back on the streets."

"I think it took them leaving me for the second time," Ivery said, speaking of Anna and his children, "for me to realize how serious it was to get my life in order. I was never going to have a relationship with them with the lifestyle I was living." He correctly sensed Anna would not give him another chance without proving himself much more convincingly.

Twerski wrote that there is a "law of human gravity," which says a person will "gravitate from a condition that appears to be one of greater distress to one that appears to be lesser distress, never in the reverse." To an addict, alcohol or drugs appear to provide relief, so the hard work of abstinence seems to be the greater distress. Abstaining from a substance that the addict thinks has made life livable seems preferable. The critical point is when the *pain and misery* of using exceed whatever *relief* it provides, and abstinence is seen as the lesser distress.

Fluker said drug counselors don't necessarily want someone to reach "rock bottom" because "it could mean death or jail. Nowadays, they're talking about many paths to recovery." She said that at an addiction treatment center where she worked, some clients there by court order "had as good a chance as the rock-bottom person." Ivery had a hefty list of bad consequences of his addiction, but would their gravity lead to sobriety? Rock bottom for one addict may be, for another, just another step toward misery, jail, or death. There may or may not have been a lower bottom for Ivery, but he finally reached a low enough point that seeking treatment, however difficult it might be, was better than where he found himself.

Ivery recalled October 28, 1998, vividly: "I had been using cocaine," he said, "and something happened. I can't tell you what it was. For the first time, I said, 'God, please help me.'" He had realized before that he needed help, but something about this plea was deeper, more certain. "I was sick and tired of being sick," he said in an interview in a "Packers Alumni Spotlight" video on the Packers website.

After pleading with God, he pleaded with Stacy Robinson.

Robinson, who played on two Super Bowl winners (the team's leading receiver in the first) during a six-year career with the New York Giants, faced Ivery in December 1986, in Ivery's final NFL game. It was the only time Ivery was an NFL starting wide receiver, and he led the game in receiving.

Now working for the NFLPA, Robinson oversaw steroid and drug policy issues. Ivery reached out to Robinson, asking if they offered support for drug addiction. Robinson told him that they didn't have a drug rehab program for *former* players. Ivery hung up, disappointed and then angry. "Why *won't* they help a former player?" he fumed. "All those pain meds they gave me!"

That anger likely saved his life. He called back and pleaded again, this time sobbing. He shared how he had lost his family and money, pawned possessions, stolen, and manipulated those who loved and admired him. "Please help me," he begged.

Robinson said he would see what he could do.

October 28, 1998, was the last day Ivery used drugs.

Through Robinson's efforts, he was referred to the Oakhurst Recovery Program (ORP) at Oakhurst Baptist Church in Decatur, just east of Atlanta. This predominantly White, liberal Baptist church was originally part of the Southern Baptist Convention but was ousted for welcoming gay people as equal members. Notably, they held a baby blessing ceremony for a lesbian couple's newborn in 1990.

Oakhurst Baptist Church has garnered a reputation in Atlanta for its open-minded theology, inclusiveness, and activism. The ORP began in the 1980s as a ministry to unhoused people, providing overnight shelter for men picked up by the church van in downtown Atlanta. These individuals were taken to the church for a safe night's sleep in unused Sunday school rooms.

Funded by grants and donations, ORP evolved into a residential addiction treatment program that reflected the church's commitment to serving the community and addressing critical social issues.

Church volunteers cooked meals, took residents to appointments and movies, and taught creative writing, drama, and painting. They also led exercise sessions, provided tips on living on a budget, offered job-seeking advice, and held spiritual gatherings. When church volunteers prepared dinners for the residents, they shared those meals as friends, fostering a strong sense of community.

The church welcomed the men warmly, integrating them into their community. While the residents joined weekly Wednesday night dinners, attendance at church activities was not mandatory. Some chose to participate; others did not. All were treated equally with respect and kindness.

One church volunteer taught tennis lessons and took pictures for the fellowship hall bulletin board. When residents graduated from the ORP, a grand celebration took place in the fellowship hall.

Former ORP director Mayo Funderburg remarked that Oakhurst Baptist "was the heart and soul of everything that transpired" at ORP.

The *Beyond Addiction* authors point out that addicts in recovery need to do more than unlearn destructive behaviors (using drugs, living on the streets, stealing); they must also learn new behaviors, such as how to relax or find pleasure without drugs or alcohol. Taking the drug away leaves "a hole to fill," so addicts need to discover other ways for the brain to produce dopamine. So, ORP volunteers taught residents healthy ways to enjoy themselves, such as tennis or painting lessons, which provided a break from the heavy emotional and mental tasks mandated by the program while also demonstrating that there are ways to enjoy oneself that won't kill you.

Former ORP resident Chester Dixon, who later became a volunteer and then a paid staff member, said his interactions with church members helped him get clean. He said, "Mary Jo Crawford used to talk to me in a motherly way. That helped soften me up. She and her husband, Andy, were volunteers. She wasn't a trained addiction counselor, but I thank God for her. She *carried* me a few days."

Sometimes, healthy and compassionate interactions with another person helped residents see themselves anew—as human beings deserving of care and love.

"I thank God for Oakhurst," Dixon said. "You didn't have to pay them anything. You didn't have to do anything but change your life." He learned that those relationships, not only knowledge about addiction, could make a difference in his life.

"Where I came from, I was hardened. Now I find myself crying," he said. "I never did that. Back then, that was a sign of weakness, but in reality, it's a sign of strength. It was a simple lesson, but hard to get." He added, "Some think it's too soft if you change, but in reality it's strength."

Fluker said real recovery means long-term abstinence: not only whether addicts can stop but can they *stay* stopped. Addicts need to not use at all. Moderation will not work for nearly all of them. "Abstinence is not using," she said, "but in the treatment world, that's not enough. You need to do the emotional work to manage your life. Alcoholics Anonymous calls it 'emotional sobriety,' staying sober and being in healthy relationships."

ORP offered a safe residence, a private bedroom, meals, clothes, and other necessities—at no charge. It was highly structured and demanding. "A byproduct of addiction is becoming comfortable with chaos and confusion," Funderburg said, "so we provided a very clear and significant routine. Doing that allowed a person to work away from that chaotic and confused lifestyle and become accustomed to order and routine."

ORP leaders required discipline, honesty, humility, and obedience—none of which characterized Ivery's life as an addict. Funderburg said early on, ORP residents tested the rules and made excuses. "They cut corners when they could because they had *always* done that. We had to give structure that none of them had in the past."

New residents usually agreed to whatever was asked of them. They'd done that for years—if it meant getting what they wanted. But would Ivery stick to the ORP way if it *didn't* mean getting what he wanted? Addictive, manipulative thinking gets ingrained in the mind. Recovery is hard. Addiction is what they know, what has satisfied—even if only minimally and fleetingly—that aching demand for the next high that the addict's brain craves.

Many residents were expelled for breaking rules—some for getting drunk or high. Many left on their own. The undisciplined drug life may seem better than stifling demands that impede getting high. Funderburg said that wasn't surprising because most addicts in recovery—including him—had failed at it several times. Don't make their bed neat enough? Leave a messy room? That's extra kitchen duty. Do that too many times, and they're out. Any resident away from the place alone was immediately drug tested upon return. Fail it, they're out, immediately, any time of day. There's the train station, a block away.

Funderburg said the most challenging time for ORP residents was when they were alone and quiet at night: "Getting through quiet moments alone. That's when the disease starts to work its way in. You've had a tough day, the guys pushed you, then you're alone at night. It wouldn't be during the day that people would bolt and disappear, but at night when it got quiet, and the only voice they heard was their own. The key was, 'What was that voice telling you?'"

Would the voice tell them to find someone and say, "I'm having a hard time. Can we talk?" Or would it tell them to quit? *They called you a liar. They have too many stupid rules. They can't treat you like that. This is too hard. Let's go.*

ORP followed the Narcotics Anonymous concept of "the therapeutic value of one addict helping another." In addition to trained counselors, many staff, volunteers, and board members were recovering addicts (some were ORP graduates). Funderburg said they could be blunt with the residents, tell them,

> I was where you are. Now look at me. Stick with the program, and you can be clean, too. I'm not talking about what I read or what somebody taught me. I'm talking about what I *lived.* Talk about your shame. I get it. Talk about guilt. I get it. Letting people down, pain when you feel alone in a room full of people? I get it. You say it's hard; I get it, but I can get six guys in here right now who say it was hard, but they succeeded. What are you gonna do? Complain and cry because we're being too strict, or do you want to push through and get to the other side? What's it going to be?

Recovering addicts at ORP embodied hope and resilience. They fostered a supportive community but, crucially, were familiar with an addict's relentless supply of lies and manipulations, having once mastered that devious skill themselves. Each new resident was interviewed about their substance abuse history, family background, and previous treatment experience, but each one was also sized up: How will *this* one try to bamboozle us? No getting away with "I'm going to the basement to play with the dog." They would swat that ruse away halfway through the lie. "Addict helping addict" sounds nice, but they could be tough.

Addicts could tell their harrowing, sad drug sagas to men who wouldn't be dazzled by them. (Risked your life for one smoke? Crashed your car? Risked your daughter? Ho hum, done that.)

Fluker said telling drug stories can be helpful when they are talking to a safe person trained to help them make sense of their lives, so they can develop a helpful life narrative and deal with the question, "How did I get here?" Therapy, she said, "helps make sense of the world." Ivery needed to forge a personal narrative that explained both what *happened* to him and what he *chose* to do, one that helped him get a handle on his emotions, and, crucially, accept responsibility. He had to learn that addiction is both a disease and a series of choices. That would be difficult and not happen quickly. Funderburg said recovery is about "coming to terms with who you really are and who you want to be, and how that's gotten lost. Everyone had a different story of how drugs and alcohol were the answer, but ultimately found out it wasn't." He had to acknowledge that having divorced parents who were very young contributed to his addiction, as well as his choices.

> Decisions I made at age 14 that put me in the position I was in were partly my fault and partly theirs. We said to Eddie Lee, 'You can have all the good intentions in the world, but if you don't do the work, nothing's going to change.' It clicked for him, and he started doing the work, taking responsibility for his own behavior. That was the breakthrough for him.
>
> Eddie Lee had so much success, and to fall as far and hard as he did was really challenging. Confidence and self-esteem were a big part of being able to perform like he did. He had to have the will to physically do all those things.

To admit he caused his own misery was the opposite of a hard-charging running back who ran full speed from the get-go with the confidence he would handle whatever happened next. Funderburg said, "The story was, 'Let's go back in my life and see where my decision-making wasn't the best. Was it all on me? What is and isn't on me?' He fought back when we tried to push him. We got where that was coming from, an NFL star with huge expectations who got injured. We got that, but...."

Dixon worked as night manager while Ivery was at ORP, administering drug tests and making sure residents followed the rules, and disciplining those who didn't. He was sympathetic but firm. When he first arrived at ORP as a resident, like many, he thought he would skate through. Nod in approval when they talk, eat their food, do what they say, write what they say, admit responsibility, blah blah. But when he was first asked to write about himself, addiction counselor Ray Brown, a gravelly voiced no-nonsense addict-in-recovery, wadded up what he wrote—without reading it—and tossed it in the trash.

"He said it was all lies," Dixon recalled.

> It hurt my feelings, but I didn't see it. Eventually, I realized it really *was* all lies because I was an addict, and I lie. He was an addict himself; that's why he knew. He was the same way until he changed his life. First, he had me write 12 pages, then six, then three, and he threw them all in the trash. I thought I was doing something to come up with 12 pages of what I did wrong, but I was just trying to please him. He was hard on me, and that's good.

Like Ivery (eventually), Dixon realized they weren't falling for his baloney. "They forced me to act and think different," he said. "I had to change everything, including friends. I was hardened and rough when I got there, rough around the edges and in the middle. When I was rough, they were rougher. They didn't give it to me soft. They knew where I came from."

Dixon said he wanted to leave every day. "But I didn't want to go back to where I came from, sleeping on the streets, doing drugs and alcohol, getting locked up all the time. But you couldn't come back to ORP. It was a one-shot deal." Funderburg said they sometimes debated whether to take back someone who had left or been kicked out but decided their policy was good motivation: Give it all you've got; you can't come back.

Ivery stayed. He made his bed correctly. He did kitchen duty. He willed himself to follow the rules, as he had willed himself through two knee rehabs. After a rough start, instead of scheming how to manipulate, he listened and learned. He silenced the voice in the quiet that told him to give up. The recovery community is peppered with clichés: "Take it one day at a time." "You can't help someone who won't help themselves." "Be humble." "You're not greater than others here." "Accept the things you cannot change and pray for the wisdom to know what they are." Ivery took the clichés to heart.

ORP's approach to recovery, unlike places like Hazelden, where Ivery stayed 28 days, took months (Ivery stayed 14). Funderburg said,

"It's unrealistic to think someone like me who had been using for 18 years was going to change in 28 or 90 days. Some things will *begin* to change, but that they were allowed to be there 12 to 18 months gave them the time they needed to understand what those changes were, make the changes, live the changes, and work out the challenges they had in maintaining the changes."

Dixon said, "I was there 14 months, and at one year I thought I was ready to go, but I wasn't. Those extra two months helped me see I hadn't grown as much as I thought I had." Slowly, steadily, surrounded by supportive staff and volunteers, their basic needs met, residents were guided by addicts in recovery to leave addictive behavior behind and begin true recovery.

The ORP staff were initially unsure if they should accept Ivery. Would football fans in the church, especially Tech fans, elevate him when the program adamantly treated every resident the same? The NFL donated money to ORP, so would Ivery think the staff would give him special treatment to keep the funds flowing? Funderburg acknowledged the risks but argued that *he* was alive and well only because someone took a chance on *him*.

"Otherwise," he said, "I'm not here." He insisted any addict deserved an opportunity. After a lengthy discussion, they took a chance on their first NFL star. But he needed to understand that he must leave that status behind. As staff member Major Nesby drove Ivery to ORP, he told him they were familiar with his outstanding college career, his record-breaking game against Air Force, and being a highly touted first-round NFL draft pick.

Ivery's mind was locked in a pattern: turn on the charm, get what you want. He began scheming how he would manipulate the staff and the church—as he had done so often and well. He was desperate and perhaps at rock bottom, but the impulse to manipulate was strong, embedded. Would he find someone to smoke weed with him behind the kitchen?

"The first thing you need to know is that we don't give a shit who you were before," Nesby said. A stunned Ivery realized: These people mean business. Nesby reviewed the rules and schedule (precise neatness standards, daily chores, tightly controlled days, intense mandatory NA meetings and individual counseling, rigid curfew) and warned Ivery he would be treated the same as the others. When he arrived, the staff repeated what Nesby said. Dixon told Ivery, "This ain't football in here, no touchdowns. This ain't about your accolades. We don't care about that. You have to change like everybody else."

"We didn't talk about football, purposely," Dixon explained.

> That would feed into his ego. We had to talk about how to manage your life. Football was never brought up. If we talked about that, he wouldn't change. He would think he's big man on campus, and we didn't want him thinking that. We wanted him equal to everyone else. He had to be and do what everybody else did. He had a certain time to work in the kitchen, and if something wasn't right, I'd wake him up at night and take him to the kitchen to straighten it out.

Ivery told his cousin Jerry later they almost expelled him promptly for rules violations, such as not making his bed correctly. According to Jerry, "The first week they'd find anything wrong. They tried to make him quit." He said they challenged Ivery on whether he was only pretending to be serious about recovery, that they didn't want him to waste their time. But they allowed him to stay, and he settled into the program.

Twerski identifies two keys to recovery. First, addicts must lose faith in their current reasoning and accept that it is distorted. Second, addicts must embrace the possibility of a different perspective on reality, supported by someone they trust. That trust is challenging because they are told *Your way of thinking, which you have practiced for years and has worked for you (albeit self-destructively), and which to you is perfectly reasonable, is faul*ty. Who wants to hear that?

For Ivery, a key insight was that he could be a vibrant, healthy person beyond just being a football player. Gradually, over months, he pieced together a view of himself that could exist drug-free. He shared his childhood experiences, poverty, and shame with his counselors, and began recounting his life story with greater honesty, acknowledging both what had *happened* to him and the choices he made. He started the difficult process of forging a truthful narrative that made sense, created hope yet remained realistic about life as an addict.

There was poverty, shame, embarrassment, and pressure to perform—but there was also Eddie Lee Ivery, the man trying to learn how to manage his life as it had become. Funderburg said they emphasized to Ivery that he couldn't change the past, couldn't change that his knee was injured; that was the hand dealt to him. But how do you now play that hand? They challenged him: Come on now, you can't say you *really* believed the route you took would turn out well.

In the "Packers Alumni Spotlight" interview, Ivery said ORP helped him realize that football was not his whole life. Football brought him fame and money, but it also provided him easy access to cocaine. He learned that football is something you *do*, not who you are. "But all my life that's all I had done, so I had no other identity whatsoever," he admitted. A key to his recovery was accepting who he was as a whole person: the great athlete and the fallible man.

While Ivery was at ORP, he cut his finger and went to Grady Hospital, the downtown Atlanta health facility for the indigent. They asked the usual background questions, including address, employment, and insurance. He recalled the pain meds he had received playing football, reminded himself of their connection to his addiction, and told the doctor he didn't want any anesthetic. Ivery didn't want to "wake up that monster that still lies within me." He had become determined enough to say no, even to a legitimate use of an opioid.

Soon, someone at the hospital, in violation of the Health Insurance Portability and Accountability Act (HIPAA), emailed sports columnist Bisher that Ivery had been there for treatment. Bisher wrote, in an August 11, 1999, column, "When a fellow signing in at the ER at Grady Hospital gave his name as 'Eddie Ivery,' the doctor asked, 'Are you the Eddie Ivery who played at Georgia Tech?' Eddie said he was now unemployed and uninsured and adrift from his family. He was treated for cuts on one of his hands."

This was an intrusive, illegal violation of Ivery's privacy by someone at Grady and an unethical, unprofessional move by Bisher, who didn't confirm the story. Ivery was progressing well in the program but was vulnerable to emotional upheaval. Public shame could evoke painful memories and arouse temptation to ease anxiety via drugs or drink. He had compulsively turned to those so many times in the past to stanch all kinds of pain. Fluker said part of the reason addiction counselors encourage compassion toward addicts is to ease the stigma associated with being an addict, which can exacerbate shame and impede progress.

Ivery and an angry Funderburg wrote a letter to the paper describing what Ivery was doing and that his rehab was proceeding well. In a follow-up column, Bisher quoted Ivery from the letter: "My present situation is not as bleak as you led people to believe. I'm in the process of putting together a pretty good life for myself."

"I think the doctor went to UGA," Ivery speculated later.

Bisher received a letter from Grady asking who supplied the information, but Bisher wouldn't reveal his source. Ivery considered filing a lawsuit against the hospital, but he said later, "I didn't give a damn. I was so sick and tired of being like that." He was too weary to be angry, to hold Grady and Bisher accountable, wary of relapse, reluctant to risk hampering the emotional and mental progress he had made, so he focused his attention on recovery. A lawsuit was an unnecessary distraction. He plowed forward.

Funderburg said this incident became a lesson about recognizing what can be controlled and what can't: "OK, that happened, some things you're powerless over, and this is one of those things. You may want control, but you have no control over it. We notified them, and they'll handle their part, but there's nothing else you can do. That's it." Ivery felt righteous anger, but, at this point, recovery was more important.

After a year at ORP, advancing through their levels of achievement—following rules, showing honesty and responsibility, earning trust and privileges—he was allowed to call family. And Ivery finally felt *comfortable* talking to family. He called Jerry, who was surprised to hear a clear-thinking, sober Eddie Lee. He told Jerry how well he was doing and that ORP had helped him find himself. Jerry told him to stay where he was, to keep it up. Bennie Mae said, "I was so happy he was getting help. He was killing my grandmother and mom. My grandmother *stayed* on her knees praying for him."

Later, when Ivery told Jerry his addiction was connected to his poverty and shame over his mother, Jerry said he was thrilled his cousin was sober but was skeptical of the poverty angle. He said he had it harder than Eddie Lee did.

"I was older," he said, "and had more responsibility. If something turned out not right, that's *my* fault. I told him we *all* had nothing. But you made it. I didn't buy 'having nothing.' We didn't either. All we did was work and play, all 12 years we were in school. And *I* didn't take any drugs."

Eddie Lee's family—weary of his dishonest scheming—could have told him to stay away, and no one would have faulted them. But they had prayed and hoped too much. Those prayers were desperate, but they were based on the confidence that God would deliver, that forgiveness is powerful. Even if Bennie Mae felt angry at church when her mother was ridiculed, she was moved and inspired by God's presence. Their aching hopes were grounded in a strong family that had survived hardship.

Jerry looked past his skepticism and welcomed Eddie Lee back to the family. He celebrated that, finally, an attempt at recovery seemed to be taking hold. Eddie Lee seemed like a different person from the one who had stolen from him, lied to him, and crashed a car while high. "He's just a genuine person," Jerry said. "He doesn't do mean things. It's drugs that made him do that."

Even if Ivery's explanation of how he crafted his life story to illustrate his path to addiction convinced no one else, it worked for him. It helped him evaluate his life and choices and create a new sense of self. He acknowledged his deceptions and lies. Fluker said, "Treatment is all about getting in touch with your feelings. Alcohol numbs you. You don't want to feel what you feel. Once someone starts using, they stop growing emotionally." When an addict begins a regimen like ORP's, they must learn to deal with emotions anew. Ivery slowly un-numbed the emotions that drugs and alcohol had suppressed. By persisting through ORP, day by day, Ivery learned how to communicate and how to be vulnerable honestly, not as manipulation. In a way, he and Jerry were both right. His poverty and shame, his injuries and performance pressure, the pain medication—they alone didn't cause his addiction, but weaving that narrative into genuine recovery is what counted. He had excuses for his addiction and had to discard them while taking responsibility. He had to learn that a trusting relationship is not about others going along with you but about being open to honest communication. He finally did.

Funderburg said ORP hammered this home to residents: We appreciate the bad things you've been through, but we're interested in what you're going to do now.

Toward the end of Ivery's time at ORP, he received a boost from the man who almost 30 years before had just about moved into Thomson to lure Ivery to Tech: Dick Bestwick. He had coached Dave Braine, Tech's athletic director, in high school and later recommended him to Pepper Rodgers, who hired him at Tech. Braine became AD at Virginia Tech before returning to Atlanta. Bestwick said, "I felt like Dave owed me."

He told Braine about Ivery completing ORP and looking for work, and then he sought a favor: Find a place for Ivery at Tech. "He needs to be at Tech, and he needs people like you in his life," said Bestwick, who knew Ivery had betrayed the trust of Tech staff more than once. The athletic department had paid for his treatment at the Peachtree Charter drug recovery program, and it didn't work. Tech connections helped him get the Russell Athletic job, and he convincingly said he was done with drugs, but he relapsed spectacularly with the all-night binge and car crash. No one would blame Braine if, reluctant to be burned again, he declined. Ivery was well loved at Tech, but who wants to be a stooge?

Thompson and Braine had lunch with Ivery in the church fellowship hall. Ivery won them over. Thomson said, "It became apparent that he wanted to make something of himself. He admitted all the problems that he had, all the things he had done, and felt like if given a second chance he could be successful. He never, ever asked to come back to Georgia Tech. That was never mentioned by him."

Thompson said, "That posed some questions and risks. I talked with Braine, and he talked extensively with Eddie Lee." In July of 2000, Tech hired him as an assistant strength and conditioning coach under the condition he be drug-tested often. He worked with athletes from several sports, including football. Thompson loved Ivery and believed his recovery was real but kept a close watch.

"He reports to me once a month," he said in an interview at the time. "He tells me where he's living, what he's driving. I want to look into his eyes every so often." After Ivery had been at Tech for a while, Thompson said, "He has done well, and we're proud of him. He renewed his religious faith, re-connected with his children, and he's trying to do right to them."

Ivery, the player that some still consider Tech's greatest running back ever, had the humble job during football games of prowling the sidelines, waving frantically at players to keep them from entering the field when celebrating a good play, to avoid a penalty. He could not have been happier.

In addition to sobriety and work ethic, Ivery's sparkling personality returned. When Gary Lanier, Ivery's wishbone quarterback, who worked in the athletic office, brought his five children to work, Ivery charmed them. He said, "Eddie Lee makes them feel like he cares. When my eight-year-old gets here, he says, 'Is Eddie Lee going to be there?' I say, 'We'll find him.'"

Ivery assured his family he had no intention of using again. He told Jerry another story from his using days to convince him he was determined to leave that behind. He said once the power went out in a place where he was staying, and a ray of light shone through a curtain opening, reflecting on the floor. He became paranoid, delusional, and thought the reflection was a rock of crack. On his knees, he scrambled frantically for a glinting mirage. He said to Jerry, "I'd rather have cancer or AIDS than get hooked on crack again. I wouldn't wish that on my worst enemy." He said he heard whispers that he would relapse again but declared he never would. As with the whispers that he couldn't graduate from Tech or that he couldn't play after two surgeries on the same knee, he was determined to prove the doubts wrong. *I'll show you.*

Some of his dramatic drug stories Ivery parceled out to family as he felt comfortable. Jerry wasn't aware for a long time that Ivery had been homeless. He said, "Homeless? It blew my mind when he spoke about it at my uncle's funeral."

Funderburg said the key to rebuilding trust with his family was consistency. He said he "just kept doing the right thing" until they were convinced. He was especially pleased when, for the first time, his father said he was proud of his son. He said his father was "the one I felt like I disappointed the most. So many times, he was there for me. He was never *not* there for me." Many times, he had said he was clean but then relapsed; however, finally, "I wasn't just talking about it but doing it." Dixon remarked that his family began to believe his recovery was real when "I didn't have that desperate look in my eyes."

Bennie Mae knew rebuilding trust, despite hours on her knees praying, despite newly meaningful conversations, wouldn't be easy.

"It was hard to trust him," she said.

> We were on pins and needles. We'd look at him like, "Is he high or getting ready to go over in that drug area?" I had always been afraid when he came to town. We embraced him, but it was a trust thing with me. I don't want him to get on those drugs again. I think even in this small town, if you owe money for drugs, they'll kill you. From hearing what people say about addiction, they say you pick up where you left off.

She shook her head, dreading that possibility. "It was not a pretty picture. I'd see myself as big sister, and I'd pray for him, and he said he had to take one day at a time, that you're going to have people trying to get you back to old habits."

All those talks at ORP and all the lessons about honest communication bore fruit when he spoke to his family in ways they had not experienced in a long time. Drugs and alcohol had clouded his thinking, but now it was clear.

Bennie Mae said, "After he got straight and an article about him was in the paper, that was the first time we talked and shared things we had never shared before—great feelings. We talked about what it was like at home in Cherokee. The poverty, our family situation, what I went through. He said it was the first time he was sober enough to talk about it." She decided she should remind Ivery of how poorly he had treated the family. It was time to retrieve an artifact: their aunt's check that he had forged. "He thanked me. I said it was a reminder that he didn't want to ever get that low again."

The Ivery roots in Cherokee, the closeness in a cramped home, the toiling and sweating together, the learning to cope with little, the reliance on prayer that they learned and practiced in church, the shared deception about their mother—all this created a family bond that Ivery severely challenged with years of destructive dishonest behavior, yet the bond held. They knew to be wary due to many disappointments, but they also recognized their family was resilient and resourceful. They welcomed him home.

They had learned what Fluker said treatment specialists believe is crucial when dealing with addicts: compassion—plus realism. While anger and bewilderment are appropriate reactions to maddening behavior, addicts also need to be viewed as someone "whose brain has been hijacked. It is a disease of the brain, and their behavior changes." There is a powerful negative stigma associated with being a "junkie," and it's normal to judge their behavior as despicable and inexplicable, but, Fluker said, "We need to have compassion. It's hard to get families into their compassionate side, so we tell them they can be compassionate yet still set boundaries."

Free from the tight control of ORP and able to choose his path through life, Ivery passed every drug test at Tech and kept his job. A month after starting, he didn't down a Heineken, crash his car, or steal from his job. He didn't "borrow" from co-workers. Like Funderburg, Ivery consistently exhibited a clean, responsible life. Everyone could see: This time, it's for real. After several years as the strength and conditioning coach at Tech, he returned to Thomson High to work as a parent liaison and assistant football coach. He married the delightful woman with the pretty smile he met in Alabama and, in his 50s, fathered a daughter.

Ivery still receives NFL trading cards, with his picture on the front and his stats on the back, from collectors wanting autographs. One request included two cards and a letter that began, "Dear Mr. Ivery," proclaiming that the writer was Ivery's "No. 1 fan" and would be honored to receive the cards, autographed, in the enclosed stamped envelope. Judging by the letter's style, Ivery surmised the collector printed the same letter each time—after changing the name following "Dear Mr." He signed and returned them.

During a July 2000 interview with an Atlanta *Constitution* sportswriter, Ivery wept, recalling how he had mistreated his family and how they welcomed him back. He said Anna left him several times and returned until she could no longer do so. "She stayed there and tried to save me," he said. "But I found out that you can't help somebody unless they're willing to help themselves. Neither of us realized that."

Anna told the reporter she divorced Ivery when she felt she didn't know him anymore and concluded he couldn't function in a normal life, and when she feared he might be a danger to her and their children. She said, "There was a lot of trouble and heartache and pain and mental and physical abuse." Ivery said Anna had the courage to leave, which helped him realize nobody wants to live with a user, an alcoholic, an addict.

Anna expressed to the reporter none of the bitterness she was entitled to. She laughed and said Ivery repeatedly apologized to her, and she said he didn't have to. She said she never gave up on Ivery, even from Tampa. It took her a long time to realize how severe Ivery's addiction was because the Packers supported him and gave him second chances.

"That support hid the issues from me," she said. It got to be "detrimental to my health and my mental health." Now, she said, "It's clear he has God on his side." When Ivery speaks about his recovery, while he credits those who supported him—Tech, the Packers, ORP, his family—he thanks "the grace of God," particularly when he mentions the times he was one tiny change of fate from jail or the morgue. All those prayers by Bennie Mae and Katie Bell worked their way into his life.

Kent Hill, who roomed with Ivery and was a four-year teammate, said, "That's the grace and mercy of God. You have the opportunity to be redeemed that way. Eddie Lee has been such a great example of going from who I met when we were roommates in 1975, then to go through all that. Out of all our classmates who struggled with things, he is the one to make the biggest turnaround and keep it consistent."

Ivery said after his mistreatment of Anna, he learned how to be a husband. "Now I'm more involved in my marriage," he said.

> We do things together. Communication is the best part. Now I'm an active participant. I learned it through ORP, learning about me, being around ORP people, I learned to love people unconditionally. I've always been loving and caring, but I didn't know how to show it. I was embarrassed to show how much I care. I don't like upsetting people. I want everybody to like me, so I would do things so people would like me. Will they take advantage of me if I be vulnerable and show feelings? I learned it's OK to be who I am.

In November 2000, in Tampa, Ivery, for the first time, watched his son, Eddie Lee Ivery, Jr., play high school football. Wearing a Tech T-shirt under his Chamberlain High jersey, Junior, a running back like his father, rushed for a career high 181 yards and four touchdowns in a 35-16 win. Ivery Sr., also in Tech clothing, remained calm on the sidelines until his son rushed off right tackle for a go-ahead 60-yard touchdown run. He cheered madly. Ivery, Jr., a National Honor Society student, received the Guy Toph Award, for Hillsborough County's top player. He signed to play for Georgia Tech. (A knee injury ended his college career.)

In August 2003, Thomson High boosters sponsored an old-timers football game, and for the first time since 1974, Ivery and John Barnett, in their late 40s, were teammates. Barnett said, "He was on my team, and he's the reason we won. He could move around pretty good. And he caught a touchdown pass."

Chapter 19

Memorial Day

Since 1977, Ivery and many of his Black Tech teammates have gathered on the Saturday before Memorial Day in Atlanta, first at Tech on an athletic field and then at an Atlanta park. "It started innocently enough," Ivery said. "We were just kind of looking for something to do during a lull in our activities as student athletes. As time passed, we started calling everybody up and saying, 'Let's meet.'" Early on, Donnie Sewell said, "We'd run sprints, throw passes, play basketball, swim in the pool." They ordered takeout chicken, then began grilling their own food and bringing sides. When they moved the gathering from Tech to a park, they started playing softball. They've been grilling and playing softball ever since.

It started as all Tech football players, then they invited family and a few close friends. "Wives and girlfriends came early on," Kent Hill said, "and some girlfriends turned into wives." Now there are grandchildren. After the core group graduated, it became an informal college reunion. Some playing pro ball, Hill said, celebrated finishing spring camp and anticipating summer practice. NFL players arrived in their Cadillacs, Mercedes, and BMWs. Gathering on a holiday weekend was convenient for those who "got responsible, got jobs, and had families," Hill said. They began inviting "younger guys" from Tech to keep the tradition going, and many attend regularly. "As people moved away and began careers and started families, they looked forward to it," Hill said.

Although they were revered athletes at Tech, they sometimes felt like outsiders at a predominantly White university, so having a supportive community was important. That outsider feeling was absent at this gathering. As athletes in a violent sport—who together sweated and got injured, upset favorites and lost when favored, cheered and wept in locker rooms—they experienced struggle and triumph. This annual gathering was nostalgic but also a continuation of a shared narrative, with each one's story woven into the larger one. They aged, and their athleticism diminished, yet that former dynamic athleticism remained alive in their recollections, an echo of what once was, still lurking behind wrinkles, gray hair, and creaky joints.

A structure developed: In late March, they start calling and emailing. The day of the event, Sewell and a few others arrive early to set up the grill and tables and start cooking. Sewell's truck is meticulously loaded with grilling gear. (Rodney Lee said, "Sewell *has* to come. There's no cookout without Sewell.") Others arrive with sides, drinks, supplies, and softball equipment. They reminisce about Tech football, catch up on jobs, relationships, and health. They play softball, followed by a prayer to bless the food, then the meal. Tales are told and re-told.

Sewell said the cookout and softball game became important because

> it was our one time to get together. It was primarily Black athletes. I started at Tech in 1975 when having Black students was still a novelty, and most of the Black students were athletes, so it was a bonding place for us to be together. We created a family. Sometimes we don't see each other for a year, and it's like we revert to our college years. My Tech family is as important as my real family. When we stop doing it, I don't know what I'll do. Some don't come every year, but we've had people come from Miami, New York, New Jersey, Dallas. The fellowship is as good as money.

David Allen said, "It creates a brotherhood. It reiterates the diversity of Georgia Tech, having a place to remember, a landing pad to go back to and remember the good times from a Black perspective. A place to retreat as a Black student-athlete. We meet, bring our families, enjoy ourselves, and relax." They exaggerate. "Every memory," he said, "keeps getting better. A 10-yard touchdown turns into a 30-yard touchdown. The more you tell the story, the better it gets. You can create whatever you want at the softball game. It's a place to create positive memories, to keep good memories."

Rodney Lee never missed when he lived in Atlanta and attended whenever he could after he moved to Nevada. "That was a long flight," he said. "I didn't come as often." He bought a house on Mexico's west coast and, "Now I try to be in the country for it. I know it won't last forever, so it's a good thing to keep those relationships."

Henry Johnson, who intercepted the Air Force pass that allowed Ivery to re-enter the game and break the single-game rushing record, said at the 2022 gathering, "We wanted something fun that was not football. At this point now, we just want to stay connected. And some are not with us anymore."

Sometimes, a player's absence was glaring. Sewell said, "If someone who is usually there isn't, if there's a good reason to miss, they would usually communicate that. So, if we didn't hear anything, it was often a sign of trouble. If you're thinking clearly, you're there. We'd wonder where they were, what might be going on."

Kent Hill said sometimes they would tease each other, perhaps imitating someone's distinctive voice and a phrase they were known for. "We'll mock how some people talk. One had a deep voice, and we'd imitate it. Then, when one year you don't hear their voice, and they had been attending so long, you miss them."

Hill said as they met yearly, some died. "We realized," he said, "that being here isn't guaranteed, and as guys have left us, we cherish seeing each other. We appreciate we're still here and we can get together. We know that's a blessing in itself."

From the beginning, Ivery was a popular regular, considered the greatest football player of that era, so his absences during his lowest days were noticed. Sometimes former classmates mentioned his absence; sometimes they kept it to themselves. Hill said they were aware some former attendees were addicts and used the gathering as a ruse. "Some would tell their family they were going to the softball game," he said, "but would really go use drugs. It's like, 'I'm going to the game,' but they stop somewhere that they used to frequent and don't leave. You miss him and nobody knows where to find him. At that point, people knew why Eddie Lee wasn't there. We missed him."

By 2000, the gathering included memorials for those who had died—one or two each year. The memorial became a planned part of the gathering: between the softball game and the prayer. The list got longer.

When they met in 2022, the original attendees moved slower, more deliberately. Stories from their playing days surfaced. Sewell told how Roy "Sugar Bear" Simmons had told him that there was financial aid for each player, but it was sent to the athletic department, which doled it out as they saw fit. He learned to go to a certain office and fill out a form, and *his* money would go to him. Only a few knew about this. Ivery and Hill teased, "You're just *now* telling us this!" Ivery said, "My own *roommate* didn't tell me?" That led to stories about living off campus and receiving expense money, which included meals, but they would find a way to eat on campus for free, among other scams.

Ivery joked with children, stooped to their level, made funny faces, pretended to be crying, upset that he was "in trouble," as a little boy had said about him. One could see what Jerry meant about Eddie Lee establishing rapport with kids at his day care center—even as an addict. Kids loved him. (The next Memorial Day weekend, in 2023, Ivery's new granddaughter was there, and while a friend of his son held the child, Ivery teased the friend about her tattoos and piercings. He pointed at each one and instructed the baby, "No, no, no." They all laughed.)

Some talked about retirement. When Hill and Don Patterson explained how Medicare worked, suddenly attentive eyes locked on them, as they hoped for a clear explanation from a reliable source of what can be a confusing system. Hill said the NFLPA helped him navigate Medicare. This was the first year Medicare was a topic at the softball game, as they had missed two years due to Covid-19.

They told Pepper Rodgers stories and laughed. That crazy night at the Colorado Springs airport. The first time he brought Arden Zinn to lead them in stretching. His TV show. "Just don't embarrass Georgia Tech!" Ivery recalled the time Don Bessillieu completely missed him in practice. "A *lot* of people missed you," someone said. What assistant coaches yelled on the sidelines. They imitated one coach's voice, and everyone laughed. They remembered shabby cars they had in college, one they could hear blocks away, one with a fuel gauge that didn't work. Those Bessillieu parties!

In the softball game, most of the older players, including Ivery and Hill, still looked athletic, their stances in the batter's box erect and poised to uncoil for contact, their swings smooth and efficient. None "ran" the bases. Ivery, his knees showing the wear of a nine-year NFL career, shuffled between bases, barely picking up his feet. One player had a youngster run for him after he hit the ball. Easy ground balls went past a shortstop, once a fast defensive back, who made as spirited an effort as he could. Sons and grandsons were quicker and more agile. When Eddie Lee Jr. ran the bases, he *glided*—reminiscent of how both he and his father carried a football. Their competitive fire waned only a bit. They (sort of) jokingly argued over how many outs had been made and shouted outrage that one team had an extra infielder—even though he was a child. Ivery and his grandson, adorably, crouched in identical stances in the infield.

Johnson said that early on they played two softball games, and if each team won a game, they played a three-inning tiebreaker. "Now," he chuckled, "a few innings is enough."

"It went from three games to three innings," Lee joked. "After a certain point, it kept going down and down. It didn't get better each year. It got worse."

When it came time to remember those who had died since their last gathering, the list was longer than usual due to their ages and the two-year pandemic hiatus. Some memories were so strong that they recalled individuals who had been deceased for more than two years. They called out names, among them:

Don Bessillieu, Ivery's close friend and roommate, who died on Christmas Eve the previous year. He had also attended ORP but lasted only a few months.

"Sugar Bear" Simmons, who played a few years in the NFL, including a Super Bowl, and came out as gay on the *Phil Donahue Show* in 1992. He had struggled with drug addiction, contracted AIDS, became a born-again Christian, was inducted into the National Gay and Lesbian Hall of Fame, and died at 57.

Bernard Stover, who also attended ORP, died of a drug overdose.

Drew Hill, who had an outstanding NFL career in the Warren Moon-led Houston Oilers Run & Shoot offense, died of two massive strokes at 54.

Pepper Rodgers, who died at age 88, after a fall in his Virginia home caused arterial bleeding that led to a stroke and heart attack. His son Rick said before Rodgers fell,

> He was in great shape, mentally and physically. He still played golf—eighteen holes. The day before he fell, Dad was still feisty. He was railing against Trump. He was bored because everybody was still in Covid quarantine. He fell because he wore socks walking on the slick marble bathroom floor. It could have happened to anybody. Those stupid socks.

———

In 2022, Ivery, whose teams won no titles in high school, college, or the NFL, celebrated a championship. Thomson High, with Ivery as assistant, won its sixth Georgia AA state football title.

Ivery was inducted into the Georgia Sports Hall of Fame. A recorded video introduction summarized his career and showcased a beautiful clip of the wishbone going left. Gary Lanier was at his best, faking to the fullback while keeping the ball as a defender stalked him for a second too long. At precisely the right moment, he flipped to Ivery, the defender too close to Lanier to have any chance at Ivery, who dashed past him. As coached, a streaking offensive lineman crossed the field to push a defender out of the way. Ivery deftly sped to the right for a 30-yard touchdown, breaking two tackles as he dove into the end zone. The defenders had no chance. In a Packers clip, he made a clean over-the-head pass reception and then swiftly wove through defenders.

His ample range of skills was showcased on the screen in two plays.

His speech was heartfelt and humble. Animated and comfortable in front of a crowd—a long way from the shy teenager afraid to say the wrong thing the wrong way—he breathed heavily, composed himself, and expressed many thanks. He thanked God, "for allowing me to be here tonight," the Hall of Fame for selecting him, and congratulated the other honorees. He expressed gratitude to family members in the auditorium—many of whom he had mistreated in his drive to find a high.

He thanked his mom and grandmom for their sacrifices, coaches, and teammates, especially the offensive linemen, who "made it possible for me to be the player I became." He acknowledged his Thomson teachers who prepared him to attend "the best engineering school in the world."

He expressed gratitude to Dick Bestwick for saying he wanted him to play for and graduate from Georgia Tech. He mentioned that he didn't think much about graduating until Bestwick called and offered him the opportunity to finish his degree. He got a big laugh when he recounted that Bestwick told Tech if they didn't help him graduate, UGA would.

He thanked the Packers for giving him opportunities "that a country boy like me wouldn't dream of." He made no mention of injuries, without which, he would have been an even greater player.

He concluded by thanking the game of football itself for teaching him to prepare for life: "When I played with you, Mr. Football, I got knocked down and fell down, and you told me, 'Eddie Lee, get up and try again.' You told me I would face obstacles, times would get tough, and I would feel like throwing in the towel. You looked me in the eye and told me the words of Jim Valvano: 'Don't give up. Don't ever give up.'"

Sources

PERSONS INTERVIEWED

P. D. Adams
David Allen
Mack Alley
Tom Backhus
John Barnett
Bill Becker
Jim Bell
Buck Belue
Leo Benatar
Don Bessillieu
Dick Bestwick
Furman Bisher
Beau Bock
Mark Bowers
Jim Bowman
Tommy Carmichael
David Carter
Bud Casey
Cliff Christl
Al Ciraldo, Jr.
Paul Coffman
Jackie Copeland
Kory Cornum
Lee Corrick
Bill Curry
Tom Daniel
David Davidson
Lynn Dickey
Chester Dixon
Vince Dooley
Steve Drewnowski
Kelly Dude
Marvin Dyett
Dick Ellis
Janet Fluker
Larry Francois
Ray Friday
Mayo Funderburg
Bud Geracie
Bernard Grant
Bennie Mae (Ivery) Collins
Joseph Greene
Bob Harlan
Mackel Harris
Ken Hatfield
Rick Hawes
Tommy Herrington
Kent Hill
John Hunsinger
Jerry Ivery
Eddie Lee Ivery
Naomi Ivery
Ezra Johnson
Henry Johnson
Mike Kelley
Burton Kemp
Kim King
Robert Knox, Jr.
Greg Koch
John Kramer
Don Lankenkamp
Gary Lanier
Rodney Lee
James Lofton
Lawrence Lowe
Larry McCarren
Bill McDonald
Bill Parcells

Don Patterson
Tom Pigeon
Allen Potter
Dave Raabe
Matt Rank
Lee Remmell
Dale Ricks
Kelly Rodgers
Pepper Rodgers
Rick Rodgers
Calvin Sampson
Lucius Sanford
Jerry Sellers
Bucky Shamburger
Charles Shugg
David Sims
Lance Skelton
Ken Smith
Ralph Starling
Jan Stenerud
Bernard Stover
Jim Sturch
Jack Thompson
Ben Utt
Luis Valdez
Len Wagner
Len Walterscheid
David Whitehurst
Helen Williams
Reggie Wilkes
Luther Wilson
Scott Woerner
Randy Wright
Dave Ziebart
Arden Zinn

BOOKS

Christl, Cliff. *The Greatest Story in Sports: Green Bay Packers 1919-2019.* Stevens Point, WI: KCI Sports Publishing, 2021.

Dunnavant, Keith. *America's Quarterback: Bart Starr and the Rise of the National Football League.* New York: Thomas Dunne Books, 2011.

Foote, Jeffrey, Carrie Wilkens, and Nicole Kosanke. *Beyond Addiction.* New York: Scribner, 2014

Rodgers, Pepper & Al Thomy. *Pepper!: The autobiography of an unconventional coach.* Garden City NY: Doubleday & Company, 1976.

Simmons, Roy and Damon DiMarco. *Out of Bounds: Coming out of Sexual Abuse, Addiction, and My Life of Lies in the NFL Closet.* New York: Carroll and Graf Publishers, 2006.

Starr, Bart, *My Life in Football.* New York: William Morrow, 1987.

Twerski, Abraham J. *Addictive Thinking: Understanding Self-Deception.* 2nd ed. Center City, MN: Hazelden Publishing, 1997.

NEWSPAPERS AND MAGAZINES

The *Associated Press*
The *Atlanta Constitution*

The *Atlanta Journal*
The *Atlanta Journal and Constitution*
Atlanta Magazine
The Baton Rouge *Advocate*
Capital Times
The Chicago *Tribune*
The *Colorado Springs Sun*
The *Denver Post*
The *Falconews*
The Georgia Tech *Technique*
Georgia Trend
The *Green Bay Press-Gazette*
The *Los Angeles Times*
The *Macon Telegraph*
The *McDuffie Progress*
The *Milwaukee Journal Sentinel*
The *New York Times*
Sports Illustrated
The *Tampa Tribune*
United Press International
The *Washington Post*
The *Wisconsin State Journal*
USA Today

OTHER SOURCES

"30 for 30: Broke." ESPN documentary, directed by Billy Corben. 2012.
Oakhurst Baptist Church Archives
Thomson-McDuffie County Library Archives
Walter J. Brown Media Archives & Peabody Awards Collection (University of Georgia)
www.georgiaencyclopedia.org
www.giants.com/news
www.informedhealth.org
www.nih.gov
www.packers.com/news
www.vanishinggeorgia.com
www.weather.gov
www.youtube.com

Index